TECHNOLOGY, COMPETITION, AND THE SOVIET BLOC IN THE WORLD MARKET

RESEARCH SERIES/NUMBER 70

Technology, Competition, & the Soviet Bloc
in the World Market

KAZIMIERZ Z. POZNANSKI

INSTITUTE
OF INTERNATIONAL
STUDIES
University of California, Berkeley

Library of Congress Cataloging-in-Publication Data

Poznański, Kazimierz.
Technology, competition & the Soviet bloc in the world market.

(Research series, ISSN 0068-6093 ; no. 70)
Bibliography: p.
Includes index.
1. Technological innovations—Europe, Eastern. 2. Export marketing—Europe, Eastern. 3. Quality of products—Europe, Eastern. 4. Europe, Eastern—Manufactures. I. Title. II. Series: Research series (University of California, Berkeley. Institute of International Studies) ; no. 70.
HC244.Z9T4716 1987 338'.06 87-3505
ISBN 0-87725-170-3

CONTENTS

LIST OF TABLES

ACKNOWLEDGMENTS

Generous financial support from the American Council of Learned Societies and the Woodrow Wilson International Center for Scholars assisted my work. I benefited greatly from collaboration with Professor Robert Gilpin of the Woodrow Wilson School of Public and International Affairs at Princeton, and the strong encouragement of Professor Richard Nelson of Yale was most valuable to me. I am also appreciative of the friendly assistance provided by Dr. Jack Martens of the U.S. Department of Commerce, where I spent many hours searching for data. My discussions with Dr. Larry Westphal and Dr. Gene Tidrick of the World Bank were of great value as well. In later stages I benefited from helpful comments by Professor Paul Marer of Indiana University and Professor Laura Tyson of the University of California, Berkeley. Finally, I am aware that the book would not have been written without the moral and intellectual support of my wife, Joanna, who has stood by me all along.

K. Z. P.

INTRODUCTION

During the last two decades the centrally planned economies (CPEs) of Eastern Europe and the Soviet Union have reshaped some of their earlier policies, including reopening their doors to the transfer of more advanced Western technologies and external financing. Numerous changes in the CPE economic systems have been introduced, many of them aimed at their inefficient, wasteful, and conservative technological sectors. One of the goals of these reforms has been to improve the traditionally poor competitiveness of CPE exports on the world market, allowing for (among other things) some inroads into the Western market.

The CPEs have not been alone in their modernization attempts, however. One important effort is the policy of developing countries to build up export capacities in manufactured goods. This policy has resulted in the recent appearance of the newly industrializing countries (NICs) as sizable exporters of manufactured goods, many of which are based on technology supplied by subsidiaries of Western multinational corporations. The NIC effort has been extensively discussed by economists, almost exclusively in the context of possible implications for the developed Western economies. Yet it is likely to have some, possibly negative, effects on the latest efforts by the CPEs as well.

The Western economies have also been going through a series of important changes in production. The saturation of domestic demand for many traditional goods, the sudden increase in energy costs, and the recent increase of exports from the NICS—plus a fear of large-scale inflows of Western-based goods from the CPEs—have caused the West to mobilize substantial resources for restructuring industry. This effort has certainly worked against CPE plans to reduce their competitive lag toward the West. While some economists have been trying to determine the outcome of these parallel struggles, the issue awaits further detailed research.

In this volume we shall establish whether, with their latest policy changes and economic reforms, the CPEs have improved their competitiveness relative to the market economies of the West and whether they represent any match for the NICs, where the working of market forces is limited by a large public sector and extensive state intervention. In this sense we shall attempt to develop a global, three-dimensional picture of world competition, with the CPEs at the centerpoint.

While many factors affect competitiveness, we shall focus on one of them: technological level. It is our contention that technological strength—the ability to generate new inventions and to implement them in production—is the most important factor involved; here we agree with the main thrust of the neo-technological theories of trade. Consequently, we shall focus on the working of the technological sector in the CPEs and (when necessary) in the other segments of the world economy. For the same reason, we shall be concerned mostly with the technological angle of competitiveness—the age of products offered for export, the quality of those products, and the novelty of manufacturing processes employed in their production.

Our study—basically covering the period 1970-85—is divided into three major parts. In the first we shall assess in detail the latest economic reforms of the CPEs which attempt to increase the efficiency of the technological sector. The second part, representing the core of the study, is devoted to the measurement of technological performance in all three segments of the world economy, particularly in the sphere of export activities. In the final part we shall analyze the factors—of a systemic nature—that have determined the performance of the CPEs relative to that of the market and quasi-market economies.

SYSTEMIC REFORMS

We shall begin with an overview of reforms that the CPEs have introduced to stimulate technological change, mainly since the mid-1960s. The first important line of change was an attempt to merge originally separate research institutes either with associations of enterprises which manufacture similar products or with individual large enterprises in order to provide better communication between them. Another important reform throughout the region has been full-cycle planning of research to allow for a concentration of resources and a quicker application of new technologies between institutes and enterprises. For each major project, targets are now set to cover the development of technology and its full commercial application in the economy, with users and expected effects specified.

To improve the motivation for efficient research, purely administrative arrangements have been replaced by contractual ones; along with the move toward contractual arrangements, the research institutes have become business accounting units. To enable researchers to benefit from the commercialization of research in industry, several reforms have provided bonuses to supplement wages at research institutes. However, little has been done to create procedures for licensing technologies by one organization (a research institute or enterprise) to another.

From the early days of central planning, technological change in enterprises, which are the lowest level of the organizational hierarchy, has been promoted through the plan targets set by the central authorities. Recent reforms affecting planning at this level have generally been aimed at providing some kind of order in the various technological targets passed on to the enterprises. They have also been aimed at attaching a higher priority to these targets to counterbalance other, often conflicting, objectives and at improving the system for monitoring the fulfillment of the technological targets.

The focus on output maximization continues to dominate the plan targets that central authorities set for enterprises, but over the years the priority given to quality has significantly increased. State-sponsored organizations for rating quality are of some help in upgrading it. An important element of increased central pressure on enterprises to improve quality is the standardization system, which specifies technical requirements for the manufacture and performance of particular products. Some countries have also designed financial incentives to stimulate enterprises to upgrade the quality of their products. In addition, to relax the constraints of pricing rules, enterprises in many countries are being allowed to set the prices of new products higher than those of the products being replaced.

A growing appreciation for the need to eliminate obsolete or inferior products and processes has resulted in several adjustments. The prime instruments for speeding this elimination have been the production plans for enterprises. However, the central authorities have found it difficult to agree on the products and processes to be deemed obsolete, and even unanimous decisions by planners to scrap obsolete products have met much resistance in enterprises. Moreover, the CPEs have not actively curtailed production and investment in branches where an economic advantage over other countries is doubtful.

Some changes have also been made to promote the transfer of foreign technology to the domestic sectors, including revisions in the rules of ownership of new technologies. During the first years of central planning, the CPEs did not provide any protection for the Western owners of patented technology, thus discouraging the inflow of patent information from the West, and, more importantly, the licensing of Western technology in the CPEs. Nor was there any legal protection for individual inventors in the CPEs, as all new technology was considered state property. This has been changed to a degree, so that Western patent owners are provided with more or less the same kind of protection as in the West or in the developing world.

Modifications have been made in the sphere of investment which are critical for the implementation of new technologies requiring additions to existing capital stock. The state monopoly over investment decision-making has been relaxed to some degree, and more advanced techniques of project selection have been put into operation. Still, with the exception of Hungary, it is the central planners who decide not only on the allocation of investment resources to branches of the economy, but also on the construction of individual new plants, the expansion of existing plants, and any sizable purchases of machinery. Moreover, the choices of technology for projects—choices that determine capital intensity and the like—are also in the domain of planners.

As a part of the broader effort to reopen the CPEs to the world economy, some provisions have been made to allow for an integration with the world capital market. To attract foreign (particularly Western) capital, many CPEs have tried to break with the tradition of not allowing (from fear of Western influence) any investment from outside. The CPEs have been very cautious in this respect, so that only joint ventures between local enterprises and foreigners in designated areas of the economy have been legalized by most of the countries in the region (except for East Germany, Czechoslovakia, and—most significantly—the Soviet Union).

TECHNOLOGICAL PERFORMANCE

Our analysis of productivity indicators—reflecting not only technological level, but also other efficiency-related factors—seems to indicate that the policy changes have not made the CPEs more successful in reducing their long-standing lag behind the advanced Western economies. In the case of Soviet industry, a declining trend in labor productivity over more than a decade has not ceased and—according to projections by Bergson (1983)—no reversal of this trend is to be anticipated. Further evidence of lackluster performance comes from the observation that, at least in the Soviet Union, the productivity lag with respect to the Western economies has not diminished since the mid-1970s. One can speculate that the Soviet Union has approached an equilibrium technological gap, while still behind the United States, of around twelve years in productivity terms. (The productivity gap itself is extensive now—around twenty-five years; see Gomulka 1985.) Such an equilibrium gap by itself establishes that the Soviet economic system is wanting in technological ability since—as most theoretical models imply—a properly functioning economy should be able in a reasonable time span to get much closer to, if not equal, the productivity level of the leader.

Given the limitations of productivity indicators, we shall also analyze a number of foreign trade measures, including unit values for CPE exports. We shall show that all the CPEs experienced increases in their unit values in the 1970s, a combined result of world market price inflation and technological improvements in these economies. However, the increases have not been as strong as those in the Western economies, so that the difference in unit values between the centrally planned and some market economies, such as those of Western Europe, has in fact expanded. Other statistical evidence—for instance, case studies in the automobile, chemical, and computer industries—also suggests that the CPEs have performed poorly relative to technological change in the West.

Our comparison of centrally planned industries with their Western counterparts is supplemented by an analysis of comparative technological levels in the CPEs, on one hand, and a selected group of developing nations on the other. Such a line of research has been little explored, partly because of a lack of data integrating the CPEs with the NICs. However, it is a very rewarding approach since it helps to establish whether the experience of the CPEs is any different from that of other countries which also entered the postwar years with a sizable technological lag behind the industrialized West. If it is not, one should consider the inability of the CPEs to catch up with Western technology normal rather than an anomaly.

The evidence presented in this book shows that the experience of the CPEs is different from that of certain developing countries—more precisely the NICs. The NICs have been more successful than the CPEs in catching up with the Western level of technology and in the process have surpassed them in many industries where they lagged farther behind the Western economies after World War II than did the CPEs. These include not only simple technology sectors (e.g., steel-making or shipbuilding), but (as demonstrated with both aggregated and detailed data) complex technology production as well (e.g., computer peripherals and components).

We consider this aforementioned trend the most critical development in the long-standing "competition" between central planning and the market. While no proof has been offered to date that the centrally planned system could successfully replace the market mechanism as a vehicle for technological change in a mature industrial country, neither has there been any solid evidence that it would not do so for less developed economies. This lack of evidence has promoted Soviet propaganda that central planning is a solution for developing nations. With the data provided in this book, serious doubts arise about whether central planning is more suitable for the technological transformation of latecomers than the market alternative.

The combination of an unchanged CPE technological lag behind the Western economies and their diminishing advantage over the NICs has led to a substantial erosion of CPE competitiveness on the world market for manufactured goods, particularly in the West. This book provides abundant evidence of this erosion, with both aggregate data and case studies of the most important exports. The general indicator of erosion is a steady decline of CPE market share in Western imports of manufactured goods—particularly machinery—during at least the last decade. This share—traditionally low—has fallen by more than one third.

By the end of the 1960s CPE exports had been threatened in several areas of generally underinvested light industry, including textiles. During the 1970s the exports of not only intermediate goods (e.g., steel), but also of traditional machinery—continuously receiving the highest investment priority—were threatened as well. There is also some evidence that the NICs may soon make it extremely difficult, if not impossible, for the CPEs to expand the exports of advanced machinery (e.g., computers), where the region has not even begun to sell significant quantities to Western markets.

Given what we have been able to quantify, we can claim that the NICs have certainly been taking away some potential markets for CPE manufactures. More research will have to be done to determine whether the CPEs have also been forced to give up some of their already existing markets. But even if Eastern Europe (and the Soviet Union with respect to its nonenergy sales) has been able to hold up its existing markets in the West, this would not be a great relief for the region's leaders. Even with a recent slowdown in economic growth, the region has been expanding at a respectable rate, and the declining share of CPE exports in the Western market therefore means that these countries are going to find it increasingly difficult to support their industrial expansion with imports of Western goods, including technology.

One might argue that the CPEs could make up for their losses in Western markets by a vigorous promotion of trade with the developing economies. If dynamic enough, this alternative might provide the necessary support for future industrial growth in the region. For instance, it could be (as the advocates of so-called appropriate technology for the developing world claim) that the more labor-intensive and easier-to-service manufacturing processes offered by CPE exporters are better fitted to the needs of the developing economies than are the more sophisticated goods from the West. However, neither this potential attraction nor possible others (e.g., a CPE inclination to trade on barter terms) seem to matter. Most developing countries' efforts go into building ties with the Western market, and we do not find any indication that this tendency will change soon.

DETERMINANTS OF PERFORMANCE

Why has the latest wave of policy changes not greatly improved efficiency in the CPE region? The answer offered here is that the latest reforms in financing activities, pricing products, or rewarding managers and workers have at their best involved only fine-tuning. The systemic modifications have not affected the most important core elements of the central planning machinery, with only Hungary trying to change the core. Thus technological development is still governed more by the central authorities, who almost totally control resource allocation, than by the interplay of researchers and the users of research results. In sum, the waste of inputs and conservatism continue to plague the technological sector.

As we shall argue, one of the most important shortcomings of the CPEs is that resources are centrally allocated. Such an allocative mechanism puts major agents of technological change—state-owned enterprises and research institutes—in a situation where productive factors have zero prices (as understood by Kornai 1980). This situation inspires little innovation in cost reductions or quality improvements. A lack of interest in quality improvements is reinforced by the weak influence of buyers, particularly final consumers, on allocative decisions.

The zero-price situation seems a more plausible explanation of CPE failures than the fact that even under the existing planning system risks associated with technological change are not matched by commensurate rewards, as correctly stated by Grossman (1966) and Berliner (1976). Such risks are not particularly high because a number of safeguards are attached to the central plans (e.g., corrections of targets, supplementary resources, financial brakes) and because bankruptcy is practically unknown in the CPEs. It is also doubtful whether better planning—more realistic and flexible than at present—and higher rewards for technological changes would by themselves have a critical impact on the ability of central planning to encourage innovation.

In addition to the two possible explanations noted above is the fact that the CPEs, trading mainly among themselves, are closed to many technological possibilities and pressures extant in the rest of the world. The existing system—with its nonconvertible currencies, multiple exchange rates, and state monopoly in trade—isolates enterprises from external stimuli and, to make things worse, discourages foreign enterprises from direct involvement. As we shall argue, the CPEs suffer in particular from a lack of foreign direct investment by Western multinational corporations—clearly a major vehicle for technology transfer in the world economy—which find the environment in these countries intolerable.

Our main conclusion is that a centrally planned economy can obtain modest improvements in technological development by tinkering with policies and institutions, but a sharp acceleration of the pace of technological progress appears to depend on changing the fundamental principles governing the allocation and use of productive resources. Broader reforms to redesign the allocative system—perhaps along the line initiated by Hungary, probably the most technologically successful country in the region—are needed to bring about major improvements. But even the Hungarians will probably have to consider more fundamental reforms if they are to bring their performance up to the standard of the market economies, including the mixed economies of the NICs.

PART 1

SYSTEMIC REFORMS: GENERAL PRINCIPLES AND SPECIFIC MEASURES

In this part we shall discuss how the CPEs manage technological change. There is quite a literature on that subject, though most of the work to date deals with the Soviet experience alone (Zaleski 1976; Berliner 1976). We shall try to incorporate as much material on Eastern Europe as possible to fill the gap. The focus of our analysis will be on those segments of the CPE system which directly affect both the acquisition of new technology and its productive implementation. The purpose will be to show how these countries have for several decades been trying to create an alternative to the market-type mechanism, under which competitive forces and fear of bankruptcy drive producers to innovate. The latest reforms in particular will be analyzed.

We shall discuss both the basic rules of central planning as a vehicle for change and specific instruments. These will be analyzed in a four-stage sequence, following the logic of technological progress. We shall first investigate the instruments meant to promote research—i.e., the production of technology. Then we shall turn to the methods used to stimulate first applications of research results (i.e., innovations) and the means of promoting diffusion—in other words, the full-scale application of given technologies. Finally, we shall look at how planners try to stimulate economic agents to improve the quality of existing products and how they decide to eliminate obsolete technology.

Our objective in this part is to reconstruct the major technology-related segments of the CPEs and not to evaluate them in terms of comparative efficiency (i.e., compared to market mechanisms). However, in the description of these segments, we shall identify some concerns of planners which have made them correct initial systemic arrangements and/or supplement these arrangements with new ones. These concerns reflect inefficiency as perceived by the planners and not necessarily an inferiority of the existing mechanisms relative to the market system. The purely comparative aspects will be analyzed in Part 2.

Chapter 1

PLANNING OF RESEARCH AND INNOVATION

MANAGING RESEARCH ACTIVITY

DECISIONMAKING ON RESEARCH

Under the traditional scheme which evolved in the 1940s industrial research in the CPEs was performed mostly by separate organizations called institutes, expected to work exclusively for the enterprises reporting to the same industrial (i.e., branch) ministry and directly subordinated to these ministries through plans. Only rarely were there research establishments built into individual enterprises and responsible to their management. Such a scheme was expected to bring many benefits, including the effects of larger scale, the elimination of duplicate work, the extension of time horizons, and the selection of projects according to social (not private) rates of return.

This scheme continued to meet the requirements of planners throughout the 1950s, but it soon became apparent that it did not assure a full coordination of research projects with the needs of potential users. The central authorities found it too difficult to detect all the needs of enterprises or to answer them in time. Lacking much of the needed information on technological matters, they became strongly dependent on the expertise of the research institutes themselves, thus creating a bias in favor of the suppliers of technology. Several important changes have been made in the original scheme to solve this problem, with the major effort taking place in the late 1960s.

Planning Research. One important line of change throughout the CPE region was to set up clear-cut priorities for research. In the Soviet Union the first step in this direction was made in 1966, when the so-called coordination plans for research projects were instituted. Between 1966 and 1970, 246 coordination plans were recorded, covering about 3,000 projects of special importance and representing

40 percent of the total budget for research. In 1976 these plans were replaced by "scientific and technical programs," also aimed at establishing sharper priorities among projects and providing better grounds for the reinforcement of state control over priority projects (see Zaleski 1976). This program structure continues to operate; in the 1981-85 plan 170 programs were listed in addition to 41 target programs of the highest priority (Rjatsow 1982).

Another important major reform has been the introduction of full-cycle planning of research. For each major project, targets are set to cover the development of technology and its full commercial application in the economy, with users and expected effects specified. To enforce the targets the central authorities name a leading research institute to issue orders and oversee the work. (In addition, sources of finance for an entire operation are identified and usually attached to the institute in charge.)

These planning modifications force research institutes to analyze where a given technology is going to be utilized and with what effects, rather than simply looking at the possibilities of pushing forward the technological frontier. They also give the potential users of new technology the opportunity to take part in decisions on the parameters of new technology and the timing of research. Nevertheless, there is some inflexibility in the decision-making due to the large number of participants representing various levels of administration; in its present form, the arrangement gives the research institutes—not the enterprises—a dominant role in setting targets.

Contracting for Research. To improve control over the execution of plan targets in research, purely administrative arrangements (i.e., responsibility to a supervisory body) have been replaced in the institutes by contractual ones similar to those in market economies (Nolting 1976b). The 1968 reform in the Soviet Union introduced two forms of legal agreements—contracts and work orders for research, the latter drawn up by the industrial ministries. To back up plan targets with legal obligations, all contracts and work orders cover the specification of expected results, the terms and schedule of financial compensation, deadlines for delivery of completed work, and penalties for delay or unsatisfactory results. As a rule, research institutes are offered preferential payments (higher profit markups) for faster delivery or better than expected performance of inventions.

To work well this contractual system would require that the users of research institute technologies (enterprises and industrial ministries) are demanding and scrupulous in executing their agreements with research institutes. This system does not force users to be demanding, however; even if it works perfectly, the system by itself cannot assure improvements. Ambiguity about the exact definition of a final product makes it easy for institutes to claim that their projects have been completed even though they have not tried hard enough to meet the requirements set by their clients. It also makes it easy for enterprises and branch ministries to formally accept the results of a project if they are not concerned with the product (as is usually the case).

The problem with this revised (as well as with the original) type of planning is that though it allows planners to consider alternatives, it does not facilitate further corrections. The available alternatives are rather quickly narrowed down; after an authority has completed this preliminary stage, it is very reluctant to pursue more than one alternative. For the same reason there is great inertia in the execution of plan targets, partly expressed in an unwillingness, or rather inability, of the central authority to terminate unpromising projects or reevaluate the whole of an original strategy. Campbell (1976: 97-112) provides some examples of this inertia from the Soviet energy sector—for instance, handling the peak load problem in electrical power generation.

Integrating Institutes. As noted, the CPEs have attempted to merge originally separate research institutes either with associations of enterprises manufacturing similar products or with individual large enterprises in a clear effort to imitate the market system, where the management of research is organized within enterprises. This reform has been pursued most vigorously in the Soviet Union, where it started in 1965 and accelerated after 1973, when authorities decided to make the associations of enterprises a universal organizational entity in all branches of industry. Similar changes have been made by Bulgaria and Romania starting in the early 1970s (Skoczny 1982).

These one-roof mergers, called scientific production associations, are of two basic types in the Soviet Union. In one type the formal authority lies in a single (usually the largest) participating enterprise. In the second type the leading institute is in charge of all the members, including enterprises (Poznanski 1977). The first 600 scientific production associations were set up in 1970 (Bornstein et al. 1980). In 1985 there were about 4,100, with a total production estimated at 48 percent of industrial output in the country. Most of them fell into the first type. By 1978 there were some 150 associations of the second type; their number was estimated to be about 220 in 1985 (Khorzov 1982: 62).

The full merger of research institutes with industrial enterprises as pursued in the Soviet Union, Bulgaria, and Romania is a controversial issue for at least two reasons. First, if fully executed, such a move inevitably curtails the authority of the central administration (including industrial ministries), which continues to be involved in managing the research sector. A complete merger would leave these authorities with no direct power and change them into advisory bodies. Second, it is questionable whether research institutes—particularly their top management—would find a merger with production associations more rewarding than their existing relationship with the central administration. The latter, being more distant, probably allows the institutes more room for some independent action than would a full merger.

To fully merge research institutes with associations, a complete financial integration is needed, such that the cost of research is covered by the same sources as the cost of manufacturing. Consequently, the performance of research institutes operating within associations must be reflected in the same indicators as the main activity—i.e., manufacturing. Since the nature of research activity is different from that of manufacturing, this kind of full integration could hurt at least some types of research work, particularly fundamental research of general importance and longer payoff. To avoid detrimental effects, some measure of independence would have to be granted to the research institutes—such as budgetary financing by the central authorities of basic research—and separate indicators of performance would have to be applied.

In many cases full integration is merely an organizational rearrangement, under which research institutes and enterprises are not fully controlled by the scientific production associations, but continue to receive their orders from higher echelons. For instance, in the Soviet Union these are the State Committee for Science and Technology and the applicable industrial ministries (Amann and Cooper, eds. 1982). In addition, the financing of research in the associations comes largely from different sources, often at different levels of the organizational hierarchy. Moreover, merged institutes and enterprises often continue to operate according to different wage schemes and are given separate targets for (among other things) the utilization of labor, new hirings, workforce structure, and total wage bills.

PRICING RESEARCH RESULTS

Pricing Inventions. One question about managing research in any economic system is whether the results of research should be priced (in a way similar to that for manufactured goods) and if so, how. In the original CPE planning system, no prices were applied to the results of research. With the changes in research management in the 1960s the central authorities decided to promulgate regulations on the pricing of research products (including technical services for industrial enterprises). This reform has progressed particularly in the Soviet Union, Poland, Czechoslovakia, and East Germany (see Bentley 1981).

According to one line of thought, the reason for implementing prices is simply to provide users with better information on the "economic scarcity" of their technology inputs and allow research institutes to finance their expansion from current revenues. Another perspective is that prices should be directly related to economic benefits, allowing research institutes to share the advantage of applied inventions with users (as benefits from the higher quality of products are split between manufacturers and customers).

This reform has brought some improvement to the work of research institutes for reasons other than simply putting them on a more equal footing with enterprises. For one thing, the institutes have been made more sensitive to a proper calculation of the costs of particular projects and to the utilitarian value of potential inventions. For another, the introduction of pricing has complemented other new arrangements, amounting to a general shift of research institutes from budgeting-type to accounting-type organizations.

This kind of pricing system, whatever its actual design, is confronted with several problems, especially because of the special nature of research sectors anywhere, not just in the CPEs. One problem stems from the fact that a given technology is usually supplied from very few if not just one specialized source. In such a situation the new technology very often puts its supplier in a position of a natural monopolist, thus making the verification of costs—the basic component of any price—rather difficult (Poznanski 1981). This is very different from the situation in the manufacturing sector, where theoretically there are many sources of goods. If the central authorities do not try to allocate supplies independently of the user enterprises, the offer prices for manufactured products can be more accurately compared, and there is—more important—the possibility of replacing more expensive supplies with others.

There is some evidence that the conditions created by the price mechanism for an increase in research productivity are not fully utilized. A piece of evidence comes from Poland, where the pricing rules state that the price to be paid by a contracting party (say the enterprise) should cover all the planned costs plus a profit margin ranging from 10 to 20 percent, depending on the importance of the expected result. This margin can be increased to 25 percent if the result is better than planned, and no markup is offered for projects which fail to materialize or are delayed. However, the common practice is that a uniform markup is agreed upon (i.e., around 15 percent) and never changed, regardless of the results (Poznanski 1982a). Moreover, even though planners expect that enterprises will not allow for cost overruns by research institutes, it is common practice that planned costs are revised upward.

Licensing Technology. While some moves have been made to allow research institutes to charge prices for their work, little has been done to create procedures for licensing existing technologies by one organization (a research institute or industrial enterprise) to another. Potential users continue to have unhampered and costless access to domestic technologies in most CPEs once these technologies have been developed and paid for by the initial recipient, thus showing a lack of consistency in the announced policy of making technology a marketable good priced according to its costs and/or utility.

Among the few attempts to introduce domestic licensing has been a series of regulations in the Soviet Union allowing enterprises to sign contracts and charge other enterprises for the transfer of technology. In the late 1960s enterprises were allowed to charge for the direct costs of a contract—such as preparing blueprints or giving technical advice—but these changes were not intended to help enterprises recoup the actual costs of research. The original law was not precise enough on how to calculate a charge, but a series of decrees in the early 1970s made it clear that only very limited charges were permitted.

Hungary has moved further than any country in the region in instituting a domestic licensing system. Its enterprises have been given effective protection through domestic patents and the ability to charge other users (including foreigners) for subsequent commercial application of their technology. Also important, individuals not affiliated with a state agency can sign a license with a domestic or foreign enterprise. The domestic purchase of technologies has to be covered by users from their profits, thus making them at least theoretically sensitive to the price charged by sellers.

Reports from the Soviet Union and Hungary on the effectiveness of licensing are mixed. Soviet economists say that licensing has not worked because of the low sums an enterprise can charge a potential user. The Soviet media are full of complaints by suppliers that entered contracts and found returns less than gratifying. In Hungary state buyers do not try to shop around for technologies because they have found the costs of licenses too high. On many occasions workers have sabotaged technology taken from other enterprises, in part because they did not want their bonuses reduced to pay for that technology (Dezsenyi-Guellette 1983).

MOTIVATION STRUCTURE IN RESEARCH

In the original scheme for research institutes, where the crucial target was full utilization of the assigned budget, the only important incentive was the administrative correction of the basic wage fund. This simple system proved to have some shortcomings, particularly in that it did not provide a proper framework for rewarding better individual performance by some researchers. Moreover, it did not strongly stimulate research organizations to shorten the duration of particular research projects or select projects with the highest potential value for users (see Amann and Cooper, eds. 1982).

In the 1960s all the CPEs switched to more aggressive financial stimulation and imposed a number of performance indicators, including those reflecting the practical effects of new technology supplied by a given research institute. In other words, a move was made toward linking the wage and other funds with the quality and applicability of research work. This idea has been embodied in a number of financial instruments developed by all the economies in the region, but on a quite variable scale. The Soviet Union has been particularly innovative, while Poland (for instance) has experimented with some of the most aggressive motivational schemes.

The most profound reform in motivational structure has been a change in the status of research institutes from state-budget-financed to business accounting units. They work on contracts with their supervisory ministries, directly with industrial enterprises of the same branch or (more rarely) with enterprises outside the branch. This reform started in the Soviet Union in 1962 (see Berliner 1976), and soon almost all research institutes in that country had turned to a business accounting system and contracts for work. Within this system the research institutes have to cover their expenses—including wages—with the revenues from contracted work, paid not simply according to the costs of a particular project but also in some proportion to the utilitarian value of the technology delivered and the timing of work completion (see Nolting 1976a). Similar arrangements have been introduced in Eastern Europe as well, with Bulgaria making the move as late as 1981 (Maczynska 1984).

According to the current regulation of research contracts, customers are obliged by law to pay the costs of work as agreed. However, in some countries such as the Soviet Union (based on regulations from 1967 and 1968) a research institute has to pay for any additional expenses needed to improve a new technology if the initial parameters of the technique are below those stated in the contract, and it has to pay 4 percent of the actual costs of the completed project if such additional corrections take more time than agreed upon with the customer. Markups on top of actual costs of research are also tied to the timing of work involved and the quality of delivered technology, in the sense that higher than average markups are paid for faster completion of projects and better technical parameters than negotiated in the original contract (see Poznanski et al. 1977).

This contractual system has been designed in such a way that even if put in a proper setting, it should not be expected to provide strong motivation for timely and well-focused research. The critical point is that a research institute runs no risk of not being paid for a failed project, except for some minor financial sacrifices. In addition, the impact of markups on individual incomes is substantially reduced by the fact that in most CPEs a specific project does not provide bonuses to the individuals involved. Rather markup fees go into one fund, a part of which supplements basic wages. Even if the benefits of efficient work were transferred to individuals according to their contributions, the very fact that money comes from a common pot weakens motivation. If bonuses were paid on a project basis to the individuals directly involved, the attractiveness of the reward would be greater.

Only Poland has gone beyond the system of bonuses paid through a joint fund. In 1973 a special fund (called the fund of implementation effects) was introduced to allow individuals involved in research projects to participate directly in the results of commercializing the research from these projects. Research institutes were authorized to collect a certain percentage of cost reductions over the first three years and to pay individuals both in the institutes and enterprises involved. Special provisions were made to exclude employees who were involved only indirectly from receiving bonuses.

The evolution of this Polish fund is a good example of how much wishful thinking can be involved in certain systemic reforms. For instance, at one point legislators went so far as to structure the permitted payments (i.e., rates of writeoff for the fund and the duration of the payments) in such a way as to stimulate larger rather than incremental technology implementations. They also tried to focus the attention of research institutes and enterprises on product changes by writing appropriate provisions into the law. Even more ideas on how to modify the original regulation have been proposed but never implemented due to the slowness of legislation and some confusion among the central planners regarding which way to head.

It has been recently revealed that the effects of commercial applications were arbitrarily calculated and that some researchers were given astronomical sums for rather trivial technological improvements. In some extreme cases enterprises were allowing for the creation of such funds on the basis of the effects obtained from technologies which had in fact been developed without any participation of the recipient research institutes because regulations prohibited payments to individuals in the enterprises for implementations other than those based on the technologies provided by the research institutes.

Despite some positive results, the bonuses provided by such schemes as the implementation effects funds, or even contract-related payments, cannot compete with those that continue to be offered by supervisory bodies for compliance with traditional plan targets—particularly the utilization of the annual budget for research and the number of projects to be completed in a given plan period. As Amann and Cooper, eds. (1982: 31) report, the research budget remains a key criterion in the Soviet machine-tool industry—one of the few branches on the forefront of the reform movement—and the most important bonuses paid to institutes depend on the fulfillment of this target. This is partly because the branch ministries, having a firm control over institutes, find it easier to execute these rather formalistic targets than to enforce the efficient use of resources for research.

IMPLEMENTATION OF TECHNOLOGY BY ENTERPRISES

PLAN TARGETS

From the very early days of central planning technological change in enterprises has been promoted mostly through direct plan targets set by central authorities. The evolution of decision-making on technological changes at the enterprise level has been generally aimed at providing some kind of order in the various technological targets that enterprises receive. It has also been aimed at attaching a higher priority to these targets to counterbalance other, often conflicting, objectives and at improving the system for monitoring the fulfillment of the technological targets.

A good illustration of this process of providing order to technological targets is in East Germany. Up to 1960 state enterprises were receiving three separate plans—one for adopting finished designs and processes, one for standardization, and one for organizational improvements. In 1961 the list was expanded to include another three sections—covering the introduction of research results, the implementation of inventions designated as important, and the goals for automation of manufacturing processes. In 1962 these plans were split into two sections—one for product changes and the other for process technologies. These technological targets remain a main vehicle for central intervention into technological changes at state enterprises (Bentley 1981).

Technological targets in the CPEs are supplemented by other plan targets intended to pressure enterprises to make additional technological improvements and adopt additional rationalization measures. From early on, enterprises had been given targets for annual reductions in the total costs of production, changes in labor (or total factor) productivity, and savings in the use of inputs such as energy. While almost continuously used by the central authorities, these targets have been particularly high priorities in periods of economic stress (for example, the most recent campaign on energy savings).

PRICING OF GOODS

The technology policy implemented in the first years of Soviet planning directed technological changes without the intervention of prices. Prices were seen as useless except for their computational function. Accordingly, most prices were set by the central authorities on the basis of data provided by enterprises and were calculated as a sum of costs of production. For a given type of product, they were set on the basis of average cost for a number of enterprises (not on the basis of the marginal supplier's cost).

The pricing mechanism has undergone many changes since, but not in the locus of decision-making. In some countries, decision-making authority has partly been passed down to associations and to enterprises themselves in the course of simplifying the procedures for approving certain price revisions. However, with very few exceptions (e.g., farm markets in Bulgaria, Poland, or the Soviet Union) prices continue to be set centrally in all countries in the region except Hungary. In Hungary enterprises decide most prices themselves, with some prices having to conform to limits determined by the central authorities in order to avoid too drastic changes in prices for individual goods. Enterprises are excluded from pricing decisions for only a few goods of special importance (to allow the authorities to protect lower income groups or keep inflation low).

The centralization of all decisions on product prices limits how flexible prices can be to follow changes in supply and demand. The amount of administrative work involved in price revisions and registration of new prices is such that even a sizable central agency is (as evidence suggests) not able to make all the decisions in time and/or properly check the reliability of the calculations submitted. To ease these limitations, the price commissions in most CPEs are supported by many research institutes, design bureaus, and the like (e.g., almost 200,000 such organizations in the Soviet Union), which are obliged to gather necessary data and perform time-consuming calculations. Most of these organizations represent the interests of industry, making the problem of reliability great.

For the most part, the major effort in price reforms has gone not into the reallocation of the decision locus, but into methods of calculating prices. Some changes have been aimed directly at having prices promote technological change. The most important reform was in the late 1960s in the Soviet Union, giving state-owned enterprises the right to apply above-average profit markups (i.e., above average for all the producers of a similar product) for new goods (Berliner 1976). The price of new goods can be changed by an innovating enterprise only for a certain period—usually three to four years—after which the price (in practice, the markup) has to come down to the average for the given group of products. All decisions within this system are set by the central authorities, and they are responsible for enforcing the yearly reductions to the final lowest level.

There is not much evidence that the attempt to use price rules to stimulate technological change has proved successful. A common practice among state enterprises in Poland and the Soviet Union has been to apply temporarily higher prices for goods which often represent a very minor or insignificant improvement over their predecessors. Moreover, due to the slowness of decisions by state pricing bodies, the gradual reduction of preferential prices to the product average level is not fully executed. In the Soviet Union, for instance, many preferential prices remain at a higher value indefinitely. Although of little help in promoting technological changes, preferential prices are seen by many as a vehicle for inflation.

MOTIVATIONS FOR INNOVATION

Personnel Policy. All CPEs run a "nomenklatura" system for appointing industrial managers and other top officials. This centralization of top personnel decisions is a powerful instrument for directing the economy since the threat of displacement or removal of officials allows the leadership to exert effective influence over the motivation of managerial staff. Even if given some leeway to decide specific matters in daily production, centrally appointed managers may be not only responsive to central commands, but also work to motivate their employees toward approved behavior. In other words, if well handled, the centralized personnel policy may provide strong support at the enterprise level for targets in the national plans.

Throughout the region there has been a continuous trend toward replacing political appointees, who dominated the picture in the first years of central planning, by professional staff, most with a technical education. Professionals with an education in economics, accounting, and organizational theory have also made it to the top in industrial management. The preference for technocrats has made state-owned enterprises operate more according to technological considerations, which in itself should have some positive impact on innovation in production.

There have also been some attempts at basing personnel decisions on an explicit evaluation of technological performance, such as the policy by Yuri Andropov and Mikhail Gorbachev of firing managers unable to maintain a sufficiently high quality of production. This policy has some limits, however, because the managerial group is a part of the political structure which the central authorities have to canvass for support. So harsh personnel decisions can backfire if managers find sanctions unacceptable and react by refusing to support central authority.

Financial Bonuses. The complement to central personnel decisions is a system of monetary rewards for good technological performance. It has clear advantages over the personnel-decisions mechanism since it is at least potentially less antagonizing to the relationship between the central authorities and management. Also, it provides the central decision-makers with more flexibility because monetary rewards (i.e., bonuses) can be more easily attached to individual projects and better related to their actual outcomes. By its nature, the personnel mechanism has to focus on a long-run evaluation of managerial performance, while bonuses can be used to turn the attention of managers to short-run targets as well.

Until the mid-1950s there was no explicit system of centrally supervised financial rewards aimed specifically at technological innovation in enterprises. Since then explicit systems have been developed in all countries of the region. These schemes have gone in several directions, linking general bonuses (particularly for managers) with the fulfillment of technological targets. They also use separate funds to reward individuals for successful technological projects sponsored by the central authorities or undertaken by enterprises.

While the number of financial bonuses is quite substantial in all the CPEs, the payments to individuals are generally small. This is well documented in the studies of the Soviet Union by Berliner (1976) and Freris (1984). They show that all technology-related bonuses, except those paid for from funds tied to a general performance indicator, represent not more than 2 percent of total wages and around 5 percent of salaries of non-line personnel (i.e., supervisory staff, design engineers). For individuals who actually receive such bonuses, respective shares are higher, and they weigh more in relation to salaries since only a small percentage of all employees is rewarded that way. As Berliner's (1976) study shows, however, even individual payments are not high.

CPE planners have been quite creative and persistent in modifying the planning machinery for research and innovation. For the most part, they have focused on providing micro-level organizations—research institutes and enterprises in particular—with material incentives to stimulate better use of resources and promote changes, while at the same time improving the control of central authorities over these agents. In the reform process the planners clearly have been trying to imitate some market-type mechanisms without allowing the market to infringe even slightly on the control powers of the central economic leadership. Thus the real sense of these reforms has been to rationalize or routinize the planning machinery and not to move away from the systemic principles of firm central control over all economic matters. Central planners remain the sources of key decisions, while research institutes are assigned to supply the inventions required by the state planners, and enterprises are forced—or stimulated—to implement the results of research; thus in the CPEs research and innovation are driven by the supply side. This arrangement still differs fundamentally from that under a market system, where research is mostly done in response to demand from enterprises, whose decisions on whether to innovate or not are in turn motivated by changing demand conditions or by the enterprises' market strategy.

Chapter 2

SYSTEM FOR DIFFUSION AND QUALITY UPGRADING

THE INVESTMENT MECHANISM AND DIFFUSION

LOCUS OF DECISIONMAKING

Under the traditional CPE system—unlike in the market system—investment decisions, one of the main functions of planners, are highly centralized. Central planners decide not only about the allocation of investment resources to branches of the economy, but also about the construction of new plants, the expansion of existing plants, and any sizable purchases of machinery. Moreover, the choices of technology for projects—choices that determine the appropriate capital intensity and the like—are also in the domain of planners. Enterprises generally have decisionmaking power only for minor projects, though they influence decisionmaking through informal channels—say, by manipulating data used to evaluate investment projects.

Under the traditional system, state enterprises have no right to acquire other enterprises, either in the same branch or outside it, by purchasing all or some of their assets. This means that innovative enterprises cannot make capital acquisitions that would promote the diffusion of a given innovation—a common procedure in the market systems. Nor are there substitute mechanisms—such as centrally decided mergers—that would enable enterprises to propagate technological change through organizational fusion. Most of the central decisions about mergers are motivated by criteria other than diffusion, such as considerations of scale and simplified procedures.

Such bureaucratic machinery for investment decisions makes it difficult for planners to respond flexibly. To ease this problem, some of the countries have tried to delegate some investment decisions to managers, a reform that has succeeded only in Hungary—and only half way even there. Under this reform in Hungary, enterprise managers are permitted to seek investment resources from banks. In fact, however, investment credits are not distributed purely on the basis of how profitable a project may be. Banks are given very specific instructions by planners about who deserves what. (Reportedly they are given more than a dozen different criteria of project evaluation, one of which is profit.) Because enterprise resources are not sufficient for financing most projects—it is estimated that only 10-15 percent of enterprise projects are fully covered by such resources—managers have to supplement these means with the heavily overregulated bank credits (and occasionally resources obtained from the budget). This gives the planners strong leverage in the decision process for "decentralized" investments. Thus there is much sharing of investment decisions by Hungarian enterprises and investment planners.

Thus far there has not been much interest in Eastern Europe to get the private sector—where it still exists—more involved in investment decisionmaking. Only the Hungarians have introduced a viable package of policies in recent years to attempt to reverse the drop of the private sector's share in total employment from 24 percent in 1960 to only 4 percent in 1970 (Tardos 1982). The expansion of private enterprises has been encouraged particularly in services, including restaurants and small stores. In most cases state establishments have simply been leased or sold to private individuals, and flexible arrangements have been made concerning pricing, bookkeeping, and sales.

This does not mean that the Hungarian government has embarked on a large-scale reprivatization of the economy, however—certainly not in the key manufacturing industries. Instead it has decided to promote cooperatives by allowing mixed forms of production, whereby state enterprises subcontract elements of their work to domestic cooperatives. The government recently decided to allow small cooperative groups to operate within state-run farms. Moreover, similar cooperative groups with separate accounts can be established within state-run industrial enterprises to manufacture products of their own choice and price. The financial rules applied to them are the same as those for state-run enterprises.

FINANCING OF INVESTMENT PROJECTS

Budgetary Financing. The logical complement of the traditional investment system has been sole budgetary financing of projects. Under such a scheme central planners have had both the authority to initiate projects and the financial means to carry them out. Not much has changed in the financial rules considering that the locus of decisionmaking has not changed either (as we have noted).

Budgetary financing has done little to promote technological change because it does not provide strong incentives for investors to search for optimal projects or economize on scarce resources. Though not limitless, budgetary investment funds have a zero price to associations and enterprises for which a plant or production line is built. Due to the obvious scarcity of investment resources handled by the central authorities, lower-level organizations have to compete for them with other units within the same branch of industry. This competition is resolved not by the economic benefits of projects, but by connections and bargaining power.

To make investors sensitive to completion schedules and costs of projects, central planners have been experimenting with various instruments, including financial penalties for overruns. In Poland, for instance, the banks are responsible for overseeing particular projects, and they penalize investors for overruns by withdrawing specified amounts of money from their calculated annual profits. Another instrument, also tried in Poland, has been to tighten the cash flow to enterprises that do not comply with centrally determined deadlines for depreciating budget-financed projects (Glikman and Poznanski 1976).

Nonbudgetary Financing. Because a standard setting and similar measures have been of little help, many countries in the region have looked for nonbudgetary means for financing investment, including a wider use of discretionary funds by enterprises, on the assumption that enterprises would be more careful in allocating their own funds. Such a line of reforms has been tried by almost all the countries in the region, though the specific arrangements have not been uniform (e.g., methods vary in how enterprises accumulate resources for their own investment).

Most of these discretionary investment funds have been short-lived or only marginal sources of investment resources. As a rule, the funds accumulated at the enterprise level have been partially confiscated whenever an economy was going through difficulties. In Poland, where every shock has led to the short-run expansion of budgetary financing at the expense of enterprise funds, the share of these funds in total investment has only occasionally exceeded 10 percent. Enterprise funds have also been cut back during difficult periods because of attempts by the central authorities to exploit the tensions which emerge at such times so as to restore their previous power and avoid what they see as confusion resulting from independent decisions by enterprises.

Another line of changes has been to expand the role of bank credits, but in almost all cases these reforms have failed. Most CPEs have instituted some form of pseudo-credit system, under which the selection of investment projects has remained fully centralized while their financing has simply been shifted from the state budget to the state banks, carefully following the detailed decisions by central authorities for the extension of projects. By and large, no interest rate has been charged—or none with any relation to the current scarcity of investment funds. The only country in the region to radically reduce the role of budgetary financing has been (as noted) Hungary.

Recently there has been some interest in instituting a capital market in Hungary to stimulate a more efficient use of investment resources by state enterprises. The government announced in 1982 that a limited bond market would be opened. Bonds are available only to state enterprises and cooperatives, but the government intends to allow private citizens to buy them as well. (Bonds offer a higher yield than most available bank accounts.) This reform is still in an early phase, but there is no indication that it is intended as a first step to shift responsibility from the state bureaucracy to a capital market.

Despite continuous political calls for improving technological performance, almost none of the countries in the region has experimented with an investment fund aimed exclusively at financing risky technological changes. Funds for narrowly defined activities have been created to stimulate export-oriented production (as in Hungary and Poland) but not to promote technological change. An exception is a recent Hungarian decision to set up a special fund (with the participation of the finance ministry) to promote innovations. However, only state enterprises can apply to the fund, which is much smaller than the fund for export promotion.

The way that planners in Hungary operate financial instruments reduces the innovative stimulus which can be generated. Economic rules are frequently modified or replaced by new legislation. During 1968-76 the government made more than seven hundred changes in the existing financial rules, and the number of "legal interpretations" and "internal instructions" from branch ministries was probably very high as well (Szabo 1974: 1-9). Such constant modifications make profits more dependent on revisions and additions to existing laws than on genuine enterprise efforts, thus reducing the motivation for technological change.

Also reducing enterprise motivation is a heavy tax on profits. The burden of taxation has been fluctuating in the past years due to changes in tax legislation, but taxation is always at a very high level. In 1972 about 63 percent of profit increases were collected by the state, with another 4 percent collected as reserves. Only 33 percent of the incremental profit was kept by enterprises to provide them with resources for investment (17 percent) and wage increases (16 percent). This means that the growth of profits had only a marginal impact on wages, though the maximization of wages is a major objective of Hungarian enterprises—as it is for all CPE enterprises (Balazsy 1979). The most recent reform has allowed Hungarian enterprises to retain a larger fraction of their profits.

In addition to heavy taxes, the effect of financial rules on the behavior of state enterprises—in Hungary as well as in other CPEs—is "softened" by the fact that most financial instruments are highly individualized. For example, all taxes and levies linked to wages are differentiated by branches of the economy, or even by segments of particular branches. The motive is to help unsuccessful enterprises—particularly to finance their wage needs. But this reduces the pressure on inefficient enterprises to come up with technological improvements, especially if they can count on the planners' good will to collect lower (or no) taxes over longer periods of time. At the same time, efficient enterprises are discouraged from undertaking some needed changes in production because these offer small returns.

INVESTMENT AND CONSTRUCTION

The choices made centrally are translated into concrete projects mostly by specialized organizations called investment project bureaus. Subordinated for the most part to the branch ministries, their function is to formulate the designs for new plants and production lines and to specify the machinery that is to be installed and the sources of that machinery. Thus the bureaus have an important voice in influencing the way new technology embodied in machinery is spread through the economy, though not necessarily in line with what is desired by or is optimal for enterprises for which new capacity is built. This separation of project activities from enterprises clearly has some impact on technological change. For one thing, the investment project bureaus lack much of the detailed information available in enterprises, particularly on incremental changes undertaken by enterprises without assistance from the bureaus. For another, the enterprises lack the power to push the bureaus in a desired direction since the bureaus are financially independent of enterprise management.

Since the beginning of central planning, most construction work—i.e., the step after design—has been assigned to special organizations, with only some left to the industrial enterprises themselves. These construction organizations were originally subordinated to various central bodies, particularly the branch ministries, local authorities, and special central bodies responsible purely for construction work. The organizations have a statutory obligation to provide services for a given branch of industry or geographical territory and are only exceptionally assigned jobs outside their administrative unit.

This system of construction enterprises has slowed the diffusion process by placing these enterprises in a monopolistic position, enabling them to pursue their interests at the expense of customers. In general, the construction enterprises prefer routine projects (Schroeder 1979: 323-24). They also tend to prefer large projects which make them look better and require less supervision. For the same reason, they prefer projects with longer building periods (thus reducing the diffusion of smaller projects and taking money away from machinery and equipment outlays).

QUALITY UPGRADING AND PROBLEMS OF OBSOLESCENCE

PRODUCT IMPROVEMENT

Output maximization continues to dominate the plan targets that CPEs set for enterprises, but over the years quality upgrading has significantly increased in priority. Several devices (such as the pricing changes noted above) have been built into enterprise plans to promote high quality. In addition, in the 1960s most of the countries introduced obligatory quality rating systems for all products; central authorities used these systems to determine targets for enterprises and discontinue certain products. For instance, since 1968 one part of Soviet industry has operated a rating system for all products in three categories every three years (Hill 1984a, 1984b). Relying on these ratings, the central authorities give yearly output targets for products classified in the highest category, while those in the lowest category are targeted for discontinuation.

Some countries have also designed financial incentives to stimulate enterprises to upgrade the quality of their products. Generally the product quality targets—they are not standards—are associated with preset bonuses and sanctions. However, few specific funds are designed to pay such bonuses. Instead the fulfillment of product quality targets is one element in the performance evaluation of an enterprise, determining the bonus payments to managers. The only important attempt to create a direct link between quality and incentives has been an experiment in the Soviet Union with additional profit margins for new products classified in the highest ratings category.

The more accurate an assessment of actual quality, the more effective product improvement can be. The most objective assessment would be one made by an institution independent of the supplying enterprise but certainly including a representative of the latter. The presence of the customers is needed too. In some countries, such institutions exist (for example, Soviet state rating commissions; Gustafson 1981: 33), comprising the principal customer, the branch ministry, and representatives from other central administration agencies (e.g., the Ministry of Domestic Trade). These institutions face many problems, however—among them the preponderant influence of the interested branch ministry, which also has the best knowledge and equipment needed for quality testing.

An important element of quality upgrading is the standardization system, which specifies technical requirements for the construction and performance of particular products. In the Soviet Union it is the State Committee for Standards that sets requirements for manufactures. Since 1968 the realization of standards has been one of the targets of annual enterprise plans. While the standardization system allows the central administration to put some pressure on enterprises to upgrade their products, its effectiveness is limited. For example, as Hill (1984a, 1984b) and others report, the standards in many branches of the machine industry tend to follow those of Western models. However, enterprises have considerable opportunities to make the central authorities soften the requirements. Moreover, the practical execution of the standards in force is not easy to achieve (Martens 1986).

The state-sponsored institutions for rating quality cannot fully protect consumers from shoddy goods. Only strong consumers can do so. Consumer protection as a means of ensuring high quality has been recommended by many CPE economists (e.g., in Poland by Mujzel 1981). In all the CPE countries the voice of consumers is heard through the official media, which frequently publish criticisms of low quality goods and their manufacturers. Generally, however, there are no journals exclusively devoted to consumer opinion, and the institutionalization of the consumer movement is embryonic. The exception is Poland, where a formally independent consumer protection organization was set up in 1982 with a widely available weekly magazine completely devoted to quality and price issues.

DISCONTINUING OBSOLETE PRODUCTION

Another aspect of quality promotion is the elimination of inferior products. In the first decade of rapid postwar industrialization, removing obsolete lines of production was by no means critical. With the vast investment programs and increases in employment, the demand for products of any quality largely exceeded supplies. This in turn made the leadership link economic advancement with output. From that perspective, eliminating technologically obsolete but physically operational lines of production was seen as undermining the main goal of maximizing output. In the early 1960s the need to eliminate older lines became more obvious, partly due to the involuntary stockpiling of such consumer goods as wool and cotton stockings and old-fashioned vacuum-tube radios. Additional pressures on old production lines came in the 1970s as a result of constraints on such inputs as energy and materials.

The growing appreciation for the need to eliminate obsolete products and processes has resulted in a number of adjustments. Enterprise production plans have been the prime instruments for speeding up this elimination. As noted, the production plans in most CPEs specify which products are to be discontinued in a given period. The targets are set on the basis of detailed information that enterprises provide to branch ministries. Products of a certain age are classified in a separate category, and interested ministries select the ones to be discontinued. (Usually there is a desirable average discontinuation age for a given group of products; Berliner 1976.)

Decisions to scrap products cannot be based simply on an assessment of their relative technological level, and there is no economic rationale for the complete elimination of all older products and processes on purely technological considerations. By the same token, the extended use of some old technology should not in itself be considered as evidence of an industry's lack of interest in rapid technological modernization. A number of studies have shown that even in industries which have gone through dramatic modernization, older and newer technology coexist. For instance, virtually every large, fully integrated steel mill in the United States had open-hearth facilities in operation in 1974, after more than a decade of the rapid expansion of the more technologically advanced basic oxygen furnace (see Rosegger 1980).

Decisions to eliminate obsolete production lines are usually controversial. Often there are strong forces operating on the enterprise level against discontinuation. For instance, workers tend to push for the continued use of traditional machinery and products since they are familiar with them. Managers may feel uneasy about eliminating some production lines that still provide some benefits (such as serving as buffers in periods of stress). For similar reasons central authorities do not easily reach unanimous conclusions about obsolescence. They tend to prefer partial changes in existing plants and (if need be) complete restructuring to closure. In general, every agent from the branch ministry to the single enterprise is responsible for absorbing employees who lose their jobs due to the replacement of old production lines. This policy greatly reduces the concerns of workers about the replacement of old machinery or a shift to new products. However, the policy is not without cost since partial changes or restructuring can be more expensive than other choices (such as building a completely new plant).

Thus far the region as a whole has not actively restructured its economy to eliminate branches where the technological advantage over other countries is doubtful. To introduce such a policy would require many new instruments which are not widely developed (if they exist at all) —e.g., retraining programs, compensation schemes, cross-industry placement offices. Hungary is introducing some of these instruments to make its recently announced structural policy work properly (see Poznanski 1983). Poland has introduced compensation schemes and some other instruments to reallocate labor and other resources to priority industries.

Reforms in the investment field—critical for diffusion processes—have been more conservative than have systemic changes in other areas of the economy. Moreover, decentralization measures have most frequently failed in this area after a short time, giving way to earlier, centralized arrangements. Although CPE planners are more determined to create incentives for quality upgrading and the prompt discontinuation of obsolete technologies, here (as with research innovations) competitive forces have not been allowed, nor have provisions been made to increase the role of consumers as a form of pressure on producers.

In sum, decisions on the full-scale application of any technology are still strictly determined by the central investment plan, which covers investment projects, the type of technology applied, and the requisite financing. Under these circumstances, the scope and speed of diffusion is of course up to the central planners. It is also in their domain to decide when a technology must be phased out to make room for a newer product or process. In contrast, in market systems decisions on both the adoption and discontinuation of technology belong to market enterprises, with state administration, even in publicly owned industries, playing a decisively smaller role.

PART 2

TECHNOLOGICAL AND TRADE PERFORMANCE: THE CPES COMPARED TO THE WEST AND TO THE NICS

In this section we shall try to determine whether the reforms described in Part 1, combined with a shift toward Western technology imports, have helped the CPEs improve their technological performance relative to market-type economies. (We shall leave aside a related issue— namely, by how much [or how far] these policies have allowed the CPEs to accelerate their absolute technological development.) As noted, our primary interest is in analyzing possible changes in technological gaps, a more demanding criterion for technological success.

To obtain a comprehensive picture of the relative performance of the CPEs, we shall use two different types of analyses. First, we shall compare the changes in technological levels of the CPEs with those of Western market economies. We call this comparison "forward-looking" since the CPEs are set against the historically more technologically advanced countries of the West. Second, we shall turn to a "backward-looking" analysis, in which the point of reference for CPE technology will be a group of NICs which began with a clear disadvantage vis-à-vis the CPEs in the first postwar decades.

We shall employ numerous indicators of technological performance, as well as some economic measures that can serve as indirect signals for possible trends in technological development. (The latter are mostly derived from trade statistics.) Various indicators are used because none of them is perfect, as we make clear below. Consequently, our conclusions are not derived from an observation of a single indicator of technological performance, and never from tracking other indicators. Only after relating and analyzing various indicators do we make a general statement on technological performance.

The comparison is complicated by the fact that most of the East Europeans (but not the Soviet Union) have been forced since

1979-80 to terminate their ambitious growth plans. In the case of Poland and Romania an unprecedented crisis has occurred, forcing them to make radical trade adjustments, including deep cuts in imports, reductions in the volume of exports, and shifts in export composition. Many other East Europeans have taken similar steps which differ only in degree. In consequence, trade data are of less use in studying the last few years, and a larger burden of proof falls on direct indicators of technological progress.

Chapter 3

MEASUREMENT OF TECHNOLOGICAL PERFORMANCE

Economic performance can be measured in many ways. It is in itself a multidimensional concept, and most aspects of it can be quantified using different yardsticks. The measurement of technological performance represents one very important aspect of overall economic performance. Since the quantification of technological performance takes up much of this book, it may be helpful to begin with a discussion of the available measurements and their comparative value.

A country's technological level, or the difference in technological advancement between two countries—here called the technological gap—can be measured in three basic ways: the technology supplies (i.e., inventions) available; the scope of practical applications of new technology; and the economic impact of such applications. These indicators are discussed below with the focus on the measures most frequently used for quantitative purposes.

INDICATORS OF TECHNOLOGY SUPPLIES

One of the essential factors reflecting the technological performance of an economic system is its ability to supply new technology. The larger these supplies, the more opportunities become available for enterprises and/or governments to replace old technologies or enter unexplored areas. A move from lower to higher levels of technology is generally associated with increasing supplies of technology, either generated domestically or imported, and the reverse relationship is true as well.

The simplest way of measuring domestically generated technology is to establish the amount of inputs devoted to such activity (see Freeman 1974). These inputs can be expressed in financial or physical terms (e.g., number of employees), resources involved in education and research, and storage and dissemination of technological information. (The last aspect is stressed in particular by Machlup 1962). Inputs of foreign technology can be measured in many ways. An effort to acquire a foreign education, for instance, can be expressed in terms of expenditure on overseas studies by nationals of a given country (including payments by host countries) or the number of people involved. Spending on research activities abroad (e.g., by subsidiaries of multinational corporations) can be used as a measure of the available supplies of foreign technology, as can the number of agreements to license technology from foreign companies or the payments (i.e., royalties) involved in such transactions.

The shortcomings of such input-type indicators are multifold, particularly where comparative analysis is concerned. The same inputs in domestic research by two countries can result in different supplies of technology if domestic productivity varies. Productivity can vary not only because the skills of the respective research workers may be different, but also if inputs are allocated differently. (E.g., if one country does not spend enough on the developmental stage, fewer potentially commercially valuable discoveries are likely to result; the same is true if the country is more heavily involved in research in industrial sectors which offer fewer opportunities for technological discoveries.) Moreover, countries differ in the way they define and report inputs into technological production. Generally statistics on such inputs are much less developed than many other economic indicators. (In the United States, where research statistics are well advanced, companies have fully reported their expenditures only since the late 1970s. Previously official figures were based on sample survey sources.) Many countries—especially the CPEs—use very broad and imprecise classifications under the category of research, while others are more restrictive.

To avoid the drawbacks of input-type indices, indirect measures of technology supplies can be used. Publications such as doctoral dissertations, patent descriptions, and professional articles provide one set of measures. Since these publications can differ in quality, the data they present may not fully reflect the actual supplies of technology. This shortcoming is at least partially resolved by supplementary indicators (e.g., in the case of a citation index, an independently designed ranking system for journals or publishers can be utilized).

Another useful indirect indicator of supplies is the number of patents granted to nationals domestically and internationally. This is a useful measure since patent statistics are well developed and have a long tradition (antedating the modern industrial system in the United States; Schmookler 1966). However, patents at best reflect a minor part of technology supplies since few developments of commercial value, and almost none involving basic discoveries, are subject to patenting. In addition, the propensity to patent differs substantially from one sector of industry to another—clearly a factor distorting any comparison between countries with different industrial structures (Pavitt 1983). International patent comparisons can also be imperfect because (as with professional publications) patents can differ in terms of quality (e.g., a patent on a major discovery vs. a patent for a minor improvement, not to mention a patent for an object or process which ultimately proves useless). In addition, patent laws are not equally restrictive in all countries, allowing those with very "soft" requirements regarding novelty and relevance to show relatively higher figures. (Reportedly patent legislation in the United States is more demanding than in many other Western countries; not only are fewer patents granted, but it takes longer as well.)

Given the aforementioned factors, foreign patents (granted by the patent office of one country to a national of another country) seem to be better indicators than domestic ones. Such data reduce the interference of legal differences among various patent systems. Also, since patenting abroad usually involves more effort and payments in foreign currency, it discourages at least some inventors from seeking overseas protection for irrelevant technologies that have nonetheless been patented domestically. (This would be the case particularly with countries, such as those of Eastern Europe, suffering from shortages of foreign currency.)

INDICATORS OF TECHNOLOGY APPLICATION

For an economy to benefit from technology supplies, production applications of new developments are essential. Thus changes in the technological level of production have to be measured independently of the technology supply measures discussed above. Only with these application indicators can one properly evaluate the practical significance of the data regarding technology supplies. In this sense, the application indicators are more important for good quantification of technological levels in various countries and of the gaps that may divide them.

Several basic indicators of technological levels are available, including listings of new products and processes introduced in a given time span. Such listings are available in most of the Western industrialized countries and in the CPEs, where they are routinely used for the evaluation of enterprises (as we noted in Chapter 2). These listings are very imperfect, particularly because standards for classifying "new" products and processes are not clear. (These data are particularly inflated in the CPEs for reasons indicated above.) Of help here are statistics of major innovations such as are prepared in the United States and regularly cited by the National Science Foundation's *Science Indicators*.

Another shortcoming of such data is that even if they present multiple listings for applications of a given technological innovation in more than one enterprise, the information is still not sufficient to judge on the exact scope of application. The scope can be precisely established only if we know the weight of the innovation compared to the weight of older technologies used in the same area of production. The shares can be established with several kinds of diffusion indicators, which we view as a second basic measure of applications. This measure deserves special attention since many economists (including the author) consider diffusion indices a very valuable tool.

The phenomenon of diffusion—i.e., the expanding use of a particular technology over time—can be quantified (among other ways) in absolute terms by determining the increasing number of new products made or the stock of new processes in use. This is a particularly valuable way of measuring diffusion when a new technology has no close substitutes (e.g., television in the early days). However, when there are close substitutes but no data on them are available or the data are too fragmented, the absolute indicator of diffusion of the new technology is the only appropriate measure. To make these absolute indicators suitable for cross-country comparison, the relevant data have to be normalized of course (e.g., number of new products per capita or per industrial worker).

An alternative measure is to use relative indicators of diffusion that include the following three procedures. First, the relative weight of the adopters of new technology (e.g., consumers, industrial enterprises) in the total population of potential users can be determined. Second, one can look at the share of a new technology, either by product type or process, in the total output of a particular branch of production (assuming that this production is heterogeneous). Third, a similar share can be calculated for final consumers of a new product (i.e., share of the product in a total stock). Of these three indicators, the second and third are the most reliable in terms of revealing the actual scope of application. (The first method does not capture this scope properly; see Poznanski 1983.)

With any of these indicators several diffusion parameters can be calculated, providing a base for estimating technological levels. One of the parameters is the so-called diffusion lag—i.e., the time elapsing between the first application of a new technology in a pioneer country (where diffusion begins) and adoption of the same technology in another country (for instance, see Cooper 1984). Another parameter is the speed of diffusion, expressed either in years (e.g., the time needed for a country to reach a certain level of application of a particular technology) or as an econometric coefficient, along the lines of several available models (e.g., Griliches's 1957 study of hybrid corn; Stoneman 1980). Finally, the "diffusion cycle" parameter, referring to the time needed to move from the starting point to full saturation of a technology, can be determined.

The technological level of production is determined not only by the frequency of new applications and the speed of their diffusion, but also by how fast an obsolete technology is removed. As an economy can benefit from the prompt innovation and rapid spread of technologies, so can it gain from the appropriate phasing out of inferior technologies. (The opposite is true as well: the retention of obsolete technologies can damage an economy.) This process of scrapping obsolete technology—to which we refer elsewhere as an "extinguishing process"—is ignored in technological evaluations; moreover, extinguishing is not likely to be fully revealed in a diffusion analysis alone (Poznanski 1986b).

In an analysis of extinguishing processes the critical parameters are analogous to those of diffusion, though their meaning is different. The "extinguishing lag" parameter measures the time difference between the saturation of diffusion of a particular technology and the point at which it begins to decline. (In a stylized world the scrapping of technology follows the peak point of diffusion, but this does not have to be the case.) Then an extinguishing speed can be established using years and coefficients as yardsticks. So can an extinguishing cycle—i.e., the time span between the beginning of a process and its complete phaseout (or the time when it reaches a very low, marginal level of use since many technologies tend to persist in small niches; see Rosegger 1980).

The major problem with the aforementioned indicators of technology applications is that the existing data base does not allow for full coverage of even the most important technologies that are being spread, or squeezed, into an economy. For instance, it is easy to analyze diffusion in the steel industry, but difficult in the case of automobile production. In addition, even the best data are generally highly aggregated, so that only some basic technological alternatives can be analyzed—for example, computers of three different generations. Due to this high aggregation, we cannot determine the pace of changes within basic categories, though the smaller improvements are often of great importance for the development of production in specific areas.

INDICATORS OF TECHNOLOGY IMPACTS

PRODUCTIVITY INDICES

Since technological changes bring quality improvements and/or lower manufacturing costs, they lead to changes in output/input ratios—i.e., in the productivity of inputs. Economists typically consider productivity changes as cost-reducing changes in the technology of production because the issue of product quality is not in the mainstream of economic theory. This has been in part a result of a lack of well-developed methods of measuring quality changes, though lately more work has been done in this area (e.g., Griliches 1985, etc.). However, there are no logical reasons for reducing productivity improvements to cost-saving changes in technology, nor does it make practical sense since the impact of quality improvements on actual—not necessarily fully measurable—output, and therefore on productivity, is economically important.

Depending on what type of input (i.e., production factor) is involved, we can distinguish several basic productivity indicators. Labor productivity relates output to inputs of labor (i.e., man-hours, number of employees), while capital productivity relates output to expenditure on capital. The ratio of output in a given period to combined inputs of labor and capital is called total factor productivity. Of these three measures, the most frequently used is labor productivity, apparently because it has been established in a number of studies of market economies that the productivity of capital tends to be constant over a longer period of time.

The first question to be considered here is what a productivity index really measures. Two important points must be kept in mind. First, productivity indicators, like many other aggregate measures, reflect a number of factors that in actual economic life affect input-output ratios, and the relevant technology is only one of them. Thus when the productivity of one input—labor or capital—is measured, changes in this indicator will reflect parallel changes (if any) in the magnitude of complementary inputs. For instance, the labor productivity indicator will reflect (among other things) a changing capital-labor ratio, with or without technological improvements in machinery.

Second, productivity indices reflect (again indirectly) changes in *average* technological level rather than at the technological frontier (i.e., best-practice technology). The aggregate represents the weighted productivity of individual plants and industries, usually operating heterogeneous technology. In other words, it is sensitive to structural changes in production—i.e., to a reallocation of resources from industries of lower productivity to those where inputs generate larger outputs, or the opposite (and to such reallocation within individual plants as well)

This is an important point which applies to many other aggregate indicators of technological level as well. Since a productivity index measures average technology, the productivity pattern for a country can indicate trends different from those suggested by indicators of best-practice technology. This is one reason, for example, why the productivity analysis by Gomulka (1971), concluding that the CPEs were successfully catching up with Western technology in the first three postwar decades, seems to be contradicted by (say) the study of Soviet technology in the same period by Amann, Cooper, and Davies (1977), which was based on best-practice indices, particularly diffusion measures. However, given our discussion above, these results may not be inconsistent at all.

Yet another complication with productivity indices stems from the fact that it is hard to get comparable data on total production and inputs of labor and capital in various countries. The methodology for calculating production is often different from one country to another. Considerable problems arise from the difficulty in measuring the underutilization of labor and capital. Some problems arise from inaccuracies in valuing capital stock due to changes in prices of consecutive vintages. These drawbacks should be borne in mind in interpreting changes in productivity.

TRADE INDICES

Another area in which the technological level of an economy is reflected is foreign trade. The relationship between export capabilities and technology has been discussed frequently in the theory of international trade, including the works of the so-called neo-technology school (i.e., a technology-gap model by Posner 1961 and the product-cycle theory of Hirsh 1965). There is now substantial empirical proof of these theories (e.g., Soete 1981; Pavitt and Soete 1980). There is also some work relating the foreign trade prices of one country with the technological level of its trading partners, and supporting quantitative evidence has been found here as well (e.g., Saunders 1984).

The technological factor is reflected in (among other things) the product structure of exports and imports of a given country. If products were classified according to their technological content (as they can be), then by comparing the shares of more advanced products in a country's exports or imports at different times, or by comparing exports (or imports) for a number of countries, one should be able to assess the respective levels of technology. There are several specific ways of measuring the technological content of trade goods and thereby the technological level of a country or group of countries.

The simplest method, frequently used in international comparisons, is to determine the share of machinery and transport equipment, or a broader category of manufactures (including chemicals, textiles and footwear, and others), in total transactions. A more sophisticated measure is based on lists of selected manufactured goods considered to represent high technology. Such a list has been developed by the U.S. Department of Labor for use with two-digit trade data. More detailed specifications are available as well, including those used by Martens (1986) in his calculations of Western technology transfers to the CPEs (including China and Yugoslavia).

Yet another way of detecting changes in comparative technological levels is to measure the balance of trade in specific products between given countries. In a way this indicator is a derivative of the product structures of exports of these countries to each other. If one country runs a negative balance in a particular advanced product, it could be interpreted as evidence of its technological inferiority. However, it could also reflect insufficient production capacity in the net importing country, in which case the negative trade balance could be associated with either inferior or superior technology. Such ambiguity clearly reduces the practical value of this indicator in technological comparisons.

The unit value—i.e., price per unit or weight of an export (seen as a proxy for costs of production)—is another indicator used for technological comparisons. It can be so used because usually the more technologically advanced models of a product earn higher prices per unit than the less sophisticated ones (e.g., color versus black and white television sets) and because technological progress by and large helps to improve the price-materials ratio for successive models—e.g., most new models of passenger cars are lighter than old ones, and so are radio receivers. (Here as in other consumer electronics there is a strong trend toward miniaturization.)

The unit value yardstick is not without shortcomings, however. Unit values do not reflect just the pace of technological change. The two most important other factors they reflect are the marketing ability of an exporting country (i.e., the ability to capture best prices or best markets) and the degree of discrimination faced by that country abroad. Since these two factors can differ substantially over time for one country, as well as among countries, any technology comparison based on trends in unit values is likely to be distorted. To make things worse, there is no easy way to separate the impact of marketing abilities and trade discrimination from that of technological change alone.

An additional shortcoming is that movements in unit values reflect not just quality improvements and material savings, but often purely inflationary trends as well. For that reason one should work with deflated unit values, as advocated by Montias (1983). To be precise this procedure requires price statistics as detailed as the trade data on units and values used for the calculation of this indicator. Such price data are not easily available, so an alternative means must be used for controlling the analysis for pure price movements (e.g., taking trade data for a single market, relying on relative indicators—relative unit values for specific countries—rather than on absolute measures).

There are a large number of indicators reflecting various aspects of technological sophistication, but there is no single yardstick to measure it. Any comprehensive analysis of comparative technological levels has to employ a number of indicators so that the limits of some can be overcome with the help of others. Moreover, with a greater number of measurements based on different indicators, one should be able to determine a dominant pattern among quantitative results that will very likely conflict to some degree.

Given the advantages and shortcomings of particular indicators and considering data availability, the most suitable sources for cross-country comparisons appear to be foreign patents (applications or grants), foreign license payments, diffusion indicators (particularly those reflecting the transformation of outputs), and trade indicators (in particular measures of the technology content of exports and export unit values). These are the measures which we shall use in our analysis below.

Chapter 4

EAST-WEST COMPARISONS OF TECHNOLOGICAL LEVELS AND TRADING ABILITIES

To evaluate the impact of the recent policy changes in the CPEs we turn now to an analysis of the technological gaps dividing these countries from Western market economies. This is an ultimate test because it should establish not just whether the technological performance of the CPEs has improved in the last decade and a half compared to earlier years, but also whether the improvements have measured up to performance in the West. The period covered in this analysis is long enough to permit us to generalize on long-run trends in the technological development of the CPEs.

For our analysis we have had to construct most of the technological indicators. Several studies have recently been published on CPE technological levels, but they could not easily be integrated to permit an overall assessment. For instance, the valuable study of Soviet technology in the 1970s by Cooper (1984) is not matched by a corresponding analysis of Eastern Europe. The pioneering work commissioned recently by the OECD Directorate for Science, Technology, and Industry provides data on current changes in East European technology (i.e., Fallenbuchl 1983; Levick and Skolka 1984; Marer 1985), but it does not contain data on the technological levels of Western economies.

Our analysis is based on three basic types of indicators. First, we shall analyze the relative levels of productivity in the CPEs and selected Western economies, although productivity is not the focus here. The bulk of the relevant information is generated from our second and third indicators, foreign trade statistics and case studies of three important sectors of CPE industry (autos, chemicals, and computers) respectively. For the case studies we employ a number of statistics, most of them measuring the application of particular technologies in production. For the comparative analysis of technological levels we focus on 1970-85 to allow for a proper assessment of the impact of policy reforms that were taken since the mid-1960s.

COMPARISON OF PRODUCTIVITY CHANGES

HUNGARY

Probably the best data available on Eastern Europe are those on the comparative labor productivity of Hungary. Hungary was one of the first and very few East European countries expressing an interest in a continuous observation of changes in its productivity level relative to other CPEs and to Western economies as well. Among the latter, the best point of reference seems to be Austria, not only because of its historical ties with Hungary, but also due to the countries' similarities in economic potential and demographics (i.e., almost stagnant and mature populations). For this reason, most of the comparisons done on Hungary to date include data on Austrian labor and capital productivity.

Data on labor productivity show that during the first decades of its postwar development Hungary was lagging behind West Germany and Austria in terms of annual increases in the productivity of labor. During 1950/52-1967/69 labor productivity increased by 3.9 percent annually in Hungary, 4.6 percent in West Germany, and 5.0 percent in Austria. Total factor productivity (relating production to joint inputs of labor and capital) also grew more slowly in Hungary during this period, although the difference was much smaller in this case: Hungary-2.4 percent; West Germany-2.7 percent; Austria-2.9 percent (Roman 1980; Boguszewski 1981).

During the early postwar years Hungary did not benefit much from Western transfers of technology, so we can speculate that the lags in its productivity increases may reflect the negative effect of very limited imports of Western technology. But it is difficult to verify this hypothesis in a satisfactory way. It is also clear that to quantify a positive effect of accelerated transfers of Western technology we should look at the data on the 1970s, when Hungary sharply increased such imports. Unfortunately the latest data on the relative productivity of the Hungarian economy cover only the early 1970s, thus making any firm conclusion essentially impossible.

Data for 1971 show that labor productivity in the basic industries of Austria represented 140 percent of that in Hungary. (By this time labor productivity in France was 208 percent of that in Hungary [Hungary, KSM 1971].) The biggest difference was in the mining industry, where Austrian productivity amounted to 253 percent of the Hungarian. The corresponding figures were 170 percent in the gas and electricity sector, 152 percent in machinery, and 135 percent in chemicals (including the rubber industry). The smallest difference was in textiles, where Austrian productivity was only 115 percent of the Hungarian. The only important sector where Hungary had an edge—of 15 percent—was in the food processing industry. (See Table 1.)

Table 1

HUNGARIAN LABOR PRODUCTIVITY COMPARED TO LABOR PRODUCTIVITY IN AUSTRIA, CZECHOSLOVAKIA, AND FRANCE: 1971 AND 1975

(Hungarian Index = 100 percent)

	1971			1975
Industrial Sector	Austria	Czechoslovakia	France	Austria
1. Mining	253.6	351.2	319.6	221.0
2. Clothing	--	--	--	140.0
3. Leather	--	--	--	136.0
4. Food processing	85.4	115.7	134.3	146.0
5. Textiles	114.8	133.2	139.2	151.0
6. Timber, paper	153.8	115.0	129.4	177.0[a]
7. Building materials, glass	146.4	140.8	198.6	209.0
Subtotal: Light industry (4-7)	108.4	128.0	144.0	--
8. Chemicals	136.5	99.3	98.4	120.0
9. Metallurgy	125.4	147.0	202.8	91.0
10. Machinery	152.2	184.1	289.0	174.0
Subtotal: Heavy industry (8-10)	149.0	165.7	243.7	--
11. Electricity and gas	170.2	162.2	413.8	--
Total	140.3	166.1	208.4	--

Sources: For 1971-Hungary, KSM 1971; for 1975-Nyitrai 1977.

[a]Timber only.

The data for 1971 can be compared with those for 1975, again from Hungarian sources. As Nyitrai (1977) reports, the disparities in labor productivity between Hungary and Austria in 1971 had not been reduced by 1975, despite increased inflows of Western technology into Hungary since the late 1960s. In some industries the gaps had even widened drastically. For instance, in building materials Austrian labor productivity was 146 percent of the Hungarian in 1971 but 209 percent in 1975. In the timber and paper industry the figures were 153.8 percent in 1971 and 177 percent in 1975; in the machinery sector, 152 and 174 percent respectively. However, Hungary reduced the gap in the mining industry and chemicals, in the latter by a small margin only.

A closer look at these two economies suggests that the lack of any visible improvement in relative labor productivity in Hungary during 1971-75 should not be interpreted as resulting from factors other than the persistence of technological gaps between Hungary and Austria. For instance, we could speculate that Hungary's labor productivity was increasing more slowly than expected because the country was investing less in new machinery than Austria was. However, data show that during these years Hungary was investing more than Austria. We could also speculate that the real impact of Western imports was not properly reflected in the labor productivity indexes for Hungary because its labor force was growing faster than in Austria. But such was not the case since in both countries the labor force has been stagnating for more than a decade.

SOVIET UNION

Substandard productivity has also been established in a series of studies devoted to the Soviet Union. The most valuable of these is Bergson (1978a). According to Bergson, the Soviet rate of productivity growth (measured in real national income per unit of factors) in 1955-70 was 2.4 percent per year—somewhat higher than in the United States (1.6 percent) and Great Britain (1.8 percent), two relatively advanced countries. However, the Soviet Union falls short of Japan (5.9 percent) and Italy (4.4 percent), representative of the so-called industrial latecomers. More important, the Soviet rate was lower than that of France (3.9 percent) and West Germany (3.4 percent), even though these two nations began to industrialize earlier. Bergson's (1983) comparison of the Soviet Union with the Western economies also reveals that Soviet productivity increases were very close to those of the Western leaders in productivity growth only during the early postwar years, after which the Soviet performance began to lag. By the 1960s the Soviet Union was experiencing systematic declines in the annual rates of productivity growth, whereas among the Western leaders rates continued to increase rapidly or showed smaller drops. The Soviet rate of productivity growth per worker dropped from 5.5 percent per annum in 1950-55 to 3.7 percent in 1955-64, whereas in Italy it increased from 5.3 to 5.4 percent and remained at 4.7 percent in both periods in France (Bergson 1983: 63).

The deterioration of productivity growth in the Soviet Union has continued, with the rates for the late 1970s well below 1.0 percent yearly—i.e., 0.9 percent for the material sector and 0.6 percent for the entire economy. According to Bergson (1983), by projecting from past experience, we can argue that the Soviet Union should find it difficult in the future to raise its rate of growth of total factor productivity much above the very modest rate that has prevailed in the last several years. As Bergson points out, in view of certain trends, it is more likely that there will be a further decline.

The declining rates of Soviet total productivity and labor productivity cannot by themselves be considered definite proof that the recent economic reforms have not worked. Similar (though not necessarily equal) declines have taken place in Western countries, including the United States, and no one is attributing this downward trend to the poor functioning of market institutions (except for the claim that a contributing but not critical factor has been overregulation). If, despite a later decline, Soviet rates of growth remained higher in absolute terms than those of comparable Western countries, then Soviet industry would continue to catch up with Western productivity levels—which in itself would be a good reason to call the Soviet performance a success. If, on the other hand, the catching-up ceased, one could argue that the degree of Soviet decline was excessive and probably the result of some systemic deficiencies.

The above reasoning follows from neo-technology theories of growth, including a superb analysis by Gomulka (1971). In Gomulka's model of stages of economic growth, provided certain conditions are met, a latecomer is in a position to achieve faster growth than the leader in technology for a period of time simply because of having access to the technology accumulated by the leader. However, this faster growth, accompanied by a more rapid productivity increase, will not result in the ultimate elimination of the initial gap in productivity levels unless the latecomer develops his own capability to produce original technology. If this capability does not develop, the latecomer will be able to reduce the productivity gap only partially and will reach an equilibrium technological gap. Therefore, if a country is in an equilibrium technological gap, it is owing to systemic weakness.

A comparison of Soviet with U.S. productivity provides some evidence that the Soviet Union may be such a case. After years of gradual catching up, it has come to the equilibrium technological gap. Gomulka (1985) reveals that up to 1975 Soviet rates of labor productivity growth, while declining, were still high enough to bring Soviet industry closer to the productivity level of the United States (see Table 2). However, since that time the rates in both countries have equalized, but the absolute level of Soviet labor productivity remains around twenty-five years behind that of the United States. About thirteen years are attributable to overmanning (i.e., a higher number of workers operating comparable equipment) and a lower rate of machinery utilization due to supply bottlenecks, poor organization of production, and the like. Gomulka ascribes the remaining twelve years to inferior technology—narrowly defined, a technological lag—of Soviet industry. These twelve years could well be the size of the equilibrium technological gap.

Enough time has passed since the 1975 turning point to support the claim that this is a steady rather than temporary situation in relative Soviet productivity. Of course this technological state does not have to last forever: it could turn into either another period of effective catching-up by the Soviet Union or a phase in which the productivity gap widens—depending on whether or not an effective reform package is introduced by the regime. Our comparison of productivity suggests that by preserving the existing economic system Soviet industry (and possibly East European industry as well) will certainly be unable to take full advantage of accumulated stocks of Western technology and turn them to the task of eliminating the historical gap in productivity.

COMPARISONS FROM FOREIGN TRADE STATISTICS

THE TECHNOLOGICAL CONTENT OF EXPORTS

Changes in the technological levels of the CPEs can also be measured by looking at the evolving technological content of their

Table 2

AVERAGE ANNUAL RATE OF GROWTH OF OUTPUT, INPUT, AND PRODUCTIVITY FOR THE SOVIET UNION AND UNITED STATES: 1950-83
(Percent)

Category	1950-55	1955-60	1960-65	1965-70	1970-75	1975-80	1980-83
Output (Soviet data)	13.1	10.4	8.6	8.5	7.4	4.5	3.6
Output (U.S. data)	11.3	8.7	7.0	6.8	6.0	3.6	--
Capital stock (U.S. data)	12.0	11.3	11.2	8.7	8.7	7.5	7.1
Labor inputs in man-hours (U.S. data)	4.2	1.1	2.9	3.1	1.5	1.4	0.6
Total productivity (Soviet data)[a]	5.8	5.2	2.4	3.2	3.0	0.7	0.4
Total productivity (U.S. data)[a]	4.0	3.5	0.8	1.5	1.6	-0.2	--
Technical progress (Soviet data)	9.7	8.7	4.0	5.3	5.0	1.2	0.7
Technical progress (U.S. data)	6.7	5.8	1.3	2.5	2.7	-0.3	--
Labor productivity (Soviet data)	8.5	9.2	5.5	5.2	5.8	3.1	3.0
Labor productivity (U.S. data)	6.8	7.5	4.0	3.6	4.4	2.0	--

Ratio of U.S. to Soviet labor productivity growth (1975 = 100)

	1950	1955	1960	1965	1970	1975	1980
Soviet data	256	202	149	131	116	100	98
U.S. data	188	154	122	114	109	100	103

Source: Gomulka 1985: 8.

[a] Assuming capital share = 40 percent.

exports. Some indication of structural evolution can be obtained from an analysis of the share of machinery (including transport equipment) in total exports over time. Since the technology incorporated in various kinds of machinery is generally more complex than in most other broad categories of goods traded internationally, any increase in the share of machinery in total exports can be interpreted as an indicator of the exporting country's growing technological strength, as well as of its improved competitiveness.

Data on exports from the CPEs to the OECD show that with two notable exceptions, the region was drastically lagging in technology behind its Western competitors in 1965. (See Table 3.) The share of machinery and transport equipment (SITC Section 7) in East German and Czech exports reached 20.4 percent and 15.9 percent respectively, but in all other countries in the region this share was in the range of only 1-4 percent (while it was 43.7 percent in West Germany and 16.6 percent in Austria, the least advanced in our sample). By 1970 the share of machinery had increased slightly for the two CPE leaders and other countries had made some progress as well, reaching a 5-7 percent share of machinery in total exports—still very low by Western standards.

The improvements by 1970 could be at least partially attributed to the first technological deals with Western countries, but the fuller impact of technology transfer cannot be detected until later in the 1970s because only then had the cluster of Western technologies bought in the late 1960s and early 1970s begun to make an impact. Surprisingly the data for 1970-80 do not show any further significant increases in the share of machinery in total CPE exports. This suggests that the benefits from technology imports were not substantial enough to allow the CPEs as a whole to rely more on the sales of machinery than they had in the early 1970s.

Only Hungary and Poland were able to significantly increase the share of machinery in their total exports to the OECD from 1970 to 1980: Hungary from 6.3 to 12.7 percent and Poland from 5.8 to 13.9 percent. In Bulgaria and Romania the share increased only slightly, and it remained low even by Eastern standards. In East Germany and Czechoslovakia the share was lower in 1980 than in 1970 or even 1965. In East Germany the decrease resulted from a drop which took place in 1978-80, but in Czechoslovakia it reflects a long-term trend. The share of machinery also dropped in the Soviet Union, but this has to be attributed mostly to a sudden increase in its supplies of oil and gas to the West.

Table 3

TOTAL EXPORTS, EXPORTS OF MACHINERY AND TRANSPORT EQUIPMENT (SITC-7), AND SHARE OF SITC-7 IN TOTAL EXPORTS FROM EASTERN EUROPE, THE SOVIET UNION, AND WESTERN EUROPE TO OECD: 1965-84

(Millions of dollars in current prices)

1965			1970			1975			1980			1984		
Total Exports	SITC-7 Exports	Share of SITC-7 in Total	Total Exports	SITC-7 Exports	Share of SITC-7 in Total	Total Exports	SITC-7 Exports	Share of SITC-7 in Total	Total Exports	SITC-7 Exports	Share of SITC-7 in Total	Total Exports	SITC-7 Exports	Share of SITC-7 in Total
							Bulgaria							
$ 160	$ 3	1.9%	$ 240	$ 17	7.1%	$ 392	$ 36	9.2%	$ 993	$ 92	9.3%	$ 744	$ 27	3.6%
							Czechoslovakia							
440	70	15.9	723	135	18.7	1,642	287	17.5	3,235	440	13.6	2,725	403	14.8
							East Germany							
285	58	20.3	410	93	22.7	1,039	228	21.9	2,102	411	19.5	2,349	359	15.2
							Hungary							
286	12	4.2	536	34	6.3	1,250	116	9.3	2,821	359	12.7	2,565	277	10.8
							Poland							
667	16	2.4	1,061	62	5.8	3,174	367	11.6	5,471	765	14.0	3,895	1,432	11.1
							Romania							
288	2	0.7	554	30	5.4	1,692	123	7.3	3,504	271	7.7	3,789	171	4.5
							Eastern Europe, Total							
2,126	161	7.6	3,524	371	10.5	9,189	1,157	12.6	18,126	2,338	12.9	16,067	1,669	10.4
							Soviet Union							
1,785	48	2.7	2,554	92	3.6	8,494	369	4.3	23,788	666	2.8	25,893	450	1.7
							Western Europe[a]							
45,969	14,504	31.5	82,735	28,261	34.1	199,268	65,299	32.8	445,748	136,504	30.6	384,788	123,427	32.1

Source: Calculated from OECD, *Foreign Trade by Commodities*, various years.

[a]Austria, Belgium-Luxemburg, Great Britain, Italy, the Netherlands, Sweden, Switzerland, and West Germany.

Since 1980 there has been a continuous across-the-region deterioration of the relative role of machinery and transport equipment exports, except for Czechoslovakia, where it increased from 13.6 percent in 1980 to 14.8 percent in 1984. A dramatic decline was reported by East Germany in these years: from 19.5 percent to 15.2 percent. Among the countries that were on an upward trend prior to 1980, the most severe declines befell Poland, once an aggressive importer of Western technology (from 14.9 percent in 1980 to 11.1 percent in 1984), as well as Bulgaria (from 9.2 to 3.6 percent).

If one evaluates the trends over 1970-84, there appears to be a significant difference in trade performance between the conservative and aggressive importers of Western technology. Thus the 1984 shares for conservative Bulgaria, Czechoslovakia, and East Germany were below the 1970 levels, whereas the remaining economies showed higher shares in 1984 than in 1970. However, this by itself is not sufficient proof that the difference in technology borrowing is fully or even mainly responsible for the poorer trade performance of the conservative East Europeans. It is possible, for instance, that the decline in the share of machinery and transport equipment in total exports of particular CPEs could have been a result of an especially high rate of expansion in the sales of other products that also benefited from imports of Western technology. Chemicals are a good example of a priority sector in a conservative technology importer such as Czechoslovakia. It could be that Czech exports of chemicals to Western markets increased, thus depressing the share of machinery and transport equipment in the total figures. If true, this trend in the export of chemicals could be considered as an indication of a positive impact of Western technology acquisitions on the overall trade performance of the CPEs.

A look at the data indicates that in almost all CPEs the share of the exports of chemicals (SITC Section 5) in total exports to the OECD rose during 1970-80. For the group as a whole the share increased from 5.1 percent in 1970 to 6.2 percent in 1980. This change was rather modest in magnitude. Only a few of the countries reported significant changes—notably Czechoslovakia (5.4 percent in 1970 and 10.0 percent in 1980), Hungary (4.9 percent in 1970 and 10.5 percent in 1980), and the Soviet Union (3.0 percent in 1970 and 4.5 percent in 1980). Only Romania showed a declining share.

Even the limited data presented above can serve as evidence that the imports of Western technology have probably strengthened CPE exports of chemicals. However, these gains cannot be considered an important reason for the very modest improvements (or lack of improvements) in the export share of machinery and transport equipment. While it is likely that a very rapid expansion of chemical exports from Czechoslovakia contributed to a drop in its share of machinery and transport equipment, this is not the case for East Germany, where the drop was also very significant but where an increase of only 0.2 percent (from 15.8 to 16.0 percent) was reported in its share of chemical exports to Western countries from 1970 to 1980. With the exception of Czechoslovakia, Hungary, and the Soviet Union, the changes in the share of chemicals were too small to affect the share of machinery and transport equipment in total exports.

The data on market shares pose questions other than on the relationship between the scale of technology imports and trade expansion. Among them is the consideration of why, regardless of the difference in the scale of technology imports, the CPEs have uniformly reported a sharp decline in the share of machinery and transport equipment in their exports to the West. Is this because of reductions in OECD investment that caused a deeper decline in OECD demand for CPE capital goods? Or is it because of a reduced supply of these goods from the region—a possible result of a peculiar strategy of adjustment to foreign debt which primarily involves cutting investments in capital goods sectors (Tyson 1986)? These are important questions which we shall address below.

DYNAMICS OF EXPORT UNIT VALUES

Unit values have to be used more cautiously in East-West comparisons than in most other comparative work because the two nontechnological factors that can contribute to cross-country differences—trade discrimination and marketing abilities—play a greater role in these comparisons. Specifically the CPEs are subject to stiffer discriminatory measures on Western markets than most other suppliers and they lack much of the marketing ability of Western exporters. These factors will not only cause gaps in technology (as implied by unit value comparisons) to appear bigger than they are, but also will make the unit value comparison itself more sensitive to changes in these factors (e.g., a liberalization of trade restrictions against the CPEs).

Unfortunately there is no easy way of factoring out the impact of the nontechnological factors, so that we do not know precisely how significant they are at a given point. Most available figures are speculative, such as those of Marer (1984b), who claims that one can safely attribute two thirds of the difference in unit values between CPE and Western exports in the 1960s to price discrimination and poor marketing techniques. This claim has been accepted, though reluctantly, by Marrese and Vanous (1983, 1984) in their study of implicit Soviet subsidies to Eastern Europe. (Earlier they had ignored nontechnological determinants of unit values; e.g., Marrese and Vanous 1983).

The lack of precise information on nontechnological factors should be of less concern when changes in unit values in the CPEs and the West are compared over time rather than for one point in time (i.e., a given year). This kind of intertemporal comparison can be distorted only by changes in the relative price discrimination and marketing skills in the period analyzed. There are no grounds to claim that there has been a substantial change in the marketing expertise of the CPEs relative to that of Western countries in the last decade and a half. However, in this period many discriminatory measures against the CPEs have been relaxed (see, for instance, Wolf 1982). Consequently we could expect the overall trend in unit values for these economies to "overshoot" the technology-related movement in unit values, though it is not clear by how much.

There is still another methodological problem (raised, for instance, by Amann and Slama 1976)—namely, the possibility that the comparison of unit values (precisely price per weight) in the East and West is going to be additionally distorted because the CPEs operate bureaucratic pricing systems where all materials are relatively underpriced (e.g., the price of steel has not been changed much in the Soviet Union for the last twenty years). As a consequence, the differences in unit prices paid to Western and Eastern exporters will not really reflect gaps in technology between the two groups of countries but only their different interests in saving materials.

This argument, although based on an accurate description of the difference in factor price proportions in East and West, does not provide sufficient grounds for rejecting the export unit price methodology for comparative purposes. To reject it one would have to accept two implications: first, that the CPE economies are sensitive to the relative prices of production factors, and second, that these price relations are the only determinants of their attitude toward material-saving changes in production. Neither implication is apparently correct in the light of the existing literature on technological changes in the CPEs (or indeed any type of real-world economy in the case of the second implication). The current literature suggests that price considerations are not important in the decisions made in the CPEs on technology because firms are very cost-insensitive (see Kornai 1980). Consequently there is no good reason to expect the CPEs to compensate for a possibly lower pace of material-saving changes by relatively more dynamic improvements in other cost areas (e.g., the energy or labor used) which cannot be detected by the export unit prices. If true, this argument suggests that the unit price methodology can be used in East/West comparisons without fear of obtaining misleading results.

A comparison of export unit prices paid to Western and Eastern countries for sales to the Common Market in 1970 shows that the CPEs were most likely selling less technologically advanced machinery and transport equipment than their Western competitors. On the average for their products they were getting 45.0 percent of the OECD countries' unit values and 51.8 percent of that of all West European countries (see Table 4). None of the CPEs was receiving prices even close to the average for the OECD countries; Hungary, East Germany, and Czechoslovakia were paid the highest prices in the region as a whole.

In 1970-80, the CPEs increased their export unit prices more than twofold. The most successful were Romania and Poland, who in 1970 had been paid prices per kilogram much below the average for the region. By 1980 their prices were higher than those paid to all other countries in the region except Hungary. A comparison with Czechoslovakia and East Germany is particularly instructive. For instance, in 1970 Polish unit prices amounted to 76 percent of those obtained by East Germany, whereas they were 104 percent in 1980.

Of course much of the increase in the unit values was caused by inflation that plagued the OECD countries in most of the period under discussion. One can assume, however, that the impact of the inflation was probably uniformly distributed among the sample countries, in both the East and West, unless the trade of some of them was focused on country markets experiencing inflation different from the average for the OECD. It also might be that the CPEs intensified their dumping practices in these years; however, this does not seem very likely, at least not during 1970-79, when the region's leadership did not feel much pressed to balance its trade with the West while being provided with sufficient financial help from outside. Nonetheless, the matter remains to be studied in more detail (Tyson 1986).

Table 4

EXPORT UNIT VALUES OF MACHINERY AND TRANSPORT EQUIPMENT SOLD IN COMMON MARKET COUNTRIES, 1965-80
(Dollars per kilogram)

Region/Country	Year and Value						
	1965	1970	1972	1974	1976	1978	1980
World	2.15	2.51	2.99	4.04	4.89	5.12	7.91
OECD countries	2.17	2.53	3.05	4.10	4.97	5.17	7.93
Western Europe	1.93	2.20	2.73	8.36	4.48	5.03	7.11
Eastern Europe (including Soviet Union	1.07	1.14	1.25	1.43	1.84	2.24	2.96
United States	4.99	8.65	8.94	11.03	13.83	15.17	20.40
Japan	3.15	3.68	4.14	4.99	5.40	6.49	7.17
Western Europe							
Austria	1.64	1.96	2.90	4.14	5.28	7.22	10.91
Belgium-Luxemburg	1.67	1.94	2.31	3.24	3.86	5.25	6.52
Great Britain	1.95	2.31	3.09	3.49	4.29	5.73	9.60
Italy	1.83	1.96	2.44	3.10	3.60	4.52	6.46
Netherlands	2.55	2.68	2.93	4.34	4.94	5.18	6.02
Sweden	2.23	2.77	3.16	3.98	5.08	7.90	8.44
Switzerland	3.97	4.94	6.75	8.96	11.31	14.51	16.60
West Germany	1.84	2.24	2.94	3.71	4.61	5.97	7.77
Eastern Europe							
Bulgaria	0.68	1.00	1.37	1.52	1.86	2.11	2.68
Czechoslovakia	1.02	1.15	1.31	1.61	1.77	2.29	2.79
East Germany	1.23	1.20	1.42	1.77	2.11	2.17	2.68
Hungary	1.64	1.81	1.97	2.08	2.49	3.43	4.89
Poland	0.77	0.92	0.94	1.09	2.03	2.99	2.79
Romania	0.79	1.00	0.98	1.43	2.03	2.58	3.58
Soviet Union	1.00	1.09	1.25	1.16	1.40	1.78	2.35

Source: Calculated from OECD, *Foreign Trade by Commodities*, various years.

It also might be that the differences in relative unit values between the CPEs themselves, as well as between East and West, simply reflect a shift in product mix rather than changes in relative technological levels. If some countries more rapidly expanded the exports of goods with lower material intensity or of higher quality within the same material-intensity group than did their counterparts, they would show a better performance in terms of unit values. However, it does not seem likely that such structural changes could have been possible without a stronger technological effort by the countries that reported above-average unit value increases. (We shall present evidence below with the help of disaggregated data; for Poland, see Poznanski 1986c.)

The increases in CPE export unit prices were not fast enough to help the countries narrow the initial gap with the West. On the contrary, the average prices paid to Western countries by Common Market importers increased more rapidly still during 1970-80 so that the gap widened. Specifically, the CPEs were paid 37.3 percent of what OECD countries were offered for their exports in 1980. Hungary received the highest prices in the region—still 38 percent less than the average for Western exporters.

The higher unit prices received on average by Hungary do not seem to reflect just its particular interest in promoting the exports of less material-intensive goods. Another reason seems to be Hungary's ability to supply many products of a higher technological level than can other exporters in the region. Almost 40 percent of Hungarian revenues for exports of machinery and transport equipment come from products which receive prices higher than those paid to other Eastern economies. These products include power generating equipment, steam boilers, agricultural machinery, machine tools, and office machinery—all with a high content of recently imported Western technology.

It is worth noting that Hungary also fits certain general patterns. For example, it appears that smaller economies are usually paid relatively higher prices than larger economies. Hungary is a small-scale economy, as are Austria, Sweden, and Switzerland. For their exports to the Common Market the last three obtain unit values higher than those paid to other Western countries in the sample (except the United States). However, this rule does not apply to other small-scale Eastern economies. Bulgaria, for instance, was obtaining lower prices than the much larger economies of Poland and Romania during 1976-80 but moved ahead of them in 1982 (most likely owing to the serious difficulties of the more heavily indebted Poland and Romania).

If valid, this pattern implies that the performance of such countries as Hungary and Bulgaria should be compared with that of small-scale Western countries such as Austria. In such a comparison, the Hungarian performance, although very good by Eastern standards, appears much less impressive. Hungarian export unit prices increased much more slowly than those of Austria during 1970-80. In 1970 Hungarian prices for machinery and transport equipment were only 7.2 percent lower than the Austrian prices, whereas in 1980 Hungarian exports were worth 45.2 percent less per kilogram than those from Austria, and in 1984, 46.9 percent less. The initial gap in unit prices paid to Hungary and Switzerland has widened over the last decade as well.

TEST FOR TRADE PREFERENCES

Among several methodological objections that can be raised in regard to our analysis is that of the likely misrepresentation caused by bias in the data sample. It can be said, and is often said, that the goods offered by the CPEs do not necessarily represent the most advanced models available because the best products are predominantly directed either to domestic markets or sold to partners within the region. Consequently data on domestic sales or intraregional trade could provide a more appropriate basis for technological assessments than information on CPE trade with Western economies.

The supposition that the CPEs might prefer domestic markets seems at first glance to be consistent with the generally accepted notion that they are inward-looking. They might be expected not only to be trade-averse, but also to offer goods abroad that are least wanted by domestic customers—in some cases because of a product's technological inferiority. Since these economies allocate their exportable goods through predominantly bureaucratic procedures, it is quite possible that domestic agents can use more informal pressures to extract advanced goods than can Western partners relying mostly on economic instruments.

To determine to what extent (or whether) the sales of CPE goods to Western countries are biased against the most advanced exportables, we conduct the following test. With the help of the very detailed data on foreign transactions published by the Common

Market (EEC, various years), we calculate the shares of selected technologically advanced manufactures in the total sales of a given product category for particular CPEs. (These shares are established for both values and volumes—i.e., units—of products sold.) Then we compare the respective shares for exports with the shares of selected advanced goods in the total output of a specific product category. Any differences between export and output shares will indicate the existence of a trade bias.

Let us consider the case of machine tools. Two types have been distinguished: conventional and numerically controlled, the latter representing the latest stage in machine-tool technology. In 1982 numerically controlled machine tools represented 31.3 percent of production in unit terms in Hungary, 5.1 percent in Czechoslovakia, and 5.6 percent in East Germany. For Poland the share was 0.6 percent (after reaching 1.3 percent in 1977), one of the lowest in Eastern Europe. Since prices for numerically controlled models are generally substantially higher than for conventional units, the share of the former in the total value of machine-tool production was considerably higher than their share in terms of quantity. We lack the data to determine the shares in value terms.

From trade data we observe that the share of numerically controlled machine tools in the volume of Hungarian exports to Western Europe was 38.2 percent in 1982, while it was 25.5 percent for Czechoslovakia and 20.7 percent for East Germany; Poland sold none that year. Given export price differentials for conventional and numerically controlled models, these value shares translate into the following shares in quantitative terms: Hungary—19.1 percent; Czechoslovakia—5.3 percent; East Germany—11.5 percent. As can be seen, only in Hungary did the sales represent a smaller share of the total number of exported units than their share in domestic production. In Czechoslovakia the difference was insignificant, while in East Germany the share in exports was much higher than in production.

The statistical data allow a similar comparison for washing machines. Two types can be distinguished: conventional and automatic models. In 1982 automatic washing machines accounted for 31 percent of the total number of washing machines made in Hungary and 40 percent of those in Poland. This compares with exactly a 100 percent share in value (and obviously quantity) of automatic models sold by both Hungary and Poland to Western Europe in that year. Czechoslovakia and East Germany were exporting conventional models only, but information is lacking on their production of automatic machines, so an assessment of their trade preferences is not possible.

Certainly a sample of two export products is not sufficient to allow for a generalization, even though machine tools at least represent relatively important exports for Eastern Europe to Western Europe. (The share of these goods in the total imports of Western economies was around 3.2 percent in 1982; Poznanski 1985.) This sample does not indicate that Eastern Europe tends to sell more advanced products outside the Western market, though this is not unusual for some countries in the region. Rather the data imply the opposite pattern, indicating that our above analysis of market shares and input prices was not distorted by the sampling factor.

CASE STUDIES OF SELECTED INDUSTRIES

Aggregate analyses such as the one presented above seem to be adequate for an overall assessment of technological performance, but they cannot provide fully satisfactory grounds for judging a narrower issue—i.e., the impact of technology imports on the gaps separating the CPEs from the West. One important reason is that Western technology has been implemented only locally in some production lines and over a relatively short period, so the results, even if substantial, might not be accurately reflected in aggregate indicators. For a more precise picture one has to look to case studies of industries that have received heavy injections of Western technology in the recent past. In the following analysis we take a closer look at three such industries: automobiles, chemicals, and computers.

ALTERNATIVES TO WESTERN IMPORTS: AUTOMOBILES

The automotive industry represents one of the most interesting cases for analysis because it provides an excellent opportunity to compare the outcome of different CPE approaches to the imports of Western technology. Among these is a policy of aggressive technology borrowing by Poland, the Soviet Union, and (to a lesser extent) Romania, versus a passive policy by Czechoslovakia and East Germany. A comparison of the two groups helps to answer the question of whether or not relying on domestic technology offers a genuine alternative to large-scale technology imports.

In the mid-1960s, when some CPEs began reconsidering their policy toward the development of an automotive industry, Czechoslovakia (with 78,000 passenger cars manufactured in 1965) and East Germany (with 95,000) were much ahead of the other CPE producers (United Nations, Economic Commission for Europe, various years). This edge was not a result of their greater interest in the expansion of production in the first postwar decades because at that time all the Eastern planners equally neglected this industrial sector. These two countries had a lead mostly because they inherited much larger production capacities from the prewar years.

Czechoslovakia and East Germany were also the only countries in the region in which passenger cars dominated in the production of motor vehicles during the first postwar decades (Baranson 1979). In 1965, for instance, when East Germany produced 95,000 passenger cars, it produced only 15,000 commercial vehicles, reflecting the prewar pattern of production. In contrast, the Soviet Union, Poland, and Romania focused more on commercial vehicles. The Soviet Union manufactured 420,000 commercial vehicles and only 196,000 passenger cars in 1965, reflecting its planners' long-standing lack of interest in consumer needs (see Parker 1980)—especially those asssociated with the Western way of life, of which cars were a prime example.

In 1965 Czechoslovakia and East Germany were also regional leaders in automotive technology (Bauer and Soos 1979). This too was a result of their prewar leadership. In the first half of the century Czech motor vehicle production had been rated as one of the most technologically advanced in the world. After World War II Czechoslovakia terminated its traditional production relationships with Germany and Italy, formerly large suppliers of parts and accessories. Nonetheless, it was still able to hold an edge over the other CPEs because of the slow modernization of their domestic products. So was East Germany, despite being completely cut off from traditional production partners.

The Soviet automotive industry entered the 1960s with a technology badly outdated by Western standards, as did the East European producers which tried to expand automotive production with Soviet assistance (e.g., Poland). The first postwar Soviet models were "rough" copies of Western vehicles, such as Pobeda and Moskvitch, which were copies of the German Opels of 1939 vintage, and several truck models copied from American vehicles of 1940 (including the General Motors diesel engine; Parker 1980). Moreover, the Soviet copies lacked the quality and precision of the Western originals and they continued to get more obsolete due to a near stagnation of the whole automotive industry in the two decades after the war.

These trends in the CPE automotive industry were not reversed until the mid-1960s, when the Soviet Union decided to give priority to motor vehicle production in its eighth five-year plan (1965-70). The sums invested in this period were greater than all previous investment in the industry (since 1928) combined. The ninth five-year plan (1971-75) focused even more on the automotive industry, and planners continued to favor this sector during the tenth five-year plan (1976-80). Poland also embarked upon a major development of the automotive industry in 1965 (Edwards and Fraser 1977).

In their effort to modernize motor vehicle production, both the Soviet Union and Poland turned to Western countries for new technology. They acquired most of the technology needed to switch their production from traditional processes to integrated, automated methods with elements of computer control. Soviet industry received this technology primarily through two huge projects. One is a passenger car plant based on Fiat (Italy) licenses, equipped by Fiat, and with a capacity close to 700,000 cars. The second is a plant for eight-ton trucks; they are of Soviet design, but the plant is equipped with machinery from several Western countries, including the United States, which supplied computers for production control.

Like the Soviet Union, Poland bought a license for economy passenger cars from Fiat, initially for a sedan model. It subsequently extended car production to a whole line, including a small car (licensed by Fiat as well) and a luxury model designed by Fiat specifically for Poland. In addition, Poland has started assembling two Fiat models: Fiat 121 and Mirafiori (for official use). The truck industry also received large supplies of technology, including licenses from Stayer-Daimler-Puch of Austria, Volvo of Sweden for heavy trucks, British Leyland for truck engines, and some licenses for parts. Poland acquired the technology for short-distance buses from Berliet (France).

Due to these investments, the Soviet Union and Poland have multiplied their production, as has Romania, which also coupled its motor vehicle industry to Western technology (provided by Renault [France] in particular). The Soviet Union produced 230,000 passenger cars in 1967, when the first cars of Fiat design were launched. In the next several years output skyrocketed. In 1972 almost 730,000 units were produced, and in 1980, more than 1,300,000—more than five times the 1967 level. Polish output jumped from 65,000 cars in 1970 to 364,000 in 1980—more than a fivefold increase (see Table 5).

Czechoslovakia and East Germany, more conservative in their attitude toward Western imports, did not follow the aggressive Soviet and Polish policy. Although they declared their intention of modernizing their production, they decided to rely on domestic technology. Their initial plans were to multiply production by assembling a jointly designed model. This venture did not materialize during 1970-80; only recently has it gained some momentum. However, the latest plan does not call for as close cooperation as the original plan did. The countries will cooperate only in the production of parts and components, while the manufacture of national models will continue (*Quarterly Economic Review* 1980).

It is interesting that in this more modest program both Czechoslovakia and East Germany intend to match their own new technology with Western methods. For example, East Germany is trying to redesign its passenger cars (the Wartburg models) with technical assistance from Porsche (West Germany). A new front-wheel drive model, scheduled to be launched in 1985, contains several parts and components based on Western technology (e.g., drive shafts from a plant built with the help of Citroën [France]). Czechoslovakia has completed work on a new model of Skoda whose body is designed by Bertoni of Italy (*Financial Times*, 9 October 1985).

Both the Czech and East German industries increased production by a marked margin during the 1970s, although these increases have been much below those reported in the 1960s. Czechoslovakia almost tripled its production of passenger cars during 1960-70, from 56,000 to 143,000. However, in 1970-80 production increased to around 182,000 cars—i.e., by only 27 percent. Most of this increase took place in the early 1970s, after which production almost stagnated. Similarly East Germany doubled its capacity over 1960-70, but car production then increased to only 175,000 units (or by 35 percent) in 1980.

If these data are compared with the statistics noted above on car output in the Soviet Union and Poland in 1970-80, it becomes clear that the latter two have surpassed both Czechoslovakia and East Germany. Soviet output represented 127 percent of combined East German and Czech output in 1970 and 367 percent in 1980. In 1960 Polish car production represented only 24 percent of the combined output of the Czech and East German industries, whereas

Table 5

PRODUCTION OF PASSENGER CARS IN THE CPES, 1970-85
(In thousands)

Country and Car Model	1970	1975	1976	1977	1978	1979	1980	1981	1982	1983	1984	1985	Index 1980/1970	Index 1985/1980
Eastern Europe	366	591	655	706	779	799	828	718	707	--	--	--	227.1	--
Bulgaria	8	15	15	15	15	15	15	15	15	15	15	16	153.3	106.7
Czechoslovakia	143	175	179	159	176	182	184	181	174	177	180	187	128.7	101.6
East Germany	127	159	164	167	171	171	177	180	183	188	202	198	139.4	111.8
Poland	65	174	229	294	340	357	364	251	231	283	279	265	429.3	72.8
Syrena	25	37	35	40	35	35	36	19	14	--	--	--	--	--
Warszawa	16	6	0	0	0	0	0	0	0	0	0	0	--	--
Romania	23	68	68	71	77	74	88	92	104	90	--	--	382.6	--
Soviet Union	344	1,201	1,239	1,272	1,312	1,314	1,327	1,324	1,307	1,318	1,330	1,400	385.7	--
Zaporozhets	80	130	146	145	140	145	150	155	180	145	150	--	187.5	--
Volga	100	80	95	100	100	115	125	130	130	125	130	--	125.0	--
Moskvitch	150	300	315	310	320	225	230	235	205	205	200	--	153.3	--

Source: World Automotive Market, various years; United Nations, *Yearbook of Industrial Statistics*, various years; *Biuletyn Statystyczny* (Warsaw), no. 1, 1985; United Nations 1982.

in 1980 Poland made almost as many passenger cars as those two countries together. With the recent decline in production—reflecting the overall economic crisis—Poland has fallen behind by a large margin, although it is still much smaller than before.

More important, a lack of sufficient investment has left Czechoslovakia and East Germany with badly outmoded cars, which technologically lag greatly behind the major Soviet, Polish, and Romanian models. While the last three countries have moved to highly automated production of Western models of mid-1960s vintage (mostly abandoned by the West), Czech and East German models are at best from the late 1950s. Thus the early CPE leaders in car technology have been surpassed by the Soviet Union, Poland, and Romania, and they have lost their lead in several related industries as well—e.g., electrical equipment for cars, diagnostic instruments, and car service (*Business Eastern Europe*, 6 June 1980).

The technological level of Czech and East German passenger cars is similar to that of a few old domestic models which are still manufactured by Poland and the Soviet Union. For instance, Poland continued to make the old-fashioned Syrena until at least 1982. In fact its production was higher in 1980 than in 1967, when the first Western-licensed passenger cars were launched; however, its market share was well below 10 percent. The Soviet Union is more involved than Poland in the manufacture of old models (Gutman 1980). In 1984 about 36 percent of production comprised outdated cars—for example, the Zaporozhets, with a rear, air-cooled engine and body copied from the German NSU of the late 1950s; the ill-designed and fuel-inefficient Volga; and the Moskvitch, whose production is about to be terminated and replaced with a front-wheel-drive model after a complete factory retooling.

While the aggressive technology policy has helped the Soviet Union and Poland to become large-scale exporters, Czechoslovakia and East Germany have remained marginal suppliers of cars to the world market. This means they have lost their initial lead in exports. In 1961 Czechoslovakia exported 34,000 cars, while the Soviet Union sold 33,000 and Poland exported only a few hundred. Czechoslovakia increased its exports in the following years, but during 1970-80 no significant growth was reported, and total sales stabilized around 80,000 units. In contrast, the Soviet Union increased its exports from 85,000 in 1970 to 380,000 in 1980—almost five times Czech exports in that year.

The technological stagnation of the Czech and East German industries over the last decade has undermined their exports to

Western countries. Although fuel inefficient, highly polluting, and lacking many safety devices, there is still a market for their cars among the CPEs, where there is a permanent shortage of passenger cars. But on Western markets their products have been unable to maintain their market share. For instance, the Czech share in the British market dropped from over 0.5 percent in 1970 to less than 0.3 percent in 1980. East Germany had 0.52 percent of the British market in 1974 but disappeared from the market in 1979.The Czech share in the Common Market went from 0.24 percent in 1970 to 0.14 percent in 1980 to 0.20 percent in 1983; the East German share remained negligible throughout the period.

In contrast, Poland and the Soviet Union have increased their shares of Western markets during the last decade. Poland was almost absent from these markets in 1970, representing 0.02 percent of OECD imports, but in 1980 its exports rose to 0.35 percent. This share was even higher for just the Common Market members of the OECD: 0.76 percent in 1980, but down to 0.29 percent in 1983. The Soviet Union increased its share among Common Market imports from 0.05 percent in 1970 to 0.65 percent in 1980 and to 0.79 percent in 1983. None of these shares is particularly high, but in a few cases the exporting countries have been able to obtain a significant piece of individual Western markets. For instance, Soviet exports accounted for 8.1 percent of total automotive imports by Finland in 1979, versus 2.6 percent in 1970 (calculated from OECD, *Foreign Trade by Commodities*, various years).

From the above comparison we can conclude that the imports of Western technology have not reduced the initial lag between the automotive industries of the aggressive importers (i.e., Poland and the Soviet Union) and the West. At the same time, the only alternative to large-scale imports of Western technology has been a deterioration of CPE industries. The conservative economies have been unable to upgrade domestic technology even close to the level of technology imported by others in the region. Czechoslovakia and East Germany have paid the price in a stagnation of production and losses of exports to Western countries in the 1970s.

MODERNIZATION OF PRODUCT STRUCTURE: CHEMICALS

The chemical industry in the CPE region has received more Western technology than most others, implying that this sector should also have been one of the most successful in catching up with the Western level of technology. For this reason many specialists on East-West technology trade choose it as a subject for analysis (e.g., Hanson 1981). Most of them agree that the CPE production of chemicals has been deeply transformed with the help of Western technology and that the capacity lag behind Western industries in many product areas has been reduced.

The CPEs entered the 1970s with capacities in traditional chemicals close to those of major Western producers. (For example, see the data on the production of sulphuric acid in 1970 presented in Table 6.) However, the region was lagging greatly in modern chemicals at that time. With the exception of synthetic rubber, where most CPEs approached the production capacities of Western countries, CPE capacities were one half or one third as large as many major Western producers. For instance, Czechoslovakia, the CPE leader, produced 1.5 kilograms of synthetic fibers per 1,000 inhabitants in 1970, while the corresponding figure for West Germany was 4.7 kilograms.

The production of many traditional chemicals seemed to reach a saturation point in several CPEs by the end of the 1960s, and in the following years only limited investment was devoted to these products. For instance, in Czechoslovakia the per capita production of sulphuric acid increased slightly in 1970-78 and then stagnated in 1978-82, while in East Germany it even declined during 1970-82. In others, production has been increasing, with Bulgaria and Poland making the most substantial progress. Most of the new capacity was constructed with the help of technology available in Eastern countries because in many cases the CPEs had achieved substantial expertise in manufacturing equipment for the traditional chemical processes (e.g., Poland in the construction of sulphuric acid plants).

In recent years all the CPEs have made a tremendous effort to increase their capacity in modern chemicals, mostly by purchasing large quantities of Western technology. They have had to turn to Western countries because their early attempts to develop a number of modern chemicals most often resulted in high-cost and relatively low-volume installations clearly inferior to Western counterparts. Even the most advanced countries in the region—namely, Czechoslovakia, East Germany, and Poland—lacked the necessary expertise in many modern chemicals. Moreover, their production capacities were evidently insufficient to meet the region's demand, even in those product areas where they had achieved substantial technological expertise (e.g., ammonia plants constructed by Czechoslovakia).

Table 6

PRODUCTION OF SELECTED CHEMICALS PER THOUSAND INHABITANTS IN WESTERN EUROPE AND THE CPES: 1970, 1978, AND 1982

(In kilograms)

Region/Country	Year	Sulphuric Acid	Ethylene	Polyvinyl-Chloride	Propy-lene	Synthetic Fibers	Synthetic Rubber
Western Europe							
France	1970	69.5	--	8.1	11.2	1.6	5.9
	1978	135.0	42.0	11.6	--	1.6	8.6
	1982	76.9	34.3	14.2	18.5	1.2	7.2
Great Britain	1970	59.3	18.0	5.7	8.3	3.0	5.5
	1978	58.5	18.5	6.9	11.3	3.1	4.9
	1982	46.1	19.2	5.6	13.8	1.2	3.4
Italy	1970	64.6	16.8	9.2	9.1	1.8	2.8
	1978	54.5	22.7	12.4	13.8	2.4	4.6
	1982	38.7	15.2	12.0	7.8	3.0	3.7
West Germany	1970	76.6	34.5	13.3	14.5	4.7	5.5
	1978	75.9	54.5	16.3	27.7	5.5	6.9
	1982	78.2	42.7	14.0	24.0	5.2	6.5
Eastern Europe							
Bulgaria	1970	41.8	6.6	1.7	5.2	0.3	0.4
	1978	110.6	9.2	3.3	7.0	1.5	2.9
	1982	162.9	22.7	10.5	13.6	1.9	2.8
Czechoslovakia	1970	72.3	8.6	2.8	4.3	1.5	3.4
	1978	79.1	15.2	14.5	7.2	3.5	3.9
	1982	81.4	34.7	12.9	16.0	5.8	4.2
East Germany	1970	64.9	5.2	--	--	0.8	6.9
	1978	58.2	--	--	--	3.2	9.3
	1982	54.7	--	--	--	4.7	9.2
Hungary	1970	45.3	0.2	1.4	0.7	0.5	--
	1978	66.3	23.6	8.9	12.3	1.8	--
	1982	56.0	23.9	15.4	12.3	0.7	--
Poland	1970	46.6	0.8	2.6	0.7	0.6	1.9
	1978	90.6	2.8	3.6	2.7	2.3	3.6
	1982	75.9	4.9	2.2	3.3	2.1	2.8
Romania	1970	41.5	5.5	2.8	2.9	0.9	3.0
	1978	75.9	12.9	8.9	8.4	1.4	6.7
	1982	83.5	13.1	9.3	6.4	1.8	6.2
Soviet Union	1970	--	--	--	--	--	--
	1978	85.8	--	--	--	1.2	--
	1982	--	--	--	--	1.3	--

Source: Calculated from United Nations, *Yearbook of Industrial Statistics*, various years, and *Statistical Abstracts of the U.S.*, various years.

The Soviet Union has been the region's prime importer of Western equipment, not only because of the large scale of its industry, but also due to its planners' special interest in the industry—always among the most favored sectors of the Soviet economy with respect to purchases of Western machinery. Although the Soviet Union has invested much in such equipment, it has remained heavily dependent on imports. Since 1958, when Soviet planners declared chemicals one of the priority sectors, the share of imported equipment in new capacity installed in the chemical industry has remained in the range of 34-40 percent (see Rushing 1976).

For a time after 1958 most of the imported Soviet chemical equipment was from East European producers, but later the Soviet Union became interested in more sophisticated Western technology. Annual orders of Western equipment averaged $140 million during 1961-70, then increased to over $700 million in 1971-75. By that time, Western supplies surpassed those from Eastern Europe, with Italian corporations the primary source of Western technology during 1971-75. The Western equipment ordered in this period represented one fourth of the total equipment expenditure by the industry, while the East European share was only one sixth (Hanson 1981).

Soviet planners were interested in a rapid expansion of the chemical industry mostly because of their strong desire to help the troubled agricultural sector. Consequently Western equipment was purchased for the production of agricultural chemicals and related facilities. On a value basis, about 42 percent of all chemical equipment imported from Western countries went to this subsector, with ammonia plants and urea fertilizer installations absorbing most of the resources. It is estimated that in 1980 almost 60 percent of the ammonia and close to 40 percent of the complex fertilizers manufactured in the Soviet Union were produced in large plants incorporating Western technology (Soviet Chemical Equipment 1978).

Western equipment has also become very important in the recent modernization of the East European chemical industry. In Poland, for example, equipment for the industry represented 0.6 percent of total imports in 1970 but 1.5 percent in 1979. Almost 90 percent of the equipment was purchased from Western countries (*Rocznik Statystyczny Handlu Zagranicznego* [Warsaw] 1981). Chemical equipment has become one of the most important items among total machinery imports from Western countries. By the end of the 1970s it ranked third, preceded only by machine tools and heavy trucks respectively.

The chemical industry has not only been one of the major recipients of Western equipment during recent years, but it also acquired a large share of the licenses purchased by the CPEs from the West. One example is Poland, where more than 25 percent of all licenses went to the chemical industry during 1970-80 (Monkiewicz 1980: 6). Hungary is also a good case in point. By 1975 its chemical industry had 61 Western licenses in force, while the major recipient—the machine industry—operated 188 Western licenses in that year (Juhasz 1980: 98). Pharmaceuticals were the major chemical beneficiary, with 32 license contracts. Due to Western imports, the ratio of license-based products in the total output of chemicals increased from 3.2 percent in 1971 to 5.9 percent in 1975 (Kiss 1980: 85-86). This ratio was higher in the production of pharmaceuticals (8.6 percent) and highest in the manufacture of synthetic rubber (34.3 percent).

The purchase of Western technology by the CPEs has taken place without clear-cut coordination but rather according to the needs of individual countries. In the years of cheap oil, East European planners tried to expand chemical production in many directions. After 1975, when supply conditions changed and the Soviet Union started charging higher prices for oil, they found it difficult to scale down their imports of Western technology and focus on fewer product areas. Only more recently have they made some moves toward specialization, not without additional pressure from the Soviet Union, which is interested in being an exclusive supplier of certain chemicals to Eastern Europe (Fernhout 1978: 5).

There is clear evidence that most of the CPEs have substantially narrowed the lag in relative production capacities of those modern chemicals for which they have focused their imports of technology (United States, Department of Commerce 1974). One of the areas of most impressive progress is petrochemicals, such as ethylene and polyvinyl chloride. In 1970-82 Czechoslovakia virtually closed its initial gap in the production of these chemicals relative to Western producers, including West Germany. Hungary was also able to catch up, even though it started from a much lower relative level of production of both. In both products Hungary has surpassed Great Britain and Italy, although it is still behind West Germany, the West European leader in petrochemicals. Admittedly, a look at the output data alone gives an exaggerated picture of East European progress because much of the West European capacity is idle.

The CPEs have also eliminated their previous lag in the production of synthetic fibers. (Romania has been the slowest to catch up.) A recent expansion in synthetic fiber production has helped the CPEs to radically improve the structure of their chemical fiber production. For instance, in Czechoslovakia only 44.5 percent of total production of chemical fibers consisted of synthetic fibers in 1969, but in 1978 it reached 75.3 percent, the balance being cellulose fibers. In 1969 the Czech structure of chemical fibers was backward relative to that of West Germany, but by 1978 it partially closed the gap. Hungary also made progress, increasing the share of synthetic fibers in total chemical fiber production from 56.0 percent in 1970 to 71.0 percent in 1978.

The CPEs have achieved the greatest progress in the production of fertilizers—in particular ammonia (a key input for nitrogen fertilizers). For instance, Poland increased its production of ammonia from 1.4 million tons in 1970 to 2.0 million tons in 1977. Romania surpassed these figures, increasing its output from 0.9 million tons in 1970 to 2.8 million tons in 1980. The most radical changes have taken place in the Soviet Union, where in 1975-80 alone ammonia production almost doubled, from an initial 12.0 million tons to over 23.0 million tons. Several ammonia plants are still under consideration, so Soviet output may increase further in the coming years (Wharton Econometrics 1984).

Although the CPEs have sharply increased the share of modern chemicals in their total production, the major products of the industry are basic and intermediate chemicals with little value added, such as methanol, ammonia, ethylene, and propylene. These products also dominate CPE exports to Western markets, especially in the case of the Soviet Union. It is estimated that in 1976 low value-added chemicals accounted for 75 percent of the value of total chemical exports from the Soviet Union, while products with higher value added (e.g., fertilizers, plastics) represented only 17 percent. The share of the latter was similarly low in Soviet exports to Western countries alone (Fernhout 1978).

The limited capability of the CPEs in the area of specialty chemicals is also reflected in their substantial trade deficits with Western countries. While they are able to supply large quantities of basic and intermediate chemicals (used as feedstocks for highly processed Western products), they have to buy even more from the

West—mostly highly processed chemicals. These deficits are characteristic of both Eastern Europe and the Soviet Union, but there are some differences in the degree and structure of the imbalances.

In 1980 Eastern Europe alone sold chemicals to the OECD countries for $1.4 billion—which equaled 40 percent of its total imports from those countries. The 1980 deficit in chemicals was higher than in 1970, when exports represented 46 percent of imports. Trade deficits measured as a proportion of imports were 53.3 percent in 1970 and 59.5 percent in 1980 (Table 7). The differences in both years were even more dramatic than these data suggest because data on OECD trade with Eastern Europe do not include intra-German trade, in which East Germany continuously runs large deficits with West Germany (Oechsler 1981: 1332).

A more detailed analysis shows that all the CPEs were running deficits by 1980. The traditional East European leader in chemicals, East Germany, was a net exporter to Western countries in 1970 but ran a substantial deficit in 1980. All the remaining CPEs had deficits in 1970, and none was able to eliminate them by 1980. Among the largest net importers of chemicals in 1980 were the Soviet Union, with a $1.3 billion deficit, Poland ($678 million), and Hungary ($486 million). In relative terms the most dependent on Western imports were Poland, whose exports represented only 26 percent of the value of chemicals imported from Western countries, and Bulgaria, with a ratio close to 29 percent. (The average for Eastern Europe was 46 percent.)

Since 1980 the trade balance in chemicals has improved for the East Europeans, however. In total trade in chemicals with the OECD countries, the ratio of East European exports to imports increased from the 40 percent reported in 1980 to 61 percent in 1984. The deficit-import ratio declined to 38.5 percent by 1984. (Similar improvements took place in artificial resins and plastics.) However, this improvement has been rather illusory since its true cause was a sharp decline in imports by Eastern Europe, whereas exports stabilized (for total chemicals, for example) or increased very slightly (artificial resins and plastics).

In the Soviet Union, unlike in Eastern Europe, there was a significant reduction in the trade deficit in total chemicals in 1970-80. The deficit represented 69.7 percent of Soviet imports from the OECD in 1970 and 48.6 percent in 1980—despite a sharp increase in imports (a tenfold increase, compared with a sixfold increase in Eastern Europe). Clearly the Soviet Union's exports were advancing

Table 7

CPE BALANCE OF TRADE IN CHEMICALS WITH THE OECD, 1965-84
(EX-IM/IM)

Region or Country	1965	1970	1975	1980	1984
			Chemicals: Total (SITC-5)		
Eastern Europe	134.8 / 273.1 = 49.3%	269.4 / 504.8 = 53.3%	1460.1 / 2054.7 = 71.0%	2019.3 / 3392.5 = 59.5%	907.6 / 2358.4 = 38.5%
Soviet Union	101.7 / 139.5 = 72.9%	180.6 / 259.0 = 69.7%	655.8 / 978.7 = 67.0%	1237.8 / 2548.0 = 48.6%	719.1 / 1815.4 = 39.6%
Eastern Europe + Soviet Union	236.5 / 412.6 = 57.3%	450.0 / 763.8 = 58.9%	2115.9 / 3033.4 = 69.7%	3257.1 / 5940.5 = 54.8%	1626.7 / 4173.8 = 38.9%
			Chemicals: Resins and Plastics (SITC-5.8)		
Eastern Europe	36.2 / 45.6 = 79.4%	93.8 / 115.1 = 81.5%	376.0 / 414.8 = 90.6%	460.8 / 704.2 = 65.4%	151.8 / 428.1 = 35.4%
Soviet Union	31.9 / 33.7 = 94.6%	69.8 / 75.7 = 92.2%	266.0 / 269.8 = 98.6%	504.2 / 551.5 = 91.4%	351.5 / 405.0 = 86.8%
Eastern Europe + Soviet Union	68.1 / 79.3 = 85.8%	163.6 / 190.8 = 85.7%	642.0 / 684.6 = 93.8%	965.0 / 1255.7 = 76.8%	503.3 / 833.1 = 60.4%

more than those of its East European allies, in part due to its far better endowments in oil and gas, which are primary inputs for chemicals. However, since 1980 Soviet exports have visibly declined—by at least 25 percent in current value terms during 1980-84. This contrasts with Eastern Europe's exports, even though the latter's production (as indicated earlier) depends critically on Soviet supplies of inputs. The decline in Soviet exports plus an equally deep reduction in imports allowed the country to bring its deficit to 39.6 percent of total imports in 1984—close to the corresponding ratio for Eastern Europe.

Another difference between the Soviet Union and Eastern Europe is in the trade in more complex chemicals, including artificial resins and plastics. In 1970 the Soviet deficit-import ratio was 92.2 percent, and it went down only to 91.4 percent in 1980, whereas in Eastern Europe the ratio declined sharply from 81.5 to 65.4 percent in that period. Since the 1980 trade adjustment, the Soviet ratio diminished to 86.8 percent (by less in point terms than the ratio for total chemicals), while in Eastern Europe the drop was substantial—i.e., to 35.4 percent (by more in point terms than the ratio for total chemicals). This most likely reflects the continued stronger dependence of the Soviet Union on Western supplies of advanced chemicals, linked with less sufficient production capabilities (given the magnitude of domestic demand).

This deficit situation may change in the future, at least in some of the CPEs. The Soviet Union appears more likely than other economies in the region to turn its hitherto increasing deficits into a large surplus. This may result not so much from an ability to rapidly reduce its reliance on Western supplies of specialty chemicals as to its continuing heavy investment in less complex petrochemicals such as ammonia, urea, and methanol (*European Chemicals News*, 7 February 1983: 1068; 20 September 1982: 1050), all of which serve as feedstocks for highly processed chemicals. Most data indicate that the Soviet Union is quickly becoming a leading world exporter of these basic chemicals, but there is no indication that it will soon reach self-sufficiency in specialty chemicals.

East European producers have a lower potential for chemical export expansion, and none of them seems likely to build a substantial surplus in its trade with Western countries. Even East Germany is not expected to reduce its large deficit, which amounted to $353.6 million in 1979 (if trade with East Germany is included; Oechsler 1981). However, the East European countries may be able to turn some deficits into surpluses, including those in advanced chemicals.

One example is the trade in polymers and copolymers, where Czechoslovakia achieved a substantial surplus in 1980 after years of deficits.

The case of chemicals suggests that through massive imports of Western technology, the CPEs have been able to rapidly modernize their chemical industries, but not fast enough to close the gap relative to the West. The likely reason is that the most advanced Western technology is stiffly protected for commercial reasons. The CPEs could have partially overcome this obstacle by a large-scale technology effort of their own, but none of them has done so—not even the Soviet Union, which has traditionally been interested in freeing its key industrial sectors from a dependence on Western technology (Gustafson 1981).

THE COMPUTER INDUSTRY: INTRA-BLOC INTEGRATION

In several fields the CPEs have been trying to acquire Western technology with a clear intention of integrating the various national industries, assigning them parts of more general regional production programs. Among these have been the passenger car and commercial vehicle industries, the energy industry (both conventional and nuclear power), and computers. The last is considered by many specialists as the most serious effort toward an integrated production system in the region over the last several years. The following analysis is aimed at determining the degree to which this program of integration has been an economic success.

During the first two postwar decades the CPEs made reasonable progress in building up their computer industries, but not enough either to make any of them self-sufficient in computers and related products or to facilitate intra-bloc (not to mention worldwide) trade in computers. Even by the late 1960s most of the CPEs were predominately producing for their domestic markets; the Soviet Union was the only country selling small quantities of its production to its European allies—in particular to those lacking production capacities (e.g., Bulgaria). By that time most of the countries in the region were trying to obtain additional equipment—where necessary—from the West rather than from their partners in the bloc.

One of the fundamental barriers to intra-bloc trade in computers was that early production in the various countries relied on completely different technology. The first Soviet computers were domestically designed copies of earlier Western models. Czechoslovakia entered the computer business in the early 1950s, also with indigenous technology backed by Western imports. Of all the early producers, Poland was probably the most successful, with a substantial production of small, general-purpose computers of mostly domestic design (e.g., the second-generation Odra model). The first direct imports of Western technology by Poland and Czechoslovakia, in the mid-1960s, were chosen essentially independently by national planners without any interest in matching this technology with that of other countries in the region.* Furthermore, early production turned out to be far behind the Western state of the art (including the models based on Western licenses), thus discouraging potential customers in the region from placing their orders with partner countries. The Soviet Union's independently developed Ural-10 series represented its second generation of computers (Sutton 1973: 318), while the United States had already begun large-scale production of third-generation models by the mid-1960s. The backwardness of Soviet production is reflected in the vintage structure of computers in use compared with that of the models in the United States.

The first CPE production efforts were also too small to support trade in computer systems and/or computer-related goods. Even the largest producer in the region, the Soviet Union, hardly met the needs of its domestic market, leaving marginal quantities for export (Goodman 1979a: 528). The Soviet industry experienced severe production problems, which kept its output at a low level until the late 1960s. Total production for the first Soviet upwardly compatible family of computers—the Ural-10 series—reached about 1,000 units in 1965-75, while (for example) IBM produced 35,000 units of its S-360 family during 1965-70 alone (Davis and Goodman 1978: 98).

All of these shortcomings became clear to Soviet planners by the end of the 1960s, when they realized that the Eastern computer

*Imports of Western computer technology had been severely constrained by embargoes, mostly owing to U.S. insistence. Less restrictive policies by some Western countries regarding exports of technology to the CPEs worked to their advantage. To illustrate, in 1963-67 West European countries sold more than 200 complete plants for various industries to the East, while American companies were hardly present on the Eastern market; many of these exports were forbidden by U.S. embargo listings. Although American companies were competitive in these products, they could not fully enter the race for Eastern orders. Of 80 computer systems supplied to Eastern Europe by 1966 only 13 were supplied by the United States, the unquestionable Western leader in computers, but 38 units were sold by second-place Great Britain.

industry was far from able to meet regional demand—especially the needs of the Soviet military (Goodman 1979a: 547). In 1969 the Soviet Union persuaded all but one of the East Europeans to undertake a joint production program. Few of the East Europeans were eager to do so. Czechoslovakia and Poland, each with substantial potential, did so only very reluctantly. Romania completely rejected the idea and decided to continue its general policy of loosening its economic dependence on Eastern countries (the Soviet Union in particular) and relying on Western technology supplies.

Joint production was divided among all the CPEs (except Romania). The Soviet Union was assigned the largest number of models—small, medium, and large computers (including the so-called super-large units). Some of these were to be produced in cooperation with other industries in the region (Bulgarian in particular). Poland and East Germany were to produce medium-scale computers of the Ryad family, while East Germany was also responsible for the development of large computers. Czechoslovakia was assigned small-scale computers, and Hungary, small and microcomputers.

The idea behind the joint program was not just to pool all the national resources in the region, but also to get different countries to buy different pieces of computer technology from the West. The Soviet Union was interested in this cooperation only partly in order to save on the costs of Western imports. More important, it expected the East Europeans to obtain those technologies which Soviet industry, the prime target of Western restrictions, could not purchase on its own (Tasky 1981: 313-14). Soviet planners considered Western technology essential for the program's success because their real purpose in creating the program was to obtain and imitate Western technology rather than to promote a genuine system of regional cooperation.

As expected, East European producers acquired the bulk of Western technology supplied to the region. The total (i.e., manufacturing equipment, design information, and components) to Eastern Europe amounted to $54 million during 1972-78, with Romania the largest importer ($32.4 million), followed by Hungary ($9.9 million) and Poland ($6.1 million) (Tasky 1981: 313-14). In contrast, the Soviet Union imported very little—$1.8 million in 1972-78. Czechoslovakia, East Germany, and Bulgaria have also purchased only very small amounts of technology.

Large portions of the purchases were for computer systems. Since 1969 several East European countries have decided to follow the lead of early importers—i.e., Poland and Czechoslovakia. Bulgaria entered computer production after it purchased a Japanese license for a medium-sized machine in the early 1970s. Hungary's purchase of licenses to manufacture small computers from the French Compagnie Internationale pour l'Informatique (CII) was a turning point in its computer industry. France also supplied licenses for computer production to Romania (the Felix C-256 computer). East Germany and the Soviet Union did not acquire any licenses for computer systems technology directly from the West.

Much of the technology acquired since 1969 has been in the area of computer peripherals, where the CPEs had traditionally lagged more than in any other area of computer production. For instance, in the mid-1960s disk storage was unknown to Soviet industry, and only a small number of alphanumeric line printers and advanced displays were manufactured in the country. The Soviet Union had been refused Western peripheral technology during the 1970s, but Poland, Hungary, and Bulgaria in particular have recently acquired substantial amounts of such technology. It is estimated that peripherals accounted for as much as 70 percent of all computer technology imported by Eastern Europe from the West during 1971-79 (Tasky 1981).

A large amount of Western technology for manufacturing semiconductors has also been supplied to Eastern Europe from Western countries since 1969. Poland acquired licenses for semiconductor production from several Western companies, including Westinghouse (United States) and Thomson (France). About 25 percent of all semiconductor production in Poland was based on Western licenses during 1971-75. Hungary acquired semiconductor technology from Fairchild (United States) and Thomson. However, in all cases the semiconductor technology licensed by Western countries has not represented the state of the art.

These imports of technology have helped the CPEs to scale up their computer production significantly. While the Soviet Union was producing only several hundred computers in the early 1970s, its current production is close to 2,000 units annually (Goodman 1979a: 535). It is estimated that the Soviet Union manufactures up to 1,500 Ryad models within the joint program, as well as several hundred Ryad-compatible computers based on different designs. East European data on Ryad computers show an increase from 40 units delivered in 1973 to 1,345 units in 1978, with Hungary expanding its output of mini-Ryad models from 10 to 140 over this period. A number of other independently designed computers is also manufactured by several East European countries (e.g., Poland and Czechoslovakia).

Recent efforts have also helped the CPEs to upgrade their technology, in particular to move into third-generation computers. Reportedly the Soviet Union designed its first third-generation computer in 1968—i.e., one based on integrated circuit technology (the NAIRI-3 model)—and some East Europeans also designed computers of this level around the same time (Cave 1977: 383-84). However, none of them alone was able to launch a large-scale production of all basic models. Only through coordinated imports of Western technology and extensive "reverse engineering" of Western prototypes (e.g., the American IBM-600 family) by Eastern designers in the framework of the joint program has the region been able to switch from second- to third-generation technology.

Since 1973, when the first joint model of the Ryad series was launched, the CPEs have continuously improved their computer technology. Each year they exhibit new models of third-generation computers. Poland introduced three new models between 1971 and 1978, two of them clearly third-generation computers. Relying on Western technology, Polish engineers constructed a medium-sized second-generation machine (Odra-1300) and a third-generation minicomputer (Mera-400). Moreover, a medium-sized third-generation computer (the ES-1032 model), fitting the Ryad requirements, was developed in these years.

The joint program has turned out to be a success in terms of stimulating intra-bloc trade in computers. Since the sale of the first Ryad models in 1971, the number of computers traded in the region has increased multifold, exceeding the rate of growth of trade in the previous years. Between 1971 and 1978 alone, the Soviet Union exported 400 units of various Ryad models to Eastern Europe, in addition to a large number of other models—compared with fewer than 200 units in the 1960s (Scherbina 1979). The East Europeans were exporting very small quantities of computers within the region until the late 1960s, but in 1976-80 they shipped more than 500 computers to the Soviet Union alone.

Poland's trade with the Soviet Union in computer parts and semiconductors is a good illustration of the heavy Soviet orientation of the East European computer industries. The value of components sold by Poland to the Soviet Union increased from 34 million zlotys in 1973 to 119.5 million in 1980. In 1980 exports of Soviet components to Poland amounted to 84 million zlotys, or about 70 percent of Polish supplies to the Soviet Union. In 1980 Poland sold the Soviet Union semiconductors worth 31.4 million zlotys, while it bought Soviet semiconductors for 19.7 million zlotys—i.e., 63 percent of the value of Polish deliveries.

Specialization has also developed in the regional trade in peripherals. Poland has become a major supplier of high-speed line printers, produced under the British ICL license, as well as disk drive devices and display terminals (Tasky 1981). Hungary now specializes in graphic devices, but it also produces disk and tape drives as well as card readers based on licenses purchased from the United States (i.e., American Data Products Corporation) and Sweden (i.e., Saab-Scania). Bulgaria had become the leading supplier of magnetic disk peripheral equipment by the end of the 1970s due to its aggressive borrowing of Western technology and substantial investment in that product area.

The expansion in intra-regional trade has clearly benefited the Soviet Union in several ways. For one thing, the East European imports help to satisfy its unbalanced domestic market for computers, peripherals, etc. Moreover, by importing from Eastern Europe, it saves large amounts of Western currency. Although the East European computers and other hardware have a substantial hard currency component, the Soviet Union pays for these goods in nonconvertible rubles. Over the 1970s Bulgaria alone constructed twelve new plants to make computers and peripherals, furnished mostly with Western machinery; the majority of the output is sold to the Soviet Union (Radovsky 1979).

Some Eastern European countries also appear to be beneficiaries, especially because they have apparently gained easy access to the vast and stable Soviet market for computers and peripherals. The importance of this fact seems evident if one compares Bulgaria and Hungary, which unconditionally joined the Soviet-sponsored joint program, with Poland and Czechoslovakia, which looked more toward Western markets in the 1970s. The former have built heavily export-oriented industries (up to 50 percent of total output), supplying large quantities to the Soviet Union, while the latter still produce more for domestic markets after unsuccessful attempts at working their way into Western markets.

One questions, however, whether some of the East European countries might not have been better off without investing in large computer complexes, despite the vast Soviet market for their products.

Some of them have not been able to accumulate sufficient expertise in computer technology—Bulgaria, Hungary, and Romania in particular—and the costs of putting together a modern manufacturing system in computers—especially in comparison with alternative directions of investment—are unquestionably high. Unfortunately no data can be provided in support of this hypothesis.

One could argue that some of the East European countries would have been better off if they had tried to meet their needs by importing basic equipment from Western markets. In the case of the Soviet Union, the scale of domestic needs and the serious concern with security justify a huge effort, which the country has recently undertaken. In smaller countries these considerations do not apply. These countries should have been able to pay the bills for imported Western equipment; by relying on these supplies, they would probably have acquired a more technologically advanced computer system than they developed within the joint program or were able to acquire from partners in this venture.

It is not certain, moreover, whether the East Europeans can expect the Soviet market to offer them a continuous outlet. Current Western assessments of growth in Eastern Europe are confusing. For instance, it has been stated that Bulgaria, one of the leading Soviet suppliers, would certainly continue to expand its exports and reach a level equal to its bill for Soviet oil imports (*Financial Times*, 3 February 1982). However, as Tasky (1979: 510-23) points out, it is likely that the Soviet Union will lose interest in Bulgarian (or more generally East European) supplies because its domestic production may rapidly mature technologically and soon approach the point of self-sufficiency as well.

More important in the context of the issues discussed here, even the most rapidly expanding CPE industries have not moved closer to Western computer technology in recent years. The Soviet Union—regional leader in most computer fields—was able to somewhat reduce the technological gap in the mid-1970s. However, some evaluations indicate that this modest success has recently been reversed (Goodman 1984), mostly due to a current upswing in computer technology in the West. Ongoing Western expansion in microcomputers (including personal models), rapid improvements in the capacity of electronic chips, a wide range of new applications for chip technology, and progress in software have stretched the gap back to the earlier estimate of close to fifteen years (Goodman 1984: 35).

It may be difficult for the region to gain any ground in the technological race with the Western computer industry in the years to come due to the recent cuts in imports as well as other factors (e.g., at least a temporary refocusing of national priorities on other industries). The import cuts have adversely affected the East European industry. The case of Poland is instructive here, though one should refrain from easy generalization. Faced with foreign debt problems, Poland started to squeeze its imports from Western countries, first selectively around 1977 and then across the board in 1979 and after. As a result (and for other reasons as well), the production of central processors dropped from 100 units in 1975 to 59 units in 1979 to 29 units in 1980, and the output has not recovered since (Szuprowicz 1982: 92). Forced cuts in the import of components have negatively affected other producers in Eastern Europe as well. The Bulgarian industry has been the least hurt (Tasky 1981).

In sum, there is strong evidence that through a joint research effort the CPEs, with the help of large supplies of Western technology have made progress in the computer industry. Careful specialization has provided the basis for a radical increase in intra-bloc trade in computers and related products, with the smaller economies of Bulgaria and Hungary benefiting in particular—at least on a short-run basis. However, CPE technology clearly remains inferior to and generally incompatible with that of the West, thus undermining sales outside the region.

Neither the productivity comparison nor the data on foreign trade in technology-intensive goods indicate that the CPEs have been able to narrow their technological gap with Western countries. Moreover, the statistics on export unit values suggest that the region is now lagging behind even more than at the beginning of the 1970s. All the data imply that the most conservative importers of Western technology have been the least susccessful in improving the technological level of goods they offer on Western markets—East Germany and Bulgaria being the most striking cases.

The case studies on the automotive, chemical, and computer industries indicate that even in the sectors with the heaviest injections of Western technology, the CPEs have not made much progress in catching up with the West. At best they were able to gain some ground for a period of time, only to lose it in subsequent years. This is not to say that the aggressive importers of Western technology have not been doing better in terms of technological modernization than the more conservative countries. The case of automobile production probably provides the best illustration that they have.

All our comparisons with Western countries provide partial evidence that the latest systemic reforms in the CPEs have not made much difference in terms of their effort to catch up with Western levels of technology. In addition, it seems that under the reforms even large-scale imports of superior Western technology cannot contribute significantly to the catch-up effort—very likely because the present institutional set-up reduces the potential benefits from ouside technology (a point which will be analyzed in more detail below).

Chapter 5

EAST-SOUTH COMPARISONS OF TECHNOLOGICAL LEVELS

In Chapter 4 we demonstrated that the CPEs have not continued in recent years to reduce their technological lag behind the Western economies. To fully corroborate this observation it would be useful to look at other countries that have also been trying to reduce their gaps vis-à-vis the Western leaders. Comparisons between the CPEs and such countries have been lacking, thus permitting the view that there is nothing abnormal about the persistence of the CPE gap. Here we wish to compare the CPEs with the NICs rather than with less advanced Western countries (such as Spain) because by and large the NICs—unlike the less advanced Western countries—entered the postwar period not only with a dramatic lag behind the Western leaders, but behind the CPEs as well.

Our analysis will focus on Eastern Europe (with a few references to the Soviet Union) and the following NICs: Brazil, Mexico, and Argentina in Latin America, and Hong Kong, Singapore, South Korea, and Taiwan in the Far East. The NICs, particularly the Far Eastern economies, are known for their phenomenal growth and spectacular trade achievements. For this reason, one might consider this choice of countries biased and suggest taking other, less successful economies as a point of reference. However, from a methodological point of view there is nothing objectionable about selecting the NICs. Performance aside, these countries have more in common with the CPEs—at least with the historically less advanced East Europeans—than does Eastern Europe with the most developed Western economies (which are so frequently used for comparisons with Eastern Europe). Moreover, one should keep in mind that the trends noted above in the NICs are not completely unknown to other developing countries. Indeed many economists distinguish a "second tier" of newly industrializing countries, with Malaysia, Thailand, the Philippines, and Venezuela as examples; these countries have performed well too. It would certainly be useful to look at these countries as well, or to include some of the less successful economies in the kind of comparison we are going to make. However, this goes beyond the capabilities of the author at this point. (See some evidence on an enlarged sample of developing countries in Poznanski 1982b).

This backward-looking comparison of technological levels employs most of the indicators used in our analysis of technological gaps separating the CPEs from the market-type Western economies. There is only one important methodological difference: owing to data limitations (among other reasons), we have had to forego a productivity analysis. We shall focus somewhat more on trade-type indicators, which (along with certain other indicators) are calculated for a larger number of industrial sectors than in the preceding analysis.

CHANGES IN THE VALUE OF EXPORTS

Our comparison begins with an analysis of export values for Eastern Europe and the NICs in their trade with Western economies. These cannot be considered good indicators of technological progress; indeed we did not list trends in total exports or in basic categories of exports among the indicators of technological performance. For one thing, the rates of growth in exports from any group of economies to a given market reflect a change not only in the technological levels of these economies, but also in the scale of their investment programs, trade preferences for certain markets, etc. Nonetheless, such an analysis provides some guidance in the evaluation of technological performance.

Both groups of countries reported substantial increases in their total sales to the West in 1970-83, with the NICs sharply exceeding the performance of Eastern Europe. Time series data, uncorrected for inflation or changes in cross-country exchange rates, show that Eastern Europe increased its total exports to the OECD countries from \$3.5 billion in 1970 to \$15.5 billion in 1981 and to \$14.2 billion in 1983—an increase of 405 percent. Despite the size of this increase, Eastern Europe was unable to widen its share of the OECD market. Instead this share dropped from 1.5 percent in 1970 to 1.2 percent in 1981; it had further declined to 1.1 percent by 1983. The growth index for the NICs was 1012 percent, with sales of \$9.7 billion in 1970, \$87.2 billion in 1981, and \$98.2 billion in 1983. This expansion of total exports was strong enough to allow the NICs to increase their market share from 4.2 percent in 1970 to 6.7

percent in 1981 and to 8.0 percent in 1983. Table 1 compares East European and NIC shares in OECD imports for 1970-84.

The poor performance by Eastern Europe during 1981 contributed strongly to this divergence in export trends, but by no means can it be attributed solely to recent events such as the energy crisis. In 1981 sales from Eastern Europe declined by 14.6 percent, which reduced its market share in OECD imports by 0.1 percent. Interestingly, none of the East European countries reported any marked improvements in that year, and a majority showed substantial losses. Poland, hit by a severe economic crisis, contributed much to this drop in East European exports, but Czechoslovakia, Hungary, and Bulgaria suffered too. In contrast, 1981 exports from the NICs increased by 13.4 percent, with only Argentine sales stagnating. This boost helped increase their market share from 5.7 percent in 1980 to the aforementioned 6.7 percent in 1981.

For those who perceive Eastern Europe as technologically more advanced than the developing countries (including the NICs), it must come as a surprise that it has been most outmatched in the export of manufactures—chiefly chemicals, manufactured goods by material, machinery and transport equipment, and miscellaneous manufactures. Exports of manufactures from Eastern Europe to the OECD increased by 497 percent during 1970-81, whereas the comparable figure for the NICs was 1336 percent.* As a result, Eastern Europe was able only to maintain its 1970 market share of 1.2 percent in 1981 (down to 1.1 percent in 1983), while the NICs increased their share from 2.8 percent in 1970 to 7.4 percent in 1981 (and 8.5 percent in 1982 and 1983).

The gap in export performance has been particularly drastic in machinery and transport equipment, considered the technologically most complex group among manufactures. Though the East Europeans showed above-average results for these exports, the figures still contrasted sharply with those for the NICs. The growth index for Eastern Europe in 1970-81 was 723 percent, while for the NICs it was 1861 percent. Consequently the East European share in the OECD remained 0.6 percent during 1970-81, compared with an increase from 1.2 to 5.0 percent for the NICs. By 1983 the East European share dropped to 0.4 percent, whereas the NIC share rose to 6.6 percent.

*This dramatic difference is even better illustrated by a comparison of the best performing East European—i.e., Hungary—with a 950 percent increase, and the leader among the NICs—i.e., Singapore—with a 4982 percent increase.

Table 1

MARKET SHARES OF EASTERN EUROPE AND THE NICS IN TOTAL OECD IMPORTS OF MAJOR MANUFACTURED GOODS, 1970-84
(Percent)

Import Category	1970	1980	1981	1982	1983	1984
Total (SITC - 0-8)						
Eastern Europe	1.5%	1.3%	1.2%	1.1%	1.1%	1.2%
Latin America	2.4	2.5	3.0	3.1	3.6	3.8
Far East	1.8	3.2	3.7	3.7	4.4	5.2
NIC subtotal	4.2	5.7	6.7	6.8	8.0	9.0
Chemicals (SITC-5)						
Eastern Europe	1.5	1.4	1.5	1.5	1.5	1.4
Latin America	0.7	0.9	1.3	1.1	1.4	1.9
Far East	0.2	0.8	0.8	0.9	0.9	1.2
NIC subtotal	0.9	1.7	2.1	2.0	2.3	3.1
Manufactured goods by material (SITC-6)						
Eastern Europe	1.6	1.6	1.5	1.6	1.7	1.6
Latin America	0.7	1.5	1.6	1.9	2.3	2.8
Far East	1.4	3.2	4.1	4.1	4.6	5.0
NIC subtotal	2.1	4.7	5.7	6.0	6.9	7.8
Machinery and transport equipment (SITC-7)						
Eastern Europe	0.6	0.8	0.6	0.5	0.4	0.4
Latin America	0.3	1.1	1.4	1.5	1.8	2.0
Far East	0.9	3.1	3.6	3.9	4.8	5.6
NIC subtotal	1.2	4.2	5.0	5.4	6.6	7.6
Miscellaneous manufactures (SITC-8)						
Eastern Europe	1.8	2.1	1.8	1.7	1.6	1.5
Latin America	0.6	1.2	1.5	1.5	1.5	1.8
Far East	10.2	16.1	19.8	19.1	19.8	21.6
NIC subtotal	10.8	17.3	20.1	20.6	21.3	23.4
Total manufactures (SITC - 5-8)						
Eastern Europe	1.2	1.4	1.2	1.2	1.1	1.0
Latin America	0.6	1.4	1.5	1.7	1.7	2.2
Far East	2.2	4.8	5.9	6.8	6.8	7.6
NIC subtotal	2.8	6.2	7.4	8.5	8.5	9.8

Source: Calculated from OECD, *Foreign Trade by Commodities*, various years.

The most striking comparison in the export of machinery and transport equipment is between Taiwan alone and the whole of Eastern Europe. In 1970 Taiwan's exports in this category to the OECD market amounted to $183 million, which exceeded the sales of Czechoslovakia, then the leader among the East Europeans, with a total of $135 million. In 1983 Taiwan sold $5257 million of machinery and transport equipment—almost four times the entire East European figure of $1482 million; moreover, the Taiwanese exports were three times the exports of Eastern Europe and the Soviet Union combined. It is interesting to note that the exports from Taiwan were slightly lower than those from Eastern Europe in 1977, but that since then they have more than tripled, while those of Eastern Europe have increased by only about one third (with a sharp drop reported in 1983).

Eastern Europe has been surpassed in the export of machinery and transport equipment by the three Latin American countries as well, even though these countries give more priority to domestic concerns than do the Far Eastern economies. The Latin Americans have hewed closer to the East European policy not only in their focus on domestic affairs, but also in their strong stress on heavier equipment such as ships, machine tools, motor vehicles (i.e., passenger cars and trucks), and specialized machinery (e.g., for steelmaking)—in contrast to the consumer electronics and household equipment favored by the Far East. Still the three Latin American countries—Brazil in particular—have performed much better than Eastern Europe. In 1970 Latin American exports of machinery and transport equipment to the OECD amounted to $201 million, whereas Eastern Europe reported $369 million, or 183 percent of the Latin American figure. In 1983, on the other hand, Eastern Europe sold goods valued at $1671 million, compared with $7457 million by Latin America, or only 22 percent as much (Poznanski 1986a).

Eastern Europe has also been falling behind the NICs in all other groups of manufactures—including chemicals, where many Western observers had expected massive exports of East European products. Chemicals were the only manufactures where East European exports exceeded those of the NICs in 1970: sales amounted to $235 million and $144 million respectively—i.e., three fourths as much for the NICs. In 1983, however, sales by the NICs amounted to $2093 million, whereas Eastern Europe sold only $1366 million—just the reverse of the 1970 proportion. The share of Eastern Europe in OECD imports of chemicals was 1.5 percent in 1970, and it remained at this level in 1981 and 1983. The NICs increased their share from only 0.9 percent in 1970 to 2.1 percent in 1981 to 2.3 percent in 1983.

In manufactured goods classified by materials, including various goods for further processing (e.g., steel, nonferrous metals, cotton and other types of fabric), the Far Eastern economies were already exporting more than Eastern Europe in 1970, with respective sales of $970.2 million and $762 million. In 1983 the difference in sales was much more dramatic, with Eastern Europe exporting $2.6 billion and the NICs $12.0 billion— more than four and a half times the East European total. The East European market share in the OECD dropped slightly between 1970 and 1981, from 1.6 to 1.5 percent, but increased to 1.7 percent in 1983. The NICs gained in the OECD market, increasing their share from 2.1 percent in 1970 to 5.7 percent in 1981 to 6.9 percent in 1983. The three Latin American countries alone were supplying a larger fraction of this market in 1983 than Eastern Europe, although their share in 1970 had been much smaller.

In 1970 Eastern Europe was most outmatched by the NICs in exports labeled "miscellaneous manufactures," composed mostly of garments, footwear, and furniture. At that time the exports from Eastern Europe totaled $339 million, while the NICs sold $2.1 billion, or six times as much. In 1983 Eastern Europe exported $2.0 billion of goods—only slightly more than had the NICs in 1970. In 1983 NIC sales amounted to $22 billion—eleven times more than Eastern Europe. The OECD market share of Eastern Europe did not change during 1970-81, remaining at 1.8 percent; it dropped to 1.6 percent in 1983. In contrast, the NICs increased their share of OECD imports from 10.8 percent in 1970 to 20.1 percent in 1981 to 21.3 percent in 1983, a dramatic improvement considering the high initial share.

Any comparison involving Eastern Europe and the NICs is complicated by the fact that the two groups do most of their Western trade with different partners, the former with Western Europe and the latter with the United States (and to a lesser degree Japan). Any changes in the exchange rate between the dollar and West European currencies (particularly those of West Germany, France, and Britain, which are the major partners of Eastern Europe) distort the dollar-denominated trade data on exports from the two groups. Thus, for instance, if the dollar appreciates, the dollar figure will be "inflated" for the NIC exports and "deflated" for those of

Eastern Europe. This distortion will be amplified if the NICs simultaneously shift more of their exports to the United States.

There is a need to correct the above OECD data because the dollar exchange rates have gone through considerable shifts since 1970. The dollar was declining during 1970-80, with major reductions in its value during 1971-73 and 1977-78. During the 1970-80 period the dollar lost almost 50 percent against the German mark (for instance); it also lost much against the French franc and several other West European currencies (including that of Austria, an important trading partner for Eastern Europe). Thus the uncorrected data on the OECD imports put a downward bias on the NIC figures for this period; the real value of NIC exports exceeded that of East European exports by more than is suggested above. On the other hand, the NIC advantage in 1981-83 seems exaggerated because in those years the dollar started to appreciate (e.g., by at least 30 percent against the German mark; see IMF, various years).

To check whether the OECD data seriously distort the actual picture, we shall use European Community trade data for the Common Market; these are denominated not in dollars but in the European Currency Units (ECU; see EEC). By looking at these data, we can to some degree eliminate the distortions stemming from the dollar/West European currency exchange rates. The ECU figures also show that there has been a pronounced tendency for the East Europeans to lose market shares in total Common Market imports, whereas the NICs as a group have shown clear gains. Thus between 1970 and 1980 the East European share dropped from 2.04 percent to 1.68 percent, and then to 1.56 percent in 1984 (the last most likely due primarily to the collapse of Poland's economy). The NICs increased their share in total imports from 2.53 percent in 1970 to 3.19 percent in 1980 and 3.73 percent in 1983.

The above results for Eastern Europe are in line with the numerical trends established for the OECD; according to both OECD and European Community data, the East European shares declined by about one fourth in point terms. In contrast, the gains by the NICs in the Common Market are less pronounced than those for the OECD total—a one and a half time gain against an almost twofold increase. Most likely the difference reflects a greater NIC success in penetrating non-West European segments of the OECD import market (particularly the United States). Another factor is the exchange rate.

To further test how reliable the OECD data for particular product groups are, we look at the machinery and transport equipment category alone. The East European share of Common Market imports increased from 0.80 percent in 1970 to 0.82 percent in 1980 (a marginal gain) and then fell drastically to 0.64 percent in 1984. The initial increase was smaller than what was reported by the OECD, as was the decline in the share. The NICs raised their share from 0.29 percent in 1970 to 1.98 percent in 1980—more than indicated by the OECD statistics—and then to 2.66 percent in 1984 (again more than the OECD statistics). Nonetheless, the Eurostat and OECD data show similar divergent trends between the two groups for this category. We can assume that these similarities hold for other manufactures as well.

PRODUCT OVERLAPS ON WESTERN MARKETS

More instructive than the analysis of trends in export values is an investigation of product structures in Eastern Europe and the NICs and a comparison of unit values paid to them on the same foreign market. The fact that exports of manufactured goods to the West from the NICs have been expanding much faster than sales from Eastern Europe does not in itself necessarily imply that the two groups are engaged in an open trade rivalry. This would be the case only if they have moved into the same product areas, representing very similar (but not necessarily identical) technology.

To find out whether there are strong product overlaps or not, we can look at the composition of the leading exports from these countries to Western markets. The data on manufactured exports to the OECD reveal that while there were few overlaps in 1970, they were substantial in 1980, due either to the successful promotion of new exports by the NICs in areas where Eastern Europe had earlier concentrated its export effort (e.g., steel and ships), or to the parallel expansion of new exports by the two groups (e.g., passenger cars and motor vehicle parts).

In 1980 as much as one third of manufactured exports consisted of similar products, representing major positions in total sales by particular countries. They included garments, footwear, steel, electrical machinery (particularly rotary electric plants), passenger cars and motor vehicle parts (including internal combustion engines), and ships. While there were some differences in the product structure as well, they did not change the overall picture of strong similarities. The NICs were more dependent on the sales of telecommunications equipment (e.g., radio receivers from Taiwan and Hong Kong) and office machines (e.g., Mexico), whereas several types of chemicals and machine tools played particularly significant roles in a few East European countries (e.g., Czechoslovakia and East Germany; Poznanski 1986a).

These overlaps are stronger than a comparison of the product structure of exports might suggest because it appears that within the general categories of overlap, the sales from both groups tend to be concentrated in the lower- or medium-quality segments. This is suggested by a comparison of export-unit prices (i.e., price per kilogram) obtained by Eastern Europe and the NICs compared with those paid to Western exporters. With very few exceptions, the export-unit prices paid in 1980 for ten selected East European and NIC manufactured goods to the OECD market amounted to only one half (or less) of those obtained by Western products in the same category—which clearly represented a higher level of quality (see Table 2).

There is also evidence that the NICs very rarely sell manufactured goods of lowest relative price (calculated per kilogram), whereas Eastern Europe does so quite often. In the ten product categories covered in Table 2, the lowest export-unit price was usually paid to one of the East European countries. For instance, the lowest price for passenger cars was received by East Germany—namely, $1.69 per kilogram—compared with $4.55 per kilogram for Mexican suppliers. East Germany also recieved the lowest price for its footwear—$3.15 per kilogram of exports in 1980 (compared with $17.89 for Brazil). Poland received only $1.98 per kilogram for its textile and leather machinery, in sharp contrast to the $6.25 paid to Taiwan.

This contrast in relative prices can be taken as a further indication that the NICs have technologically surpassed Eastern Europe—at least in the ten product areas under discussion. However, this can also be interpreted differently—i.e., as an indication that the NICs do not push their poor-quality goods onto Western markets and that the East Europeans often choose to sell such products (not necessarily because no higher-quality substitutes are available). This is only a speculation, but not without some merit if one recalls the well-demonstrated fact that the East European economies, with an irrational price structure and misguided incentive system, do not

Table 2

EXPORT-UNIT PRICES (PER KILOGRAM) FOR SELECTED PRODUCTS TO THE OECD MARKET FROM WESTERN EUROPE, EASTERN EUROPE, AND THE NICS, 1980

(In dollars)

	Export									
	Polymerization Products	Man-Made Fabrics	Tires	Steel (Plates & Sheets)	Internal Combustion Engines	Rotary Electric Plants	Textile & Leather Machinery	Machine Tools	Passenger Cars	Footwear
Western Europe										
Great Britain	$ 1.65	$ 7.57	$ 3.34	$ 0.77	$ 6.74	$ 6.05	$13.74	$11.19	$ 5.01	$21.06
Italy	1.37	11.30	3.59	0.65	6.76	5.96	10.51	9.88	5.29	16.68
France	1.22	12.90	3.39	0.63	7.09	7.27	10.65	8.92	5.86	15.46
West Germany	1.52	10.04	2.90	0.60	7.11	9.18	14.06	12.27	6.54	23.57
Eastern Europe										
East Germany	0.75	5.74	2.04	0.38	5.00	2.18	5.92	4.61	1.69	3.15
Czechoslovakia	0.76	5.42	2.12	0.34	3.77	1.97	8.66	3.47	2.12	6.85
Poland	0.82	5.70	3.04	0.33	3.16	2.58	1.98	3.66	3.19	9.43
Hungary	0.71	5.94	2.14	0.35	6.39	2.34	3.76	6.56	--	10.53
Romania	0.75	5.40	1.69	0.36	2.53	2.01	--	--	--	7.84
NICs										
Brazil	--	6.62	3.06	0.39	4.56	2.67	7.87	9.26	3.58	17.89
Mexico	--	--	--	--	4.43	--	6.71	--	4.55	12.28[b]
South Korea	0.93[a]	7.27	2.60	0.49	4.54[a]	8.27[a]	5.18	4.99	3.28	6.19
Taiwan	1.01[a]	5.06	2.85	0.58[b]	7.65	11.65[a]	6.25	3.47	--	7.89

Source: Calculated from OECD, *Trade by Commodities*, 1982.

[a]Exports to Japan.

[b]Exports to the United States.

optimize their trade but rather tend to target their export revenues to balance an arbitrary amount of imports permitted by planners (see Wolf 1982: 54-67).

A look at the geographical destination of exports from the two groups of countries suggests that the trade rivalry might be less severe than indicated by the aforementioned data. As noted, most exports from Eastern Europe are headed for Western Europe—the Common Market in particular—whereas those from the NICs are primarily geared to the United States and Japan. For instance, in 1980 the United States imported 50.2 percent of all NIC manufactures exported to the OECD market but only 7.1 percent of the corresponding East European exports. At the same time, the members of the Common Market purchased only 27.0 percent of manufactures from the NICs and 62.6 percent of those from Eastern Europe.

Under closer examination it turns out that Eastern Europe is facing strong competition not only in the United States, but also in Western Europe. NIC advances in the 1970s have helped them to improve their market position in Western Europe relative to that of Eastern Europe. Moreover, in many instances the NICs have captured a larger share of the market for certain goods than has Eastern Europe (e.g., garments, some consumer electronics). The highest shares obtained by the NICs for their leading exports greatly exceed what the East Europeans have been able to obtain for their most important exports (e.g., some petrochemicals, steel).

It is worth adding that the strong attachment of the East Europeans to the West European market can be a handicap in their competition with the NICs because Western Europe—particularly the Common Market countries—shows a lower propensity to import manufactured goods from all newcomers than does the United States. In 1980, for instance, the Common Market countries imported 54.8 percent of all manufactures purchased by the OECD countries, but only 39.7 percent of the suppliers were from Eastern Europe and the NICs combined. In contrast, the U.S. share in total OECD imports in that year was 17.6 percent, but the combined East European and NIC share in these imports was 50.6 percent.

ANALYSIS OF BASIC MANUFACTURES

To further test some of the above observations and bring new elements into the analysis, a more disaggregated look at the two groups of countries since 1970 is necessary. Among other tests, one should attempt to find a direct measure of relative technological performance by the two groups because (as indicated in our methodological discussion) export performance data are polluted by factors other than technological advances. Finding this additional evidence is the major purpose of this section.

A common opinion among economists is that Eastern Europe (and the Soviet Union) continues to have a technological edge over the rapidly growing countries of Latin America and the Far East. Unfortunately this view has not been derived from quantitative data since (as noted) no comparative studies of technological gaps between these regions have been done to date. This lack of data was not so essential in the first postwar years, when the relative technological backwardness of Latin America and the Far East—particularly in comparison with Czechoslovakia and East Germany—was so obvious that even casual observation seemed to provide sufficient grounds for making a reasonable judgment on the issue. However, it is possible that the last decade and a half of dynamic economic expansion in the NICs has changed their technological position relative to Eastern Europe.

We shall focus on several manufacturing sectors in Eastern Europe and the NICs from industries which cover the whole production spectrum—i.e., intermediate goods, capital goods, and consumer products; the sectors represent areas of particular importance for export promotion by both groups of countries. Our analysis of changes in competitiveness will include the following: a comparison of production capacities as one of the major preconditions of trade; an assessment of relative technological levels (seen as another trade-determining factor); and a comparison of actual export data. These will be presented so as to directly highlight the trade struggle between Eastern Europe and the NICs.

INTERMEDIATE GOODS

Eastern Europe entered the 1970s with a substantial advantage over all the NICs in the production of intermediate goods—including steel and basic chemicals (e.g., sulphuric acid and soda ash). If the quantities of key intermediate products are used as indicators of economic advancement, the NICs as a group would have to be regarded as lagging dramatically behind Eastern Europe in 1970 and as being quite inferior in 1981 and after. However, the qualitative aspects must also be considered—including the technological level of production and the competitive positions on the world market. A look at these aspects suggests that the NICs represent a comparable if not superior level of technology in such products as steel and some chemicals and that they outcompete Eastern Europe in the Western markets for these products as well.

Iron and Steel. In 1970 East European production capabilities in the steel industry were several times larger than those of the NICs. In that year the region's total output of steel ingots was 38.4 million tons, whereas the NICs (excluding Argentina, Hong Kong, and Singapore) produced less than 11 million tons—i.e., only about one quarter of the East European total. In 1981, however, this difference was substantially smaller: Eastern Europe produced 62.0 million tons and the NICs, 27.9 million tons—almost half the East European total. Due to expansion in the 1970s, Eastern Europe was able to increase its share in the world production of steel ingots from 6.7 percent in 1970 to 8.0 percent in 1981, while the NICs enlarged their share from an estimated 1.8 percent to 4.1 percent. The NIC improvement resulted mostly from a tremendous expansion of steel production in Brazil and South Korea, whose individual outputs remain small by East European standards (e.g., Brazil's production was smaller than that of Poland or Czechoslovakia in 1981).

While smaller in quantitative terms, the steel industry of the NICs now appears to be equally or in some cases even more technologically advanced than that of Eastern Europe. Much effort has been put forth by the East Europeans to modernize their industries, including substantial purchases of Western equipment. However, most of this equipment has continued to be supplied by the Soviet Union, which lags behind the West in technologies for the final stages of steel processing and in high-quality steel. In contrast, the NICs are supplied mostly by large Western corporations, particularly from Japan (Martin 1983). Partly for this reason, their steel industry is using more of the most advanced technologies than is Eastern Europe. To illustrate, in 1982 the share of oxygen-blown steel in Brazil's total output was about 68.4 percent, and it was 74.8 percent in South Korea. The corresponding share for Romania—the highest among East Europeans (and higher than that of the Soviet Union)—was around 46.7 percent, and it was only 8.1 percent for East Germany. (Table 3 shows this share for various countries.)

Table 3

SHARE OF OXYGEN-BLOWN STEEL IN TOTAL OUTPUT OF CRUDE STEEL FOR SELECTED COUNTRIES, 1961-82

(Percent)

	NICs						Eastern Europe			
Year	Argentina	Brazil	Mexico	S. Korea	Taiwan	India	E. Germany	Hungary	Poland	Romania
1961	*[a]	10.6%	*	*	*	*	*	*	*	*
1962	*	9.7	*	*	*	*	*	*	0.5%	*
1963	*	13.5	*	*	*	*	*	*	0.6	*
1964	*	21.2	*	*	*	*	*	*	0.6	*
1965	*	25.4	*	*	*	*	*	*	0.4	*
1966	*	36.5	*	*	*	*	*	*	6.5	*
1967	*	37.6	*	*	*	*	*	*	9.3	n.a.
1968	*	37.4	*	*	*	*	*	*	10.4	6.2%
1969	*	37.5	*	*	*	*	*	*	11.2	18.5
1970	*	37.1	*	*	*	*	*	*	12.7	28.7
1971	*	37.4	*	n.a.	n.a.	*	*	*	17.2	30.8
1972	*	39.8	7.9%	n.a.	n.a.	*	*	*	20.3	33.5
1973	9.4%	40.0	8.8	n.a.	n.a.	2.9%	1.2%	*	22.1	36.2
1974	23.3	39.6	12.4	52.5%	n.a.	7.4	4.1	*	22.7	
1975	19.6	44.3	13.0	55.5	n.a.	16.5	8.8	*	22.3	37.3
1976	19.5	38.0	26.8	60.9	18.8%	20.2	9.2	*	21.5	41.5
1977	10.6	56.2		58.2	35.1	22.4	9.4	*	29.4	42.3
1978	19.8	62.2	36.8	57.1	54.6	20.7	9.3	*	36.8	44.1
1979	23.6	63.4	42.7	69.7		24.6			39.1	44.4
1980	26.1	65.0	45.6	69.2	48.8	20.4	9.1	0.1%	39.2	43.6
1981	27.6	62.6	39.8	76.2	48.6	23.9	8.9	14.0	38.2	44.5
1982	21.8	28.4	41.2	74.8	63.4	23.5	8.1	33.1	42.4	46.7

[a] Asterisks indicate no production of oxygen-blown steel.

The recent increases in production and technological capacities by Eastern Europe have been of some help in the effort to penetrate the Western market, at least as far as market shares are concerned. The share of Eastern Europe in OECD imports of steel was 4.9 percent in 1970 and 1981 and had increased to 7.7 percent by 1983. In general the East Europeans—including Czechoslovakia, which has the most export-oriented steel industry in the region—export their steel not for purely profit reasons but rather because they are forced to exchange their surpluses of inexpensive carbon steel for high-quality (chiefly alloy) steels made in the West. In contrast, some of the NICs (e.g., South Korea) have clearly developed their capacities (including the capacity for specialty steels) primarily for the world market. Not surprisingly, these countries were able to increase their share in OECD imports from an insignificant 0.3 percent in 1970 to 5.1 percent in 1981 and 7.0 percent in 1983 (see Table 4).

Petrochemicals. Eastern Europe entered the 1970s with a slight edge over the NICs in the production of modern petrochemicals, a fact reflected in (for instance) the relative output of polyvinylchloride (PVC), one of the crucial intermediate products of the petrochemical industry. In 1975 Eastern Europe (excluding East Germany) produced 556,300 tons of PVC, compared to 467,400 tons for the NICs (excluding Singapore and Hong Kong). However, this gap closed a few years later and reversed in 1981, when the East European and NIC outputs were 735,600 and 985,800 tons respectively. In the production of synthetic fibers the NICs have built up an even bigger lead. In 1967 Eastern Europe produced 109,000 tons of synthetic fibers, whereas the combined output of Korea and Taiwan was 88,000 tons. In 1982, however, the latter two countries produced 583,000 tons against 259,000 tons for Eastern Europe.

In recent years Eastern Europe has significantly reduced its investment in chemicals due to the higher prices of Soviet oil since the 1985 revision of the intra-regional pricing mechanism. Many NICs (e.g., Taiwan, South Korea) have scaled down their programs as well, also due to the higher prices of oil from the Middle East and elsewhere. However, oil-rich countries like Mexico are likely to continue their expansion—as indicated (among other things) by Mexico's increasing output of ethylene (*Maly Rocznik Statystyczny* 1983) and this may give the NICs a clear edge over Eastern Europe in the coming years.

Table 4

SHARES OF EASTERN EUROPE (EE) AND NICS IN WORLD PRODUCTION AND IN OECD IMPORTS OF SELECTED PRODUCTS, 1970-83
(Percent)

Product	Region	1970	1975	1980	1981	1982	1983
Intermediate goods							
Steel (ingots)							
Share in world production	EE	6.7	7.9	8.5	8.0	8.9	9.1
	NIC	1.8	2.5	4.2	4.1	4.5	6.1
Share in OECD imports	EE	4.9	4.9	5.8	4.9	–	7.7
	NIC	0.3	0.4	4.8	5.1	–	7.0
Products of polymerization and copolymerization							
Share in world production	EE	1.9	3.3	4.4	4.7	–	–
	NIC	1.0	3.0	5.6	5.8	–	–
Share in OECD imports	EE	0.7	0.3	1.5	1.8	1.8	1.8
	NIC	0.0	0.1	1.7	2.3	2.5	2.8
Capital goods							
Ships							
Share in world production	EE	3.9	3.7	6.5	6.0	5.7	6.8
	NIC	0.9	2.5	13.2	14.6	13.1	12.3
Share in OECD imports	EE	2.3	2.8	4.4	–	–	2.1
	NIC	0.6	0.8	5.2	–	–	16.4
Machine tools							
Share in world production	EE	9.0	11.5	7.8	7.9	8.3	12.7
	NIC	1.2	1.2	2.8	3.2	3.1	2.1
Share in OECD imports	EE	4.9	4.8	3.6	3.1	2.2	2.0
	NIC	0.0	0.0	2.7	3.4	3.3	4.1
Consumer goods							
Passenger cars							
Share in world production	EE	1.6	2.2	2.8	2.1	2.2	2.4
	NIC	1.7	3.3	5.1	3.4	4.4	3.4
Share in OECD imports	EE	0.2	0.3	0.4	0.3	0.2	0.2
	NIC	0.0	0.0	0.2	0.3	0.3	0.2
Radio receivers							
Share in world production	EE	2.5	3.7	2.8	2.9	2.9	3.0
	NIC	27.5	47.9	44.7	41.4	48.1	45.6
Share in OECD imports	EE	0.3	0.4	0.3	0.3	–	0.1
	NIC	14.6	29.7	38.5	37.7	–	43.4
Watches							
Share in OECD imports	EE	0.4	0.3	0.3	0.1	–	0.1
	NIC	0.7	14.3	30.6	32.5	–	36.4

Sources: For production—United Nations *Bulletin of Statistics of World Trade in Steel*, various years; *Yearbook of Industrial Statistics*, various years; *Monthly Bulletin of Statistics*, various dates; and *Bulletin of Statistics in World Trade in Engineering Products*, various years; *Lloyd's Register of Shipping*, various years; World Automotive Market, various years; *National Machine Tool Builders' Association*, various years; *American Machinist*, various years; and national statistics; for OECD imports—OECD, *Foreign Trade by Commodities*, various years.

The expansion of petrochemicals in the 1970s was based on essentially the same sources of technology for both groups of countries—i.e., Western manufacturers of processing equipment. Most of the major installations in Eastern Europe have been imported on a turnkey basis due to a lack of sufficient capacities in the region and heavy shortages of modern equipment in the Soviet Union. Much the same is true for the NICs with one significant difference—i.e., they have relied less on purchases of complete installations than on direct investment by petrochemical corporations. There has been no significant direct investment by Western corporations in East European petrochemicals, while (for instance) more than half of the total output of the South Korean petrochemical industry comes from foreign subsidiaries and joint ventures (Koo 1982: 69-71).* This closer integration of the NICs with Western corporations is likely to give them some advantage over Eastern Europe—for instance, in the terms of access to some secrets of production technology.

Many countries in both groups have directed much of their new petrochemical output to the Western economies, resulting in a visible improvement of their market positions. For instance, Eastern Europe increased its share of OECD imports of polymerization and copolymerization products from 0.7 percent in 1970 to 1.8 percent in 1981 and 1983, even though (as noted above) its share in total imports of chemicals did not change. The largest gains were reported by East Germany, Czechoslovakia, and Hungary. Even more impressive was the progress of the NICs, whose share in 1970 was negligible but in 1983 reached 2.8 percent, with South Korea and Taiwan the major suppliers (Table 4). However, there are grounds to believe that both groups will find it difficult to go beyond their current shares of Western markets since (aside from Mexico) they are not likely to withstand the growing competition from oil-rich countries (e.g., Indonesia, Saudi Arabia). Consequently, it seems unlikely that either Eastern Europe or the NICs will be able to turn their current deficits in petrochemicals into gains, though some individual countries possibly may do so. (East Germany, for example, already shows a sizable surplus with the OECD market.)

*Koo (1982) lists thirteen foreign firms operating in the South Korean petrochemical industry, all but one of them (Dow Chemical, Netherlands) a joint venture with 50 percent or less foreign ownerships.

CAPITAL GOODS

In capital goods Eastern Europe had a clear advantage over the NICs by the end of the 1960s. This was partly due to its earlier industrial takeoff, particularly by Czechoslovakia and East Germany. It also resulted from the exceptionally high priority East European planners had given to capital-goods industries, which they perceived as a major engine of technological change in their economies. Since the early 1960s many developing countries have intensified their investment effort in capital-goods manufacturing, especially Brazil and Mexico (with their drive toward import substitution) and South Korea (mostly for strategic reasons—i.e., a confrontation with North Korea). Such efforts, have substantially reduced the original differences in output, and in some cases the NICs have surpassed Eastern Europe (e.g., ships). There is evidence that they have been even more successful in catching up with the East European level of technology (e.g., in computers and electronic components).

Commercial Ships. In the production of ships, Eastern Europe enjoyed an enormous lead over the NICs in 1970 (*Lloyd's Register of Shipping* 1971). In that year Eastern Europe (excluding Czechoslovakia, Hungary, and Romania) produced ships with a total tonnage of 849,600 GRT, compared with around 215,000 GRT for the NICs (excluding Mexico and Hong Kong). Indeed the total NIC output was only half that of Poland alone (463,400 GRT in 1970). By 1981, however, the East European figure was 1,037,000 GRT, while the NIC total was an estimated 2,200,000 GRT. By this time South Korea, with virtually no production at the beginning of the 1970s, made more ships than all of Eastern Europe. As a result, while the East European share of world output rose from 3.9 percent in 1970 to 6.0 percent in 1981 and 6.8 percent in 1983, the NIC share rose from 0.9 percent to 12.3 percent during that period (Table 4).

East European shipbuilding was also more technologically advanced in the early 1970s, with Poland the unquestionable leader in the whole sample of countries under discussion here. While the East Europeans were producing various types of vessels—including many involving complex technology—the NICs were concentrating on relatively simple tankers and other bulk cargo ships. (In South Korea only wooden vessels were made as late as 1970.) However, in the mid-1970s the NICs appear to have acquired more advanced technology than Eastern Europe, mostly due to their closer relations with Western corporations, Japanese in particular.* Now in many respects at least some of the NICs seem to be more advanced than Eastern Europe. One piece of evidence is that these countries are heavily involved in the production of relatively complex container ships and oil rigs, which Eastern Europe produces in marginal quantities only.†

Because of these trends in production capacities and technology levels, the NICs have been able to build up an export potential which largely exceeds that of Eastern Europe. In 1970 East Germany, Bulgaria, and Poland exported ships valued at $406.6 million, while Brazil, Mexico, Taiwan, South Korea, and Singapore sold only $33.6 million. In 1979 Poland and East Germany (the major exporters in Eastern Europe) sold about $1.3 billion, only slightly above the NIC exports, which were estimated at $1.2 billion (United Nations 1981a).** In 1982, however, the South Korean shipbuilding industry alone reported orders (the majority from foreigners) for a total tonnage much above that obtained by all of Eastern Europe in the largely depressed world market for ships (*Norwegian Shipping News* 1982); the same was true in 1983.

Machine Tools. Eastern Europe entered the postwar period with an unquestioned lead over the NICs in the volume of machine-tool production, with Czechoslovakia and East Germany having the largest industries. The region continues to hold an edge, but the difference in production has diminished. In 1970 the value of machine tools made by Eastern Europe represented 9.0 percent of world output, whereas the NICs (excluding Argentina and Hong Kong) accounted for 1.2 percent. In 1981 the East European share dropped to 7.9 percent while the combined production of the NICs (excluding Argentina and Hong Kong) amounted to 3.2 percent. While Argentina, Mexico, and Hong Kong continue to have limited capacities, Brazil, South Korea, and Taiwan have established themselves

*The only two Brazilian shipyards able to make large vessels are Japanese subsidiaries (see World Bank 1982).

†In 1981 Brazil, South Korea, and Taiwan produced container ships with a total tonnage of 110,300 GRT, representing 15.2 percent of the world output of these vessels, while Eastern Europe reported production of 8,700 GRT, or 1.2 percent of world output (*Maly Rocznik Statystyczny* 1983: 325-26).

**The data for Eastern Europe are presented in dollar values converted from local currencies with artificially high exchange rates, so the East European advantage is likely to be exaggerated. (Data in units are too fragmented to be used as a substitute.)

as large-scale manufacturers of machine tools in recent years. For instance, Taiwanese production in 1970 represented about 5 percent that of Czechoslovakia in value terms, while in 1981 Taiwan produced 95 percent as much as Czechoslovakia. (Comparisons with other East European countries show equally striking changes.)

The NICs have recently mostly expanded the production of conventional machine tools (i.e., multi-purpose tools for low-precision jobs), while Eastern Europe has focused on the diversification of its production and has entered the field of numerically controlled machine tools and industrial robots. All of Eastern Europe is currently involved in the substantial production of numerically controlled tools. In 1982 East Germany manufactured twenty-one types of such tools, the Soviet Union seventeen types, and Czechoslovakia three types. Most were based on Western designs and components (including complete numerical driving sets). Some of the NICs—particularly South Korea and Taiwan—have also undertaken the production of numerically controlled machine tools and on a larger scale.

We lack sufficient data on the production of numerically controlled machine tools in the NICs to determine their share in total production or to assess their technological level relative to Eastern Europe. Fortunately data are available on the most advanced machines—i.e., computer-controlled models—that obviously accurately reflect the best-practice technology in use in these countries. For Eastern Europe we have only East German data, but it should be kept in mind that East Germany is considered a leader among East Europeans in machine-tool technology, or at least among the top producers (along with Hungary perhaps). Statistics for the NICs are available in most country cases.

The output of computer-controlled machine tools amounted to 43 units in East Germany in 1981, representing 0.2 percent of the total number of machine tools made in that year (and 5 percent of the numerically controlled machines; *DDR Handbuch* 1985: 1479). In comparison, Brazil manufactured 36 such units in 1980, Taiwan, 174 units in 1981, and South Korea, 222 units in 1982 (Jacobsson 1985: 361). In Taiwan the computer-controlled models accounted for around 0.7 percent of the total number of units shipped in 1981 and in South Korea an estimated 3 percent (Poznanski 1985). These data show that Brazil, Taiwan, and South Korea cannot be considered technically lagging in the production of machine tools, though more information is needed for a definitive assessment.

Table 5 shows the production of advanced machine tools in selected East European countries and NICs.

Table 5

NUMERICALLY CONTROLLED MACHINE TOOL PRODUCTION IN SELECTED EAST EUROPEAN COUNTRIES AND NICS, 1975 AND 1981

Region and Country	Year	Machine Tools: Total Number Produced	Numerically Controlled	Computer Numerically Controlled
Eastern Europe				
East Germany	1975	19,720	581	10
	1981	16,800	935	47
Hungary	1975	12,850	--	--
	1981	10,900	363	--
Poland	1975	33,200	180	--
	1981	305,000	201	--
Latin America				
Argentina	1975	162[a]	--	--
	1981	2,361[b]	--	10-15
Brazil	1975	--	--	36
	1981	--	--	36[c]
Far East				
South Korea	1975	1,902	--	--
	1981	3,181[c]	--	222
Taiwan	1975	7,933	--	--
	1981	13,068	--	174

Source: National statistics; Jacobsson 1985.

[a]1979.

[b]1982.

[c]1980.

Despite their continued quantitative lead and strong technological effort, the East Europeans have lost much of their initial advantage to the NICs in terms of market shares of machine tools in the OECD (see Table 4). The East European share dropped from 4.9 percent in 1970 to 3.1 percent in 1981 and 2.0 percent in 1983. In contrast, the NICs (excluding Argentina) enlarged their share from less than 0.1 percent in 1970 to 3.4 percent in 1981 and 4.1 percent in 1983. To a great extent East European performance was a function of the disappointing export expansion by Czechoslovakia, the region's leading supplier to Western markets. Czechoslovakia held 2.1 percent of the OECD market in 1970 but only 1.2 percent in

1981. NIC progress was most evident in the remarkable growth in exports reported by Taiwan. This country had been a marginal supplier in the early 1970s but in 1981 had almost 2 percent of the OECD market.

Computer Equipment. The production of computers began much earlier in Eastern Europe than in the NICs, with the major breakthrough in the computer industries taking place in the 1970s, when all the countries of the region moved into the production of compatible computers and related products. At the same time, some NICs have attracted some Western subsidiaries and made an effort to establish national companies (e.g., Brazil produces minicomputers which are fully reserved for domestic companies; Tigre 1983: 39-73). Nevertheless, many NICs still do not operate sizable computer industries (as do Taiwan and South Korea), although they are preparing to launch programs soon.* There is some evidence that because of the recent buildup of its computer industry, Eastern Europe has been able to at least temporarily retain, if not increase, its original edge in the scale of computer production (though not necessarily in all segments of the industry).

By the 1980s the Soviet Union and Eastern Europe seemed to have fallen behind some of the NICs in the production of microcomputers (also called personal or home computers), however. To fulfill their plan for the computerization of high schools, Soviet leaders had to turn to Western suppliers. (Their own Agat model, a copy of one of the Apple machines, performs so poorly that it cannot be put into mass production.) Reportedly negotiations in 1985 involved a deal for around 60,000 units (*Financial Times*, May 1985). In fact the Soviet Union bought about 4,000 Japanese units that year. (Only the 8-bit machines were made available to the Soviets because the 16-32-bit systems are restricted under a COCOM agreement; *Business Eastern Europe*, 20 December 1985). Despite severely reduced imports, Poland bought 4,000 Atari models in 1985 (*Business Eastern Europe*, 10 February 1986), and Hungary bought 2,000 Commodore personal computers in the same year (*Business Eastern Europe*, 22 November 1985). In comparison, 1985 output in Taiwan reached

*Three U.S. companies (Texas Instruments, Keytronic, and AT&T plan a multimillion dollar investment in the Taiwanese electronic industry. This plan includes the manufacturing of integrated circuits (also very large-scale circuits) and keyboards. However, no sizable production of computer systems will begin in the near future (*Financial Times*, 13 September 1983: 6).

734,900 units—mostly microcomputers copied from Apple (some of the 1987 models already with 32-bit capacity; *Business Week*, 30 March 1987). The discrepancy between CPEs and Far Eastern production is substantial enough to be considered as evidence of a Taiwanese lead (see *Industry of Free China*, October 1986: 112).

While NIC computer production is smaller in scale, it seems to represent a higher technological level than that of Eastern Europe; the same is true for the manufacture of components. The newest computer models manufactured by Eastern Europe are copies of an American computer family introduced in the mid-1960s, and there are many indications that these copies are of poorer quality than the originals (Goodman 1979a and 1979b). In contrast, the NICs rely on direct supplies of Western technology not much different in vintage from that used by the leading Western (notably American) manufacturers. (Brazil is a good case in point.)* The United States is also a major source of technology for electronic components—including the technology for chips, which is generally not available through official commercial channels to the East Europeans. Instead the East Europeans have to go through a slow process of reverse engineering, with only some successes reported (e.g., recent developments in East Germany).†

Despite smaller production capacities, the NICs have clearly been able to reach a higher level of computerization than the East Europeans (see Table 6). This is mostly because of the much larger

*According to Tigre (1983), the total value of Brazil's output of computers and peripherals was estimated at $1.1 billion in 1981, less than the combined output of East Germany and Poland in 1979, which was estimated at $1.2 billion dollars (see Tasky 1981). For additional production figures, see text below.

†There is some evidence that Eastern Europe generally lacks a domestic capability to develop technology for the large-scale manufacturing of chips. However, recently East Germany opened a new plant manufacturing a new silicon base for advanced chips; it was developed by the domestic research sector (to bypass COCOM restrictions). East Germany still needs a machine to start the mass production of chips. (This kind of equipment is embargoed by COCOM; *Business Eastern Europe*, 14 April 1986.) East Germany produces around 100,000 chip elements annually, minimal by world standards and far from a level that would allow it to enter the microelectronic age (*Business Eastern Europe*, 17 February 1986). In contrast, some of the NICs are able to acquire the necessary technology from the West or develop it by themselves. Spaeth (1984: 30) reports that four major South Korean electronic companies are spending a total of $0.75 billion on their semiconductor production facilities—i.e., for the 64K chip and the next generation 256K memory chip, to be licensed by Western corporations or independently developed by Koreans.

Table 6

STOCK OF COMPUTERS IN USE (EXCLUDING MICRO-COMPUTERS) IN SOVIET UNION AND SELECTED EAST EUROPEAN COUNTRIES AND NICS, 1970-82

Region and/or Country	1970	1972	1974	1976	1978	1980	1982
Soviet Union	6,000	8,500	12,500	–	–	50,000	–
Eastern Europe							
Czechoslovakia	236	331	827	–	–	1,500	–
East Germany	300	475	1,000	–	–	–	–
Hungary	126	200	300	548	–	1,163	–
Poland	170	300	528	1,540	–	2,400	–
Latin America							
Brazil	–	840	–	–	6,641	10,000	–
Mexico	300[a]	–	–	–	4,500[b]	15,000	–
Far East							
South Korea	9	37	68	126	258	–	2,100[d]
Taiwan	–	–	–	485	–	988[c]	1,298

Source: Poznanski 1985.

[a]1969. [b]1977. [c]1980. [d]1983.

supplies of computers from Western countries. With such supplies, Brazil increased its stock of computers in use from 840 units in 1982 to about 10,000 units in 1980, while four major Eastern Europeans increased their stock from around 1,300 to 8,000 during this period—i.e., 20 percent less than the Brazilian stock alone. This gap appears even wider when compared with Mexico, where approximately 15,000 computers were reported in 1980. The total stock of computers in the Latin American countries in our sample is probably at least three times that of Eastern Europe, although the two regions possess similar industrial capabilities.

The East European countries also seem to be on the verge of falling behind some of the NICs in the application of electronics to industrial control—e.g., in the use of robots. Czechoslovakia, one of the leading CPEs, planned to increase output of robots from 348 in 1981 to around 1,000 in 1986 (*East European Markets*, 2 September

1983). In that period Taiwan increased production from zero to about 725 units (*Industry of Free China*, October 1986), by far faster than the Czechs. (All these figures have to be treated with great caution because various countries and publications use different definitions of "robot.")*

Final products of the computer industry continue to be insignificant among both East European and NIC exports to Western markets. Only Brazil recently reported somewhat more significant sales (e.g., to Japan). In both groups of countries suppliers are still too limited to allow any large-scale exports; Eastern Europe is additionally constrained (as noted) by the incompatibility of its systems with those in the West. In contrast, in the sale of semiconductors—particularly simpler devices for consumer electronics—the NICs, but not Eastern Europe, have made substantial progress in the West. For instance, the NICs exported $518 million worth of integrated circuits and microprocessors (including chips for computers) to the United States in 1981, while Eastern Europe reported almost no sales of such semiconductors. NIC sales represented fully 24.0 percent of the total imports by the United States in this product category in that year. Much of what is exported by the developing countries to the United States represents a reexport of semiconductors that are shipped to these low-wage countries for processing, particularly in the simpler stages of production.

CONSUMER GOODS

A commonly recognized fact about consumer industries in Eastern Europe is that they traditionally have received a smaller share of total investment than in many capitalist countries, although some indications of increased interest in their expansion appeared among planners during the 1970s. It is also known that consumer goods are less traded than other products in these generally autarkic economies. Not surprisingly, Eastern Europe has performed more poorly in the consumer sector than the NICs, where no particular bureaucratic constraints have been put on investment, thus making the choice between the domestic and world market less of a problem than it is in Eastern Europe. Eastern Europe was much behind in

*For instance *Worldwide Robotics Survey* and *Directory, Robot Institute of America* (1983) report that by 1982 the stock of robots in use was 285 in Poland and 154 in Czechoslovakia, but only 25 in Singapore and 10 in South Korea, indicating an East European lead.

consumer goods as early as 1970, and the gap in the scale of exports and the technological level of most consumer goods has widened since.

Passenger Cars. The production of passenger cars and parts is one of the many consumer industries in which the NICs had achieved a marked advantage over Eastern Europe as early as the 1960s, despite their lower income level. This in itself comes as no surprise if one considers the low priority given to the consumption sector in Eastern Europe in the postwar decades, but the magnitude of the advantage is striking. In 1970 Eastern Europe made only 358,000 cars, while the NICs—particularly in Latin America—supplied 560,000 (World Automotive Market 1980). In 1980 the figures were 813,000 and 1,693,000 respectively, giving the NICs an edge of almost 110 percent. The picture is the same in the production of motor vehicle parts, where the NICs have invested much more effort than has Eastern Europe, partly in response to the policy of Western multinational corporations of relocating much of their parts production to the low-wage countries of Latin America and the Far East.

In the late 1960s both groups of countries were manufacturing outdated models. In order to modernize production, at least some of them have recently turned to Western countries for more advanced technology. Among the NICs Brazil has been the most successful and has built up a large-scale production of the most advanced (i.e., fuel-efficient, front wheel, two-door) medium-quality compact cars; most of the technology is supplied by U.S. subsidiaries (e.g., Ford). South Korea and Taiwan are expanding large facilities for the newest compact cars, based on technology from Japanese multinational corporations.* In contrast, the most modern East European countries—i.e., Poland and Romania—manufacture models based on mid-1960s technology recently imported from the West, while (as noted) East Germany and Czechoslovakia retain an even more outdated technology of late-1950s vintage.

Despite initially smaller capacities than the NICs, Eastern Europe became more involved in exporting cars to the West by the early 1970s, but it has since lost this edge. In 1970 its share in OECD imports was 0.2 percent; it increased to 0.4 percent in 1980, and fell

*The largest South Korean car manufacturer, Hyundai Motor Company, had the capacity to produce 110,000 cars and trucks annually by 1984 and is expanding it to 300,000 front-wheel drive cars (*Wall Street Journal*, 1 March 1984). In 1985 the company sold almost 25,000 low-priced models in Canada, and it plans to sell 100,000 cars in the United States in 1987 (*Financial Times*, 3 October 1985).

to 0.2 percent in 1983. The recent losses by Eastern Europe are related mostly to the drastic decline in sales from the major exporter in the region, Poland, suffering (as indicated earlier) from a severe economic crisis. Other East European exporters have not been doing well either. The NIC share increased from 0.0 percent in 1970 to 0.2 percent in 1983 (see Table 4).

There is strong evidence to suggest that the NICs will soon surpass Eastern Europe. Poland, with rapidly deteriorating equipment and no fresh imports of automobile technology, will not soon expand its sales above the precrisis level (although it is negotiating a license for a new model with Renault and Fiat; *Business Eastern Europe*, 24 February 1986). East Germany and Czechoslovakia are not able to further penetrate Western markets due to the obsolescence of their cars. In contrast, the NICs seem likely to continue their rapid growth—in particular Brazil (see Dahlman 1982: 30-37) and South Korea, which has already made dramatic inroads into the largest world market, that of the United States and Canada (*Financial Times*, 3 October 1985).* The NIC advance is likely not only because of the expansion in capacity noted above and the relatively advanced automotive technology, but also because these countries are going to be helped in their export efforts by Western multinational corporations, unlike East European exports to the West.

Consumer Electronics. Already in 1970 the NICs as a group had outperformed Eastern Europe in the production of some consumer electronics products such as radio receivers and television sets, and this gap has widened dramatically since. In 1970 the NICs made 35.4 million radio receivers, while Eastern Europe produced only about 3.0 million. In 1981 the NICs reported an output of almost 74.0 million radios, compared with 4.9 million for Eastern Europe. The gap in television sets has widened even more: NIC production increased from 2.5 million units in 1970 to 19.8 million in 1981, whereas East European output expanded from 2.2 million in 1970 to 2.9 million in 1981—less than Brazil's production of 3.2 million units.† Among other products in this category, electronic calculators and watches

*According to some sources, Brazil's production of passenger cars increased to one million units in 1985, placing it seventh among the world's major producers (Motor Vehicle Manufacturers' Association 1986).

†In countries like Bulgaria a drastic drop in the total production of both radio receivers and television sets was reported in 1976-80. Output of the former declined from 227,000 in 1976 to 51,000 in 1980.

provide good examples of how rapidly the NICs have been increasing their edge over Eastern Europe.*

In the early 1970s the NICs enjoyed some technological advantage over Eastern Europe, and there is sufficient evidence that the advantage has increased since. For instance, almost all the NICs have moved to the large-scale manufacture of color television sets based on the latest Western technology, supplied particularly by Japan. In Eastern Europe only Hungary and Poland have acquired Western technology for color televisions, while the other countries either continue to manufacture black and white sets only or rely on inferior Soviet technology. (Table 7 shows the share of color sets in total television production in selected countries.) In the production of electronic watches, the leaders among the NICs (e.g., Hong Kong) utilize the most advanced microprocessor technology, while Eastern Europe has taken only the first steps toward refocusing its production on digital models.

Eastern Europe has never been an important source of consumer electronics for the world market, nor has intra-regional trade been of much significance. Only Hungary, Romania, and Poland have recently tried to launch some exports to the West, while the traditional suppliers, East Germany and Czechoslovakia, have not. Between 1970 and 1980 Eastern Europe maintained its share of the OECD market for radio receivers—0.3 percent—but it fell to 0.1 percent in 1983.† The NIC share increased from 14.6 percent in 1970 to 38.5 percent in 1980 and to 43.4 percent in 1983. Even more striking is the case of watches, where the East European share dropped from 0.4 percent in 1970 to 0.3 percent in 1980 and to 0.1 percent in 1983, while the NICs increased their share from a very low 0.7 percent to 36.4 percent (Table 4). From the early 1970s Eastern Europe had no chance against NIC competition in radio receivers, but the example of watches shows that it has been unable to grasp

*Figures for Taiwan are in order here. In 1975, Taiwan produced 284,000 electronic watches (the only kind it makes), while the leading East European producer, East Germany, manufactured 3,789 units. In 1979 Taiwanese production reached 8,018,000 while East Germany made 3,967. Total East European production was 4,486 units (United Nations, *Yearbook of Industrial Statistics* 1981; *Industry of Free China* 1980).

†In the entire category of telecommunications and sound recording apparatus (including radio receivers) the East European share of OECD imports was 0.2 percent in both 1970 and 1984, while the NICs increased their share from 4.1 percent to 21.2 percent over that period (OECD, *Foreign Trade by Commodities*, various years).

Table 7

SHARE OF COLOR TELEVISION SETS IN TOTAL TELEVISION PRODUCTION OF SELECTED COUNTRIES, 1970-84
(Percent)

Year	Brazil	South Korea	Taiwan	Soviet Union	East Germany	Hungary	Poland	Japan
1970	*[a]	*	*	0.6	2.2	*	0.1	46.4
1971	*	*	*	n.a.	n.a.	*	n.a.	n.a.
1972	*	*	*	n.a.	n.a.	*	n.a.	n.a.
1973	*	*	*	n.a.	n.a.	*	n.a.	n.a.
1974	*	*	11.5	n.a.	n.a.	*	n.a.	n.a.
1975	32.7	3.6	15.3	8.5	9.8	1.0	2.9	60.0
1976	n.a.	2.4	14.0	n.a.	n.a.	n.a.	n.a.	63.6
1977	n.a.	3.3	18.4	n.a.	n.a.	n.a.	n.a.	63.3
1978	32.8	13.7	28.9	17.2	28.5	n.a.	6.2	61.4
1979	24.9	7.7	17.0	19.2	30.9	n.a.	8.0	65.7
1980	21.1	14.0	20.1	24.9	45.6	13.9	16.3	65.2
1981	53.1	29.8	23.8	32.9	50.1	18.1	20.8	66.8
1982	46.8	35.8	25.2	34.8	49.7	24.5	32.0	81.6
1983	n.a.	48.6	36.8	39.5	48.1	n.a.	31.9	88.9
1984	n.a.	44.2	44.0	39.9	59.9	n.a.	38.1	91.7

[a] Asterisks indicate no production.

the opportunities still existing in some categories of consumer electronics.

MILITARY EQUIPMENT

As a final method of assessing the technological levels in the two regions we can compare the military sectors. Not much is known about military production in Eastern Europe, but it seems likely that it has lost some of its technological edge over Latin America. Forced by the Soviet Union into the role of second-rank suppliers of mostly conventional armaments, Eastern Europe has been unable to diversify its traditionally manufactured equipment while Latin America has had more flexibility. This can be illustrated with the case of military aircraft and the related production of civilian airplanes, both of which are reasonably well reported in the professional literature.

AIRCRAFT PRODUCTION

The two leading producers of airplanes in Eastern Europe, Czechoslovakia and Poland, were relatively advanced at the outbreak of World War II. Poland, for instance, manufactured several models in the 1930s in marked quantities. With about 600 planes (both military and civilian) built yearly, Poland could then have been considered a medium-sized manufacturer (Crane and Gilliot 1981). These aircraft were either domestically designed or licensed by major West European producers, and all were of world standard. Czech military planes were also of a quality comparable with major world producers; they were part of a sizable defense industry capable of arming the national forces and supplying other countries as well.

After falling under Soviet domination in 1945, however, the East Europeans were forced by the Soviet Union to give up independent military production and phase out the production of more complex weaponry, including combat planes. (Poland moved out of production in 1951.) The industries became subordinated to Soviet needs, focusing almost exclusively on conventional arms and mostly on parts rather than final products. Czechoslovakia has a limited production of military aircraft and training planes, as has Poland. These represent a medium level of technology, mostly of domestic design; there is some Soviet assistance but no direct transfer of the most advanced Western technology—even compared with the CPE leader, the Soviet Union. Romania, seeking political independence from the Soviet Union, has managed during the last few years to move into the production of combat planes in a joint venture with Yugoslavia, but it does not seem to be more successful in its efforts than the other East European countries.

The experience of Eastern Europe contrasts with that of Brazil, a major producer of aircraft among the NICs. Until the early 1970s Brazil was manufacturing an insignificant number of planes (even by comparison with Czechoslovakia and Poland), with almost no military models. Since then, however, it has rapidly expanded and diversified its military industry in general, producing more than twenty major models of weaponry and moving aggressively into the production of independently designed or licensed (mostly from the United States) combat planes. Brazil increased its production from 71 aircraft in 1972 to more than 600 in 1977, a large portion of them for the military (*Latin American Economic Report*, 16 February 1979). The latter are of a high standard, a fact reflected in Brazil's becoming a sizable supplier of military planes abroad, particularly to developing countries. All these are domestically designed because of restrictions on the export of licensed models.

Brazil's possible advantage in aircraft technology is also visible in civilian production. Poland is strong in two types of aircraft, planes for agricultural use and helicopters. In the output of agricultural planes, Poland is considered second only to the United States, and it is ranked fourth in the production of helicopters. According to Crane and Gilliot (1981), its production of planes is dominated by a rather outmoded AN-2 model of Soviet origin. In the 1970s Poland tried to acquire Western licenses to upgrade its models and succeeded in setting up cooperation agreements with Piper of the United States (among others). In the mid-1970s about 300 light planes close to Western standards were assembled, but the number has sharply declined since; indeed these models have never counted much in the total supply. In contrast, most of the civilian production in Brazil represents the top technology, generously provided by Western multinational corporations (including Piper).

The East European and Brazilian industries share one feature—namely, their production of civilian planes depends heavily on foreign markets. Poland sells more than 80 percent of its output abroad (compared with 25 percent before World War II); the respective share for Czechoslovakia is almost as high. Brazil has become export-oriented too, particularly due to its debt-related difficulties of the last years. However, the East Europeans and Brazil are geared to completely different markets. Almost 90 percent of Poland's sales go to other CPEs—particularly the Soviet Union (e.g., almost all agricultural planes)—and some to developing countries. It makes minor sales of high compression engines and parts to the West. In contrast, most of the Brazilian airplanes are exported to the West, particularly small commuter planes that make up more than 25 percent of the domestic sales in the United States. Clearly the East Europeans are unable to penetrate Western markets and are not likely to do so in the near future (Crane and Gilliot 1981).

The difference in East Europe's and Brazil's performance on the world market results from many factors, only one of which is that most of their production is (as indicated) most likely at an inferior technological level. The fact that the East Europeans do not use Western technology works against them because potential customers are not very familiar with CPE designs. Unlike Brazil, Eastern Europe does not import many Western parts and components that are considered most reliable by major world buyers and are certified by international agencies. This is one reason why delinking from Western multinational corporations, the major agents in the world aircraft industry, hurts the East Europeans. Another reason for Eastern Europe's inferior performance on the world market is that (unlike Brazil) its industry is not used to competition or to the continuous search for improvements which is related to it. Competition is very much absent from CPE markets, though there are reports of sporadic conflicts concerning a specialization in production (see Rice 1984).

Our analysis of market shares of manufactures on the Western market has established that the CPEs have encountered an unexpected threat from the rapidly growing NICs. (The Soviet Union relies only marginally on the sales of manufactures.) The fact that the NICs have been more successful on Western markets, despite their historical technological lag behind most of Eastern Europe and the Soviet Union, does not in itself mean that they have been narrowing the gap. However, such indicators as the product structure of exports and unit values have strengthened the impression that while the CPEs have not been gaining ground on the technological leaders, they have been losing it to these once more technologically backward economies. This can be considered the ultimate proof of the inferiority of central planning as a vehicle for technological change.

The case studies presented above provide additional grounds for concluding that the NICs have outperformed the PCEs not just, or even mostly, for cost reasons (i.e., cheaper labor) but rather because of more rapid technological modernization. NIC improvements have left many of the CPE industries behind, particularly in traditional, mature sectors such as shipbuilding, steel, and consumer electronics, even though many of them have enjoyed a lasting preference in investment. Moreover, there is some evidence that the NICs can surpass the CPE technological level in other more advanced sectors—e.g., semiconductors, computer equipment, and machine tools, some of which have lately been given priority by the planners.

The fact that the NICs have encroached upon the CPE edge in some traditional industries may come as no surprise because the Western economies have faced the same kind of challenge. However, while the Western economies have responded to this threat by speeding up their expansion of advanced industries and refocusing their exports, the CPEs have not succeeded in realigning their production in the same way. Their capacities in technologically advanced industries are too limited and their technology is not competitive enough to substitute the production of advanced manufactures for that of besieged traditional goods. Consequently the threat posed to the CPEs is going to be more serious than it is for the Western economies.

The NIC threat to the CPEs is of a different nature than that to the West for another reason as well—namely, because it is felt by the CPEs on the foreign markets while the Western economies are affected mostly domestically. The NICs do not penetrate the CPEs much and are not going to be allowed to do so in the foreseeable future. However, they drive the East Europeans (and the Soviets) out of Western markets for manufactures. Thus they threaten the CPE ability to finance vital imports of Western technology which in turn threatens their growth plans in the future (i.e., as a result of NIC successes, the CPEs run the risk that their export revenues will not suffice to pay for imports of technology needed to meet planned growth targets).

PART 3

FACTORS BEHIND LACKLUSTER CPE PERFORMANCE

In this final part we shall be concerned with the factors that have contributed to the lackluster technological performance of the CPEs. A number of general explanations are offered in the literature dealing with CPE technological development in the first postwar decades. Mentioned most frequently are the initial size of the lag behind Western economies, systemic deficiencies of the CPEs, and Western discrimination (especially a blockade on the most advanced technology), combined with the reluctance of the East to become too dependent on the West. The focus of our discussion on the last decade and a half will be the second factor—namely, the shortcomings of central planning as a vehicle for technological change.

The first factor, initial backwardness, cannot be dismissed out of hand, but there are reasons not to consider it of critical importance here. If the initial technological inferiority of the NICs to the West—even greater than that of the CPEs—has not prevented them from impressively reducing the gap over the last decade and a half and passing the CPEs on their way (as we have shown), there is no reason to argue that historical backwardness is to be blamed for the persistence of gaps between the CPEs and the West.

The mix of Western restrictions and CPE "paranoia" about becoming overvulnerable certainly have an important impact on the technological development of the CPEs. While important, this factor cannot be discussed at length here because a rigorous analysis would require more expertise than the author now has. Moreover, it is very difficult, and sometimes impossible, to establish precisely the existence of mutually discriminatory measures. In particular, it is difficult to distinguish them from individual, economically motivated decisions of Western companies—not governments—not to get involved in technology transactions with the CPEs and analogous moves by state enterprises in the CPEs to avoid contacts with the West.

In our search for systemic determinants we shall first look into the comparative ability of the CPEs to acquire technology for production as a prerequisite for technological modernization. Our focus will be on the measurable aspects of the technological behavior of their economic agents, and we shall compare these with the behavior of market agents in developing countries—specifically the NICs. Then we shall analyze the CPE capacity to apply technology in production, taking market-type Western economies as a point of reference.

We have decided to discuss cross-systemic differences in the acquisition of technology and its commercial application in the context of either developing economies or the West for two reasons. First, market-oriented developing countries are more appropriate for the comparison of technology acquisition because as latecomers, they, like the CPEs, rely more on imported technology than do Western economies. Second, the availability of data makes Western countries a better point of reference for an analysis of the application of technology.

Chapter 6

LIMITED CPE ACCESS TO TECHNOLOGY SUPPLIES

In this chapter we shall look at the ability of the CPEs to acquire technology, particularly foreign technology. This issue is discussed separately not only to avoid the unnecessary confusion of putting all systemic issues together, but also because of its particular significance (as will be shown). The primary point of reference here will be the NICs, which (as noted) share many more structural similarities with the CPEs with respect to the role of foreign technology than do Western countries.

In particular we shall compare Eastern Europe and three Latin American economies: Argentina, Brazil, and Mexico (all classified as NICs). This choice is dictated to some degree by the fact that statistical data on these countries are more abundant than for the Soviet Union or such NICs as South Korea and Taiwan. In addition to determining how accessible technology is to Eastern Europe relative to Latin America, we shall assess whether any differences in the access to foreign—essentially Western—technology are relevant. In particular, we shall attempt to determine whether openness to foreign technology has been decisive in the success of the technological effort by the three Latin American economies compared to the efforts of Eastern Europe (a point we raised in Part 2 above).

We shall begin by looking at the domestic research efforts of these two groups of countries to determine whether Latin America's more successful development during the last decade and a half has been owing to domestically generated supplies of technology which have outpaced those in Eastern Europe. An answer to this question will provide a good background for testing a hypothesis critical to our discussion—namely, that Latin America's performance is the result of more aggressive imports of Western technology.*

*The following comparison of import patterns should not be distorted by a scale factor, since a closer look at the two regions suggests more or less equal economic size during the period discussed. Clearly the three Latin American countries, with a population of around 216 million in 1980, outnumber Eastern Europe, whose population amounted to 110 million. However, the East European

RELATIVE DOMESTIC RESEARCH EFFORTS

The three Latin American countries have reported significant increases in expenditure for domestic research over the last several years. In Argentina the share of national income devoted to research increased from 0.20 percent in 1970 to 0.50 percent in 1978, while Brazil reported an increase from 0.39 percent in 1973 to 0.62 percent in 1978. However, these increases have not been significant enough to close the traditional gap in relative spending between Latin America and Eastern Europe. In 1978 Eastern Europe still spent far more on domestic research, with Czechoslovakia devoting 3.8 percent of its national income to it; Hungary, 3.5 percent; Bulgaria, 2.3 percent; and Poland, 1.9 percent. Thus on average Eastern Europe spent three to four times as large a fraction of national income on research as Latin America. This translates into the same difference in absolute expenditure given the roughly similar scales of the two regions.

In this comparison on domestic effort, one should not ignore the fact that many specialists consider CPE data greatly inflated, particularly because many nontechnological activities (such as custom manufacturing and administrative work for industrial enterprises) are included under the technology sector. Also, a comparison of expenditures does not provide a full picture because it leaves aside the matter of efficiency. For instance, it is possible that the smaller domestic sector in Latin America is more efficient since it operates without much government support, whereas in Eastern Europe all work is financed from the state budget. For this reason it is necessary to extend this comparison to some output indicators of domestic effort.

To estimate statistically the relative outputs of endogenous technology one can analyze data on the number of foreign patents granted to the sample countries in the West (patents being a proxy for technology outputs). The total number of patents (including patents granted domestically) is not used here because in Eastern

countries generally enjoy higher levels of national income per capita than does Latin America. Income per capita in all three Latin American countries was about $2000 in 1980, whereas Czechoslovakia and East Germany reported average incomes around $5000 and the other countries in the region claimed incomes close to $4000! If the scale of these economies is measured in terms of their population weighted by the income level, the regions turn out to be close to each other (Marer 1985: 112-13).

Europe and Latin America patents are given for inventions of doubtful commercial value. As we noted, it can be assumed that patents granted by foreign countries are a more meaningful basis for comparison. They are usually more difficult to obtain owing to stricter qualifying procedures, and they present other obstacles as well, such as payments in foreign currency.

Data on patents granted by foreign countries clearly indicate that the East Europeans have continuously surpassed the three Latin American countries in the development of domestic technology (WIPO, varous years). In 1967 Eastern Europe was granted 4,670 foreign patents, more than 80 percent of which were obtained in Western countries. In the same year the Latin American countries obtained 305 patents, mostly in Western countries. The Latin American patents represented only 6.4 percent of the total for Eastern Europe. The gap between the regions has changed only slightly in subsequent years. In 1980 Eastern Europe obtained 3,667 patents, whereas the three Latin American countries obtained 370 patents—or 9.9 percent of the total for Eastern Europe (see Table 1). During 1980-84 the number of patents declined in both regions, with Eastern Europe reporting 1,956 in 1984 and Latin America 183 (or 9.2 percent of the East European figure). The Latin American nations have been in the same range as Bulgaria and ahead of Romania, countries not only smaller in scale than they, but also considered the least technologically advanced in Eastern Europe.

A comparison of patents granted to Eastern Europe and Latin America by the United States alone, however, shows Latin America in a much better relative position (United States, Patent and Trademark Office 1981). With 1,030 patents granted by the United States in 1963-79, Mexico was far behind Czechoslovakia but markedly ahead of many other East Europeans—including Poland, which was granted 444 patents by the United States in that period. In addition, the figures for Argentina and Brazil for these years were closer to those for some of the East European economies. It is worth noting that in some sectors of industry Mexico surpassed all the East European countries in terms of patents obtained. These include primary and fabricated metals, food processing, and particularly chemicals, where Mexico was granted 421 patents in 1963-79, compared to 289 for Hungary, 267 for Czechoslovakia, and 75 for Poland. The three Latin American countries also appear to be relatively strong in the technology for consumer electronics and passenger cars.

Table 1

FOREIGN PATENTS GRANTED TO EAST EUROPEAN AND LATIN AMERICAN COUNTRIES, 1967-84

	Eastern Europe						Latin America		
Year	Bulgaria	Czecho-slovakia	East Germany	Hungary	Poland	Romania	Argentina	Brazil	Mexico
1967	67	1,727	1,652[a]	602	451	171	78	78	149
1968	88	1,876	1,791[b]	522	366	233	107	62	143
1969	99	1,735	1,228[a]	597	457	188	116	111	66
1970	80	1,512	1,684[b]	737	437	206	143	88	94
1971	129	1,303	2,156	878	438	235	89	62	81
1972	139	1,503	2,286	1,168	508	325	192	122	137
1973	135	1,252	2,110	1,115	416	230	193	87	146
1974	132	1,134	2,074	1,135	398	227	102	110	165
1975	168	1,039	2,430	1,260	382	150	115	109	195
1976	184	996	1,685	1,262	368	112	138	101	207
1977	251	1,185	1,469	1,295	346	97	129	98	203
1978	228	719	1,236	1,238	433	90	168	179	162
1979	--	--	--	--	--	--	--	--	--
1980	231	508	931	1,254	643	100	100	112	158
1981	--	--	--	--	--	--	--	--	--
1982	157	654	1,054	713	177	44	82	123	--
1983	101	323	499	842	137	22	34	64	82
1984	85	310	564	878	96	23	40	59	84
Subtotal, 1967-72	602	9,656	10,797	4,504	2,657	1,358	725	523	670
Subtotal, 1973-78	1,098	6,325	11,004	7,305	2,343	906	845	684	1,078

Source: WIPO, various years.

[a]Except patents granted by Austria, Great Britain, and Switzerland.

[b]Except patents granted by Austria.

The data on patents granted by the United States put the Latin American countries in a slightly different light partly because these countries are heavily oriented toward the U.S. economy, while Eastern Europe does more business with Western Europe. In addition, while Argentina, Brazil, and Mexico obtain most of their foreign patents in the United States, Eastern Europe seeks patents for a given invention in many Western countries simultaneously. In other words, it is very likely that the data on total foreign patents granted in Western countries exaggerate the East European edge because of the more frequent multiple patenting of individual inventions. However, even if the multiple patenting had been eliminated in the data on both Eastern Europe and Latin America, it would not change the general picture—i.e., Eastern Europe's large advantage in domestic technology production in the period under discussion.

The East European lead in foreign patents offers some help in determining whether there is any merit to our hypothesis (noted above) that the Latin Americans, with less government support, are nonetheless more efficient. With a total of over 28,900 patents granted from 1973 to 1978, Eastern Europe outpaced the Latin American countries by a factor of ten. This difference was considerably greater than the gap in absolute spending noted above. On average, then, the domestic effort by the East Europeans is either more efficient than that of the Latin Americans or benefits from having attained critical mass. However, some countries of Eastern Europe (e.g., Poland and Romania) seem to produce fewer foreign patents per unit of spending.

A comparison of Eastern Europe with Western countries shows—in a somewhat exaggerated way, given the generally lower propensity of the CPEs to patent—that research in Eastern Europe is much less efficient than in the West. For instance, Poland employed 83,000 researchers in 1979 and France 670,000. Their work resulted in 855 patent applications abroad by Poland and 19,276 by France—more than a twentyfold difference. Indeed the number of patent applications by France was twice as high as that for Eastern Europe and the Soviet Union combined (Maciejewicz and Monkiewicz 1982: 23).

Not only does Eastern Europe get low output from its research, but also it is well recognized that quite often the technologies supplied are not well fitted to the needs of final users. No good quantitative data are available to measure this phenomenon—only some fragmentary information of the case-study type. A number of case studies of Soviet industry presented in Amann, Cooper, and

Davies (1977) provide examples of how much slower the Soviet process is in transforming rough inventions into fully applicable ones owing to the insufficient ability of Soviet research to come up with quick solutions to the practical requirements of enterprises.

Another indicator of the low efficiency of the CPE research sector is the rather small number of CPE technologies licensed abroad. In Poland, for instance, only five technologies were licensed annually to Western countries in the whole postwar period, and annual royalties from all license agreements have been only $1-2 million dollars in recent years (Maciejewicz and Monkiewicz 1983). The annual receipts for all the CPEs were $40-50 million by the end of the 1970s; these are comparable to royalties recently paid to such Western countries as Spain ($73 million in 1978) or Sweden ($75 million in 1977) alone (United Nations 1983c).

It is reported, moreover, that a large proportion of these licenses have been granted for technologies at early stages of commercialization—another reflection of the region's difficulty in bridging the gap between rough invention and commercial application. As Kieser (1977: 20-22) reports, in a sample of fifty-seven licenses granted to the United States, West Germany, and Great Britain by Czechoslovakia, East Germany, Hungary, and Poland, only 39 percent involved technologies at the commercial production stage. Almost 35 percent were in the stage of experimental prototypes, and the balance fell into the category of production prototypes and pilot projects.

THE MAGNITUDE OF TECHNOLOGY IMPORTS

Since a comparison of domestic research efforts does not explain the success of the Latin American countries in closing the gap relative to Eastern Europe, we must look to the data on technology imports. It is theoretically possible that Latin America is better prepared for technological modernization than Eastern Europe simply because it is a more aggressive importer of technology from the West. Since Western technology is on average more advanced than the technology indigenously produced in Eastern Europe, a heavier import of Western technology could easily explain the Latin American success. This would be an even more powerful explanation if there were indications that the Latin American countries have been more efficient in adopting Western technology than has Eastern Europe.

INFLOWS OF DISEMBODIED TECHNOLOGY

International licensing statistics indicate that Latin America was buying more Western licenses than Eastern Europe in the late 1960s and that it continued to do so in subsequent years (see Table 2). While Brazil paid Western countries about $3.1 billion in royalties and other fees during 1972-79, the East European leaders in technology imports, Czechoslovakia and Poland, spent only $448 million and $404 million respectively in the same period. Mexico alone spent $2.1 billion on royalties in 1972-79, while the estimate for all of Eastern Europe was under $1.5 billion.

Interestingly the difference in license payments and related fees between the two regions has become much greater in the last few years (similar to the difference in imports of machinery and transport equipment—discussed below). In 1972, Czechoslovakia and Poland paid a total of $81 million, which represented about 25 percent of the payments of Brazil and Mexico ($321 million). Around 1977 the discrepancy began to increase: payments by Eastern Europe stagnated, while there was a sharp acceleration in spending by the Latin American countries. As a result, in 1979 payments by Czechoslovakia and Poland ($119 million) represented only 9.9 percent of those by Brazil and Mexico ($1,196 million). Since 1979 license imports by the two East European leaders have been on the decline; Poland has virtually phased out all imports, as evidenced by the statistics on signed contracts.

The above comparison cannot be accepted without certain caveats, a fact indicated by wide discrepancies among various available approximations. The trend line presented for Brazil and Mexico has to be treated as a high estimate, certainly far above the estimates of Chudnovsky (1982: 515) and the OECD (1979: 71-72). According to the latter, in 1977 Brazil and Mexico paid a total of $160 million for patents and license fees to the United States, France, West Germany, Italy, and Great Britain. If transfers from other countries are included, these payments probably amounted to around $200-210 million. This figure is only 25 percent of the sum noted alone; however, it is still larger than the corresponding amount for Czechoslovakia and Poland ($146 million).

The broad differences among estimates may result from the fact that national sources on license transactions are not based on uniform classifications. In particular, the United States has a broader

Table 2

PAYMENTS FOR IMPORTS OF DISEMBODIED TECHNOLOGY BY EAST EUROPEAN, LATIN AMERICAN, AND FAR EASTERN COUNTRIES, 1966-81

	Eastern Europe				Latin America[a]			Far East
Year	Czecho-slovakia	East Germany	Hungary[a]	Poland	Argen-tina	Brazil	Mexico	South Korea
	1. Payments/Royalties (Millions of dollars)							
1966	$ 4	--	-- (--)	-- (6)	--	$ 46	--	--
1967	5	--	-- (--)	-- (--)	--	63	--	$ 1
1968	29	--	-- (--)	-- (--)	--	70	--	1
1969	47	--	-- (--)	-- (--)	--	91	--	2
1970	46	--	$ 2 (1)[b]	-- (--)	--	104	--	2
1971	40	$8	8 (7)	-- (50)	--	132	--	4
1972	53	1	7 (5)	$28 (47)	--	154	$167	7
1973	47	2	4 (3)	30 (58)	--	166	189	10
1974	55	5	12 (10)	36 (120)	$101	212	192	19
1975	45	4	19 (16)	39 (148)	--	311	216	19
1976	65	8	12 (48)	50 (160)	--	362	258	21
1977	65	6	18 (17)	81 (17)	--	513	350	--
1978	67	--	17 (27)	72 (32)	--	591	380	--
1979	51	--	27 (6)	68 (10)	--	782	414	--
1980	42	--	33 (--)	-- (--)	--	--	641	--
Total, 1972-79	448	--	-- (132)	404 (432)	--	3091	2166	
	2. Number of Contracts Signed							
1966	62	--	--	--	--	--	--	≈5
1967	42	--	--	--	--	--	--	--
1968	71	--	--	--	--	--	--	--
1969	40	--	--	--	--	--	--	--
1970	44	--	18	21	--	--	--	≈70
1971	32	36	29	42	--	--	--	≈70
1972	44	18	35	57	--	--	--	--
1973	29	13	39	83	--	--	--	--
1974	34	14	43	67	--	--	--	--
1975	46	13	60	67	--	--	--	--
1976	58	11	59	55	--	--	--	--
1977	56	16	68	28	--	--	--	--
1978	63	--	111	30	--	--	--	--
1979	57	--	96	12	--	--	--	≈250
1980	58	--	--	6	--	--	--	≈250
1981	42	--	--	0	--	--	--	--

Sources: 1–Eastern Europe: Maciejewicz and Monkiewicz 1983; Fallenbuchl 1983; Levcik and Skolka 1984; Marer 1986; Latin America: Dahlman and Sercovich 1984; South Korea: Kim 1981; 2–Czechoslovakia: *Statisticzeska Rocenka CSSR* (Prague); East Germany: Zentraleslizenz-buro der DDR (Berlin); Hungary: Central Statistical Office, Ministry of Foreign Trade (Budapest); Poland: *Maly Rocznik Statystyczny.*

[a]Includes payments for technical consulting, management, etc.

[b]Figures in parentheses indicate the value of licenses bought.

definition of technology payments than many other Western countries. In this category it includes consulting fees and similar payments. For this reason the data on countries more dependent on U.S. technology (e.g., Brazil and Mexico) tend to be exaggerated when compared with less dependent economies such as Czechoslovakia and Poland. Brazil and Mexico seem to make more payments for transactions not directly involving technology transfers. (These make up close to 40 percent of all their payments reported by the United States.) In contrast, Eastern Europe favors pure technology transactions (see Marer 1986).

The increase in Latin American imports can be seen in Table 3 which shows payments by selected countries for licenses purchased from the United States alone. Eastern Europe and the Soviet Union paid $247 million in royalties and other fees during 1975-84, while all of Latin America paid $5.6 billion. Argentina, Brazil, and Mexico were the dominant sources of these payments. In 1981, for instance, the three paid $341 million of the $800 million total for Latin America—i.e., almost half. As noted, payments by Eastern Europe and the Soviet Union peaked in 1977 and then declined by two thirds in 1984. In Latin America payments increased until 1981 and then declined, but only by one fourth. In 1984 the purchases by Eastern Europe represented only about 3 percent of those by Latin America.

Another important Western supplier of technology that deserves a closer look is West Germany, which has traditionally provided most of Eastern Europe's imports. (For example, it provided more than 50 percent of all licenses bought by Hungary in the 1970s.) In 1967-75, Argentina, Brazil, and Mexico paid DM 728 million in royalties and other fees to West Germany, whereas Eastern Europe paid some DM 160 million—or 22 percent as much as Latin America (OECD 1981b; Deutschen Bundesbank 1984: 359-88). Thus even on the market that serves as a major source of foreign technology for Eastern Europe the presence of the Latin Americans is stronger. This is also the case with purchases of technology from Italy, another key supplier to Eastern Europe. In 1972-75 Latin America paid 11,393 million lire, while Eastern Europe paid 8,803 million lire (OECD 1981c).

Since most of the commercially valuable technology has to be protected in some way in order to be licensed, one might expect that the three Latin American countries not only purchase more licenses but also grant more patents to the exporters of disembodied

Table 3

ROYALTIES AND OTHER FEES TO THE UNITED STATES BY SELECTED REGIONS OR COUNTRIES, 1970-84

(Millions of dollars)

Region or Country	Source[a]	Year 1970	1975	1976	1977	1978	1979	1980	1981	1982	1983	1984	Subtotal, 1975-79	Subtotal, 1980-84
Eastern Europe and Soviet Union	b	$ 4	$ 14	$ 19	$ 50	$ 34	$ 33	$ 20	$ 22	$ 21	$ 17	$ 17	$ 150	$ 97
Latin America	a	318	376	299	337	372	422	589	669	590	514	513	1,806	2,875
	b	46	60	63	71	98	89	101	131	110	101	87	381	530
	a+b	364	436	362	408	470	511	690	800	700	615	600	2,187	3,405
Argentina, Brazil, and Mexico	a+b	--	--	--	110	148	195	295	341	--	--	--	--	--
Asia (excluding Japan)	a	--	345	381	362	475	508	495	661	538	764	707	2,071	3,165
	b	--	38	57	60	66	91	101	129	209	219	194	312	852
	a+b	--	383	438	422	541	599	596	790	747	983	901	2,383	4,017
Great Britain	a	--	468	471	501	637	747	814	832	819	768	813	2,824	4,046
	b	--	86	79	70	77	103	114	128	122	125	129	415	618
	a+b	--	554	550	571	714	850	928	960	941	893	942	3,239	4,664
Canada	a	--	566	633	670	715	824	--	252	--	--	--	--	--
	b	--	37	40	48	52	38	--	16	--	--	--	--	--
	a+b	--	603	673	718	767	862	--	268	--	--	--	--	--
Japan	a	--	231	257	300	318	416	406	413	303	387	394	1,522	1,903
	b	--	227	241	289	318	366	403	379	475	498	524	1,441	2,279
	a+b	--	458	498	589	636	782	809	792	778	885	918	2,963	4,182

Source: United States, Department of Commerce, various years.

[a] a = affiliated companies; b = unaffiliated companies.

technology in the West. The available data confirm this expectation, at least for 1967-74 (see Table 4). For instance, in 1968 Argentina, Brazil, and Mexico together granted 10,709 patents to Westerners, whereas Eastern Europe granted 2,996—or less than one third as many (WIPO, various years; also United States, Patent and Trademark Office 1981). Argentina alone granted 42,139 patents to Western countries during 1967-78, whereas the corresponding figure for Eastern Europe was 65,219.

By comparing East European data on license payments with those for patents granted to the West, we see that the two time series follow a similar pattern. In the late 1960s, when East European license imports were relatively low, the number of patents granted to the West was low as well. The increase in license payments during 1970-76 was accompanied by a similar increase in patenting. In the late 1970s both license payments and patent grants dropped. However, in Latin America the rapid increase in license payments in the last few years has not been accompanied by an equally dramatic increase in patenting activities. For some reason Western countries have found it difficult to patent their technology in Latin America. (One reason may be the pressure by these countries for compulsory licensing; Poznanski 1984.)

The patenting pattern in Eastern Europe differs from that of at least some of the NICs. In Argentina and Mexico there was some decline in the number of patents granted to foreigners in the 1970s, but both have become more active in patenting over the last few years. In Brazil the number of patents to Westerners was quite stable in the 1970s and then increased abruptly in recent years (e.g., 4,191 patents in 1984 versus 1,188 in 1978). In South Korea there has been a continuous increase in patenting from a very low level in the mid-1970s to a relatively high level which greatly exceeds the recent figures for each of the East European countries. (E.g., in 1982 South Korea granted 2,335 patents, compared to 1,189 for Czechoslovakia.)

TRANSFERS OF EMBODIED TECHNOLOGY

Machinery. Data on the imports of machinery and transport equipment (i.e., SITC-7) are conventionally used to indicate the transfer of embodied technology. The data (uncorrected for price changes or exchange rates) show that the three Latin American countries have imported much more such technology from the West

Table 4

PATENTS GRANTED BY EASTERN EUROPE, LATIN AMERICA, AND FAR EAST TO WESTERN COUNTRIES, 1967-84[a]

Year	Eastern Europe						Latin America			Far East
	Bulgaria	Czecho-slovakia	East Germany	Hungary	Poland	Romania	Argentina	Brazil	Mexico	South Korea
1967	109	893	1,311	379	310	914	4,319	647	--	64
1968	92	618	1,168	570	318	230	4,545	982	5,182[c]	152
1969	63	700	1,225	591	423	114	7,164	--	4,950	--
1970	266	821	1,943	594	321	63	4,798	2,042	--	--
1971	207	856	2,543	816	461	181	4,279	1,504	--	--
1972	175	674	2,358	1,269	673	454	3,552	1,302	--	5
1973	437	1,541	2,581	1,079	331	488	2,871	--	--	11
1974	337	1,379	2,850	991	775	425	3,004	--	--	95
1975	432	1,722	2,351	951	2,843	502	2,247	--	--	230
1976	266	1,438	1,867	911	2,070	439	2,635	1,410	--	288
1977	196	1,331	1,676	825	1,301	497	1,785	1,188	--	170
1978	325	1,693	1,335	705	998	628	974	--	1,413	294
1979	--	--	--	--	--	--	--	--	--	--
1980	363	1,462	1,089	795	1,663	598	--	3,494[b]	770	1,446
1981	--	--	--	--	--	--	--	--	--	--
1982	154	1,189	948	877	708	715	2,349	8,471	2,273	2,335
1983	136	731	1,520	1,026	655	792	1,319	5,155	2,002	2,177
1984	119	767	1,334	1,161	513	763	1,087	4,191	1,553	2,056
Subtotal, 1967–72	912	4,562	10,548	4,219	2,506	1,956	28,657	--	--	--
Subtotal, 1973–78	1,993	9,104	12,660	5,462	8,318	2,979	13,482	--	--	--

Source: WIPO, various years.

[a]The Western countries are Austria, Belgium, Canada, Denmark, Finland, France, West Germany, Italy, Japan, Luxemburg, the Netherlands, Sweden, Switzerland, Great Britain, and the United States.

[b]Total patents granted to foreigners.

[c]Excluding Great Britain.

than has Eastern Europe. In 1970-81 Latin America imported machinery and transport equipment from the OECD countries with a cumulative value of $105.9 billion, while imports by Eastern Europe amounted to $42.6 billion (OECD, *Foreign Trade by Commodities*, 1982). Much of this gap in imports resulted in the late 1970s, when Latin America rapidly increased its imports while purchases from Eastern Europe actually dropped in absolute terms.

The Latin American advantage does not appear to be any smaller when one looks at the purchases of industrial machinery alone (i.e., SITC-7.2, 7.3, and 7.4), even though East European planners have traditionally favored the imports of equipment for industry at the expense of other manufactured goods. The difference in total imports between the two regions was relatively small until 1976, when imports by Eastern Europe represented 93.2 percent of those by Argentina, Brazil, and Mexico. Since 1976, however, Latin American imports have been increasing at a high rate while Eastern Europe has been reducing its purchases in absolute terms. In 1981 the three Latin American countries imported industrial machinery worth $7.8 billion, whereas Eastern Europe spent $2.7 billion, or 35.2 percent of the Latin American purchases.

Data which do not go beyond 1981 may exaggerate the edge enjoyed by the three Latin American countries because in the following years they too have had to cut their imports of Western goods. Post-1981 trade statistics show that imports by Eastern Europe were further reduced in 1982 and again in 1983 and 1984. Total imports by Eastern Europe from the OECD market dropped from $20.7 billion in 1980 to $11.9 billion in 1984 (Marer 1984b: 8). Cuts in the purchase of machinery and transport equipment were of almost the same proportion (from $5.5 to $3.0 billion). Latin America reduced its imports from $38.4 billion to $24.3 billion during 1980-84—i.e., by more than one third. Machinery and transport equipment suffered similarly serious losses; there was a drop from $18.4 billion to $11.4 billion during the period—i.e., one third.

As noted above, during 1980-84 the dollar was gaining against major West European currencies, thus depressing the import figures for Eastern Europe and exaggerating the figures for the NICs. To take these gains into account we again look into Eurostat data for Western Europe, though they provide only a small part of Latin American imports. Nonetheless, data indicate that the import of machinery and transport equipment dropped in Argentina (but not in Brazil and Mexico), and it declined in all of Eastern Europe excluding Czechoslovakia and Hungary (Poznanska 1987). Thus we have further evidence that the gap in the pace of purchases of Western embodied technology which Latin America built up vis-à-vis Eastern Europe in the late 1970s has most likely not diminished.

The drop in the East European imports of Western goods in the last few years corresponds to a similar decline in the purchase of disembodied technology (illustrated above with the data on Western license purchases). This correspondence suggests—at least in the case of Eastern Europe—that most imported licenses have to be supported by related imports of Western machinery. In other words, Eastern Europe has not reached a point where its industries are able to couple Western disembodied technology with domestic machinery. Therefore we can speculate that once the region was forced to reduce its imports of Western machinery and transport equipment, Western license imports had to be reduced as well, even though the sums involved in the purchase of licenses are small compared with those devoted to commodity imports.

Foreign Equity Investment. There is a sharp discrepancy between Eastern Europe and Latin America in the number of foreign affiliates each has attracted in the recent past (United Nations, Center on Transnational Corporations 1983b). While Brazil (for instance) had more than 2,600 joint ventures and subsidiaries in 1982, the total number of joint ventures in Eastern Europe—the only type of equity investment allowed there—was 24 in 1983. (Romania had 6 joint ventures, Hungary 13, and Bulgaria 5; see Table 5.) No important ventures of this type were reported by Poland—only 380 very small firms fully owned by Polish emigrants (Gajewski 1983)—see below.

In recent years the Western multinationals have not shown a greater interest in investing in Eastern Europe. Some new ventures are being negotiated by Hungary, but in other countries no progress has been reported. No new joint ventures have been registered in Romania since 1977. In the early 1980s one important venture between Romania and Nippon of Japan collapsed, and another (with Citroën of France) was on the verge of liquidation (*Business Eastern Europe* 1982). Reportedly two of the very few large joint ventures in Hungary—with Volvo of Sweden and the Corning Glass Corporation of the United States—have been discontinued recently (see Marer 1984a).

Table 5

DIRECT INVESTMENT BY WESTERN COUNTRIES IN EASTERN EUROPE (1983) AND LATIN AMERICA (1982)

Region and Country	Number of Joint Ventures	Number of Subsidiaries	Cumulative Foreign Direct Investment *(Millions of dollars)*
Eastern Europe			
Bulgaria	5	0	$1
Czechoslovakia	0	0	0
East Germany	0	0	0
Hungary	13	0	32
Poland	0	0	8[a]
Romania	6	0	23
	Joint Ventures and Subsidiaries		
Latin America			
Argentina	780		3,300[b]
Brazil	2,600		21,200
Mexico	2,150		6,000[b]

Sources: Eastern Europe: *Business Eastern Europe*, various issues; Conference Board, various issues; Poland: Gajewski 1983; Latin America: calculated from United Nations, Center on Transnational Corporations 1983b: 32, 312, 318; *Quarterly Economic Review, EIU Brazil, Annual Supplement (1983):* 26.

[a]Author's estimate based on the assumption that an average $20,000 is invested in each of 380 small firms operated by emigrants (see Gajewski 1983).

[b]1978.

None of the recently established joint ventures in Eastern Europe involves a substantial amount of Western capital, whereas investments by multinationals in Latin America are often very large. The largest negotiations in Eastern Europe have not exceeded $100 million; one of these (i.e., Romania's deal with Citroën) has not materialized, while another (in Hungary) is still being worked out (Marer 1984a). Most of the ventures are much smaller in scale, rarely exceeding $1 million. Around $64 million had been invested in Eastern Europe by 1983, excluding money provided by Westerners for an off-shore bank in Hungary. In Argentina and Mexico more than $9.3 billion of Western foreign direct investment was reported by 1978, and $21.2 billion by 1982 in Brazil alone.

The Polish policy of promoting small businesses by emigrants has not been a success. The government has been able to convince quite a number of emigrants, mostly from the United States, to open businesses in Poland. These enterprises play some useful role in the economy, particularly in restoring the heavily unbalanced domestic market for consumer goods. However, they do not serve much as vehicles for large-scale foreign investment and technology transfers. As noted, all the enterprises are small (as required by law) and involve only limited investment. Moreover, much of the investment spending is financed from local sources—i.e., profits earned on domestic sales (Ziech 1983). There is no indication that any substantial transfers of modern technology are involved. Even if there were some, they would have little impact on the rest of industry because these small enterprises typically have only limited contact with the state-run establishments (*Business Eastern Europe*, 24 April 1980).

In place of direct investment in Eastern Europe, Western multinational corporations have attempted to substitute so-called countertrade (or buy-back) agreements, which are rather uncommon in their relations with Latin America. Instead of investing directly in the region, many corporations (and governments as well) have decided to provide it with capital and relevant technology in exchange for specified East European goods. Around 107 agreements were signed between 1969 and 1980, but since 1978 there has been a general decline in the number of new agreements (OECD 1981a: 29-30). Thus far the buy-back agreements have not become an important avenue for investment by Western multinationals, a fact reflected in the low share of exports contracted through these agreements in total East European exports to the West; the share has been estimated at 7 percent (Altman and Clement 1979).

FUTURE TRENDS IN TECHNOLOGY IMPORTS

The final step in our analysis is to determine the future trends in Western technology imports by the two regions. As noted, in recent years there has been a slowdown in such imports in almost all the countries surveyed and absolute reductions in some as well. Can a reversal be expected, and if so, when? In addition, will the three Latin American countries retain the edge they gained over Eastern Europe in the late 1970s? To answer these questions, we shall analyze the future conditions for the import of machinery and for the inflows of foreign equity investment—the two major potential vehicles for technology transfer.

IMPORTS OF MACHINERY

Among the many factors which determine an economy's ability to purchase foreign technology is its export capability—i.e., its tradable goods, particularly for Western markets. In the long run this capability plays the most important role in determining the ability to import, though other factors, such as access to trade credits, are important as well. In this section we shall analyze the conditions for export and policies toward exports. This effort is of a preliminary nature and does not claim to offer a final answer to the questions addressed here.

Above we showed that the three Latin American countries and other NICs were more successful than Eastern Europe in promoting exports to the OECD market in 1970-80 and that their edge has widened since. Below we shall try to relate their success to the differences in approaches toward debt repayment between the two regions in the last few years. Adjustments in Latin America (and the Far East) and Eastern Europe differ in two basic respects: foreign trade strategy and investment allocation. Both have implications for the future relations of these countries with Western economies—including the transfer of Western technology.

Trade Adjustments. To analyze foreign trade strategies it is useful to distinguish two particular forms: dynamic and restrictive (Poznanska 1987). Under a dynamic strategy a country generates a trade surplus to stabilize or reduce its debt through accelerated exports combined with a slower increase in imports. With this strategy there is generally no need for slowing down economic growth. Under a restrictive strategy a trade surplus is created either by a combination of accelerated exports and reduced imports (the export-oriented version) or through import reductions followed by a less drastic export decline (the import-substitution version). In the restrictive strategy some slowdown in growth is almost inevitable.

To avoid distortions from changes in dollar values, we employ Eurostat (EEC) trade data on the Common Market, reported in Eurocurrency (ECU). From these data we find that among the nations in our sample only two have clearly pursued dynamic adjustment—South Korea and Taiwan. (The latter cannot correctly be characterized as a debtor country.) In these two countries both exports to and imports from Common Market countries increased in 1979-84, with rates for exports exceeding those for imports. The export index for South Korea amounted to 165.3 and the import index to 150.8; for Taiwan the figures were

221.4 and 201.1 respectively. (See Table 6.) Both countries pursued their strategy without major interruptions in rapid economic expansion and are now back to their earlier very high rates of growth.

Eastern Europe pursued the restrictive strategy—more precisely, the export-oriented version. In all of Eastern Europe except Bulgaria (which instituted adjustments prior to the years analyzed), exports increased in 1979-84. At the same time, for all the countries except Poland and Romania import increases were reported, though in Czechoslovakia and East Germany they were rather small. In the case of Poland and Romania import reductions were at least as deep as the export increases. (For example, in Romania the export index was 187.7 and the import index 49.6 in 1979-84.) At the same time, the national product of almost all these economies has been growing at rates much lower than prior to 1979, providing additional evidence of restrictive adjustment (most pronounced in Poland and Romania).

Except for Brazil, all the developing countries of Latin America (and the Philippines in the Far East) followed the same strategy as Poland and Romania—i.e., restrictive adjustment involving both both export increases and sharp import reductions. For instance, Argentina's export index to the Common Market in 1979-84 was 127.8, and its import index was 73.6. These figures place Argentina among the extreme adherents of this strategy in Eastern Europe, particularly Poland. With a 193.6 index for exports and a 65.5 index for imports, Peru falls close to the case of Romania.

Brazil has also embarked on the export-oriented version of the restrictive strategy, but without allowing import cuts. A major difference between Brazil (and Mexico) and Eastern Europe is an extraordinary export expansion, accompanied by a strong reliance on the U.S. market, which in recent years has been far more dynamic than that of Western Europe (the major outlet for Eastern Europe's exports). In 1979-84 the export index for Brazil was 805.5 (compared with 217.3 for East Germany, the East European country with the fastest growing exports), and the import index was 111.8 (a figure close to that for East Germany). The adjustment cost Brazil only a short slowdown in the national products between 1981 and 1983, followed by strong more recent growth.

These strategies have allowed all the indebted economies, except for Bulgaria, Hungary, and Indonesia, to improve their trade

Table 6

EXPORT AND IMPORT INDICATORS FOR SELECTED COMMON MARKET TRADE PARTNERS

Region and/or Country	Index of Change, 1984/1979: Exports to Common Market	Index of Change, 1984/1979: Imports from Common Market	Cumulative Trade Balance, 1979-84: Total *(Millions of ECU)*	Cumulative Trade Balance, 1979-84: Percent of Exports
Eastern Europe				
Bulgaria	98.6	224.5	$2,726	-94.7%
Czechoslovakia	161.8	116.9	1,975	19.9
East Germany	217.3	108.0	1,876	28.4
Hungary	109.5	135.9	-689	-7.0
Poland	126.9	87.5	1,704	11.6
Romania	187.7	49.6	4,023	34.7
Soviet Union	239.7	115.8	25,250	30.8
Latin America				
Argentina	127.8	73.6	2,203	18.8
Brazil	805.5	111.8	16,179	53.2
Mexico	730.5	48.1	3,260	27.5
Peru	193.6	65.5	770	22.1
Far East				
Indonesia	139.3	254.8	-2,585	-32.8
Malaysia	161.4	185.2	3,660	33.4
Philippines	171.9	93.2	1,795	30.3
South Korea	165.3	150.8	6,911	47.0
Taiwan	221.4	201.1	9,730	58.1

Source: Poznanska 1987: 11.

balances with the Common Market countries. By and large, they turned their deficits into surpluses for 1979-84. However, despite similar strategies, the East European economies achieved relatively smaller surpluses than the developing countries. Romania achieved the highest ratio of trade surplus to cumulative exports (34.7 percent) and East Germany the second best (28.4 percent). Among non-East European countries the best performances in relative terms were in Taiwan (58.1 percent), Brazil (53.2 percent), and South Korea (47.0 percent); and even the best efforts of poorer performing Argentina and Mexico resembled the best in Eastern Europe.

While Eastern Europe's effort is less impressive in terms of commodity surpluses, it has been doing better in terms of balancing its current accounts with Western lenders. It was the only region with a current account surplus in 1980-84 and the only debtor that actually reduced its gross and net debt to the West—by at least one fourth. Even though this was mostly due to the positive impact of dollar appreciation on the nominal value of Eastern Europe's debt (denominated mostly in nondollar currencies), the reduction in its debt can nonetheless be considered a substantial accomplishment (Poznanska 1987). All other large debtor countries had to allow their debts—denominated primarily in dollars—to grow further, owing partly to the aforementioned appreciation of the dollar (Tyson 1986). By 1985 Eastern Europe joined the developing countries, however. Its gross and net debts have begun to increase as well, due both to increased borrowing and to the dramatic depreciation of the dollar since 1985 (*Economic Bulletin for Europe* 1986: 43-44).

One cannot rule out the possibility that the East European preference for debt reduction, even at the cost of trade losses to its competitors on the Western markets, might turn out to be more rational in the long run than the policy of most NICs to protect their economies from trade losses at the cost of further (though slower) increases in their debt. The final outcome of these two strategies will depend on the behavior of interest rates, on Western demand for exports from these countries, and on the political stability of the various economies. However, it is almost certain that it will not be easy for the CPEs to recover their recently incurred losses on Western markets, particularly because of their already marginal role on most of them. If the NICs—especially Brazil and Mexico—succeed in their current adjustments through a continuous increase in the exports of manufactures to Western markets, a comeback will be particularly difficult for Eastern Europe.

Investment Priorities. Divergences between Eastern Europe and the NICs may deepen in coming years owing to current differences in the investment plans of these two groups. For one thing, the NICs continue to invest heavily in many export industries despite temporary squeezes, whereas most of the East Europeans squeeze their investment programs in the industries connected with Western markets. At least through the late 1980s most of the funds allocated to investment in Eastern Europe will benefit such sectors as energy, agriculture, and housing—none of them intended or likely to improve exports in a direct way. It is also unclear whether these investments will have any strong indirect impact on export promotion (e.g., the relaxation of some import requirements which could help to increase the import of Western equipment which is needed to back up the export industries in the region).

One example of investment differences between Eastern Europe and the NICs will be in the steel industry. Most increases in steel output in Eastern Europe in the near future will come from the gradual modernization of existing mills, while most of the NICs will be building large additional capacity. South Korea planned to build a second integrated steel mill with a capacity of 2.7 million tons by 1985. It ultimately plans to increase the capacity to 12 million tons, making the mill one of the largest in the world (Martin 1983). Mexico was expected to increase its output from 7.4 million tons in 1981 to 19.2 million tons in 1990 by constructing new plants with Western help. Even with recent downward revisions the target figure is still high—around 13 million tons (*Latin America Weekly Report*, 26 October 1979).

Another example is the automobile industry. None of the East Europeans intends to invest in the physical expansion of their industries—except for Bulgaria, which plans a new factory (mostly to satisfy domestic demand in the face of low supplies from other East Europeans and the Soviet Union). Instead they will focus on retooling and upgrading their models (as is the case in Poland, for example). In contrast, countries like Brazil and Mexico are investing heavily in the construction of new plants; Mexico plans a facility for 100,000 small cars a year to be operating in 1986 (*Economist*, 14 January 1984: 59-60). South Korea has expanded its industry by adding at least 200,000 units with the help of capital and technology from the United States.*

These different responses to debt problems can be considered as an indication, as Hanson (1982, 1984) has suggested, that Eastern Europe has reevaluated its strategy toward the import of Western investment goods and is going to assign them a lower priority than in the 1970s. Hanson points out that the most visible indication of this reevaluation is Soviet policy in recent years. As he demonstrates, the Soviet Union reduced its orders for Western machinery long before encountering losses in oil and gas revenues; now it is going to be even more pressed to live with limited Western supplies.

Soviet sales of oil and gas were stable in 1982-84, then declined dramatically. The 1985 losses—related to the sharp drop in world

*General Motors (United States) plans to invest in a joint venture with Korea's second largest car manufacturer, Daewoo, to expand its output by 100,000 units which will be sold mostly in the United States (*Wall Street Journal*, 1 March 1984).

market prices for energy—are estimated at $3 billion (*Business Eastern Europe*, 15 November 1985) and 1986 losses at $5-6 billion (*Wall Street Journal*, 15 May 1986). The 1986 loss is equivalent to 15-20 percent of Soviet dollar revenues from the West. The impact of these losses has already been felt: imports from the West have slowed down sharply, and many large-scale contracts negotiated with Western companies have been either canceled or temporarily put off. The Soviet losses are going to have an impact on Eastern Europe owing to the importance of the Soviet market in East European trade.

FOREIGN EQUITY INVESTMENT

While the East European stock of foreign equity investment is minuscule compared to that of Argentina, Brazil, and Mexico, it need not stay that way unless some factors prevent a quick build-up. There are many examples of countries that have been able to multiply their foreign equity investment in a short period—for instance, Turkey in the last few years (*Wall Street Journal*, 25 April 1983). In addition, Western interest in Latin America could decline, which would result in a slowdown in the remarkably rapid rise of subsidiaries or joint ventures in the region. If the financial crisis in the three Latin American countries continues, such a possibility could become a reality.

It has been shown that foreign investment decisions are based on many considerations. However, the critical variable in the dynamics of foreign equity investment is going to be the attractiveness of local conditions for Western companies. One of the most important conditions is the permissiveness of foreign governments and the incentives offered. Consequently, the recipients of foreign equity investment will tend to compete for outside resources by designing more attractive regulations and weighing potential benefits against the disadvantages of heavier Western involvement in their economies. Thus here we shall extend our analysis of trends in foreign equity investment with a comparison of the legal arrangements in Eastern Europe and Latin America for investment by foreigners.

Direct investment has been permitted by Argentina, Brazil, and Mexico during practically the whole postwar period, but it was only in the early 1960s that they began to introduce legislation aimed at attracting Western investors. In Brazil, for instance, a greater concern for direct investment by foreigners appeared around 1960, when the government decided to get outside help for the development of a domestic car industry. In contrast, East European countries as a rule did not allow direct foreign investment during most of the postwar years, and only some of them have initiated arrangements for it recently: Hungary and Romania in 1972, Poland in 1976, and Bulgaria in 1980. East Germany and Czechoslovakia remain closed to foreign equity investment, and they are not considering any enabling legislation (Svejnar and Smith 1982).

The recent regulations on direct foreign investment in Eastern Europe and Latin America seem to be very similar in many respects. (A comparison is presented in Table 7.) For instance, regulations on ownership do not differ much. Bulgaria and Argentina set no upper limits for foreign ownership. Other East Europeans do not allow foreign assets in joint ventures to exceed 49 percent; similarly Brazil and Mexico insist on mixed ownership (also involving some state funds), with substantial local content. However, there is a drastic difference in legal practice between the two groups of countries. Thus far none of the East European governments has agreed to majority foreign ownership, whereas such ownership, including full subsidiaries, is quite frequent in Latin America. Although Brazilian laws are restrictive, thirty-nine of the two hundred largest foreign affiliates are majority foreign-owned (United Nations, Center on Transnational Corporations 1983a).

East European regulations also allow foreign corporations much less freedom in daily production decisions. There is a tendency in the region to impose upon foreigners the same bureaucratic boundaries within which the state-owned entities operate. Thus the revised Polish regulations of 1989 (Buizynski 1986) state that all joint ventures have to be managed by a board of directors appointed mostly by local authorities. Moreover, their managers have to follow a long list of instructions issued by the planning bureaucracy—including production indicators, allocations of raw materials, and wage schemes. Particularly stiff are regulations concerning payments in foreign currency. (This is the case even under the relatively liberal Hungarian rules; Marer 1984a.)

Western multinational corporations in Argentina, Brazil, and Mexico face only a very few such restrictions on daily decision-making (UNCTAD 1980). The only major restriction involves the financing of foreign trade transactions, including purchases of Western technology. All three countries require government approval for any substantial payments in foreign currencies. For instance,

Table 7

COMPARISON OF BASIC REGULATIONS ON FOREIGN DIRECT INVESTMENT IN FOUR EAST EUROPEAN COUNTRIES AND THREE LATIN AMERICAN COUNTRIES

Country	Date of First Regulations	Ownership	Restricted Investment Areas	Hiring and Wages	Profit Repatriation	Taxes and Tax Incentives	Borrowing Restrictions
Bulgaria	1980	No limits to foreign equity share	No sectoral restrictions	Key posts on boards of directors restricted to nationals	No limits, but additional 10 percent tax on profits transferred abroad	20 percent one- to three-year tax exemption possible	Not allowed
Hungary	1972	Equity share generally up to 49 percent (foreign majority in nonproduction activities and full ownership in free-trade zones)	No sectoral restrictions	50-50 representation allowed	— —	40 percent up to 20 percent of net assets and 60 percent on additional profits	Not allowed
Poland	1976	Equity share maximum 49 percent, except wholly owned small companies in service sector and handicrafts	Most service sectors excluded	Only local management permitted	Up to 50 percent of net profits, but not more than 9 percent of registered currency capital	25 percent turnover tax, may be waived for initial three years	Allowed

Romania	1972	Foreign ownership maximum 49 percent	--	Only local management permitted	No limits, but additional 10 percent tax on profits transferred abroad	30 percent on profits, 24 percent on profits reinvested for at least five years	Not allowed
Argentina	1976	Up to 100 percent foreign ownership	No sectoral restrictions	No regulations against foreign managerial control	No limits, but remittances over 12 percent of registered capital are more highly taxed	33 percent on profits (45 percent for fully owned subsidiaries); no taxes on reinvested profits	Foreigners on equal footing with local companies
Brazil	1962	Government insists on majority local ownership	Restricted areas include parts of computer industry, coastal shipping and fishing, and production of gasohol	Fully foreign management allowed	No limits, but remittances over 12 percent of registered capital are severely taxed	Generally 35 percent on profits (45 percent on excessive profits)	Bank loans restricted to small portion of bank portfolios
Mexico	1973	Foreign equity up to 49 percent, except special cases	Foreign direct investment prohibited in petroleum and primary petrochemicals, broadcasting, urban transport, gas distributing, and forestry	Limited foreign management control	Profits freely remittable after legal reserve requirements are met	Graduated rate ranging from 0 to 42 percent of taxable income	Some restrictions, especially for preferential loans

Sources: Business Eastern Europe, 27 June 1980; *Business International*, 28 May 1982; United Nations, Center on Transnational Corporations 1983a; Buizynski 1986.

in Argentina central bank approval is necessary to obtain foreign exchange for all imports, and a certificate of necessity has to be obtained for all nonessential goods (*Business Latin America*, 4 May 1983: 143). Separate regulations put serious restrictions on technology contracts in Brazil and Mexico; in Mexico all agreements have to be registered with the appropriate agencies, and a certificate of approval is needed in order to implement a negotiated transfer (*Business Latin America*, 4 May 1983: 268-69).

General rules on profit regulation and taxes seem quite similar across the two groups of countries. However, the Latin American economies go much further in offering tax preferences and other financial privileges (e.g., exemptions from import duties) by allowing for so-called industrial (or free) zones, which are generally not permitted by Eastern Europe. Mexico operates three such zones (the first of which was established in 1946) and Brazil one (United Nations, Center on Transnational Corporations 1983b). Only recently did Hungary express some interest in granting foreign investors almost full extraterritoriality and substantial financial preferences similar to those offered by many developing countries, including China. The enabling legislation was introduced in 1982, but thus far only one small extraterritorial venture has been set up; its capital value is estimated at $2 million (*Business Eastern Europe*, 10 February 1984: 41).

There is also a fundamental difference between East European and Latin American legislation regarding the access of foreign affiliates to local capital markets. All three Latin American countries allow borrowing by multinational corporations from local banks, whereas no such provision is made by most of the East Europeans. Moreover, foreign affiliates can acquire existing local companies through the stock market, and they can deposit their money in local banks in Latin America, but not in Eastern Europe, where such operations are not permitted by the law.

The unattractive regulations in some of the East European countries, along with a lack of strong momentum for changing the policy toward foreign equity investment, suggest that a rapid increase in such investment should not be expected in the coming years. There is no indication that countries which remain closed to foreign equity investment will introduce new laws soon—though in the important case of the Soviet Union, some steps have been taken under Mikhail Gorbachev's economic reform overtures. In contrast, among the three Latin American countries there is some interest in liberalizing the current rules, which have already moved far from the restrictive laws of the 1960s. For instance, Mexico has recently announced that many restrictions on investment (including the very controversial requirement of national-majority equity) will be liberalized (*Wall Street Journal*, 2 June 1984).

Our analysis reveals that the CPEs are less inclined to seek foreign (including Western) sources of technology than are some of the NICs. While this conclusion is based on an assessment of commercial channels of technology transfer, it probably applies to noncommercial channels as well (with the possible exception of the Soviet Union, which seems to rely particularly heavily on noncommercial transfers). Not only do the CPEs obtain less Western technology than the NICs, but they also have more limited access to generally newer (i.e., less outdated) technology.

Undoubtedly the greater NIC involvement in technology transfers has been facilitated by large-scale equity investment by Western multinational corporations, which are almost completely absent in the CPEs. Closer investment ties with Western countries have clearly benefited the NICs and even helped them to diminish the technological advantage the CPEs used to have over them. One can even go so far as to say that these close ties have probably been a major factor in the faster technological modernization and superior trade performance of the NICs, though other factors not specified here could have contributed as well.

There is no indication that the CPEs are trying to adjust systems to allow for greater Western technology transfer—particularly in the form of foreign equity investment by multinational companies. On the contrary, there are signs that the CPEs are withdrawing from the Western market, in part as a result of their latest trade adjustments to the debt crisis which focus on a reduction of Western imports. At the same time, the NICs are going through a round of liberalization measures to attract foreign direct investment, and they are following a trade strategy that gives priority to expansion.

To attract more foreign direct investment (and get better access to advanced foreign technology) the CPEs will have to go ahead with funndamental changes not only in their obsolete foreign trade systems, but also in other elements of their institutional mechanism. It is the rigidity of the current systems (in addition to some obvious political factors) that discourages Western multinational corporations or other private investors from entering the

CPEs. As the CPE foreign trade mechanism seems to be the least likely component of the central planning machinery to be reformed, no radical changes in the Western attitude to investing in the region should be expected in the near future.

Chapter 7

CPE DIFFICULTIES IN THE APPLICATION OF TECHNOLOGY

In this chapter we shall try to analyze another aspect of CPE technological ability—i.e., effectiveness in the commercial application of technology. In Chapter 6 we provided some grounds for arguing that the CPEs are technologically inferior in part because their producers have fewer technologies to choose from compared to open-market agents. Here we shall try to determine whether the CPE technology lag is also due to an inability to adopt new technology. Ideally we would like to determine which of the two factors is more critical—access to technology or ability to incorporate it.

Our major point of reference will be the market West—in particular the United States and Great Britain, the two best researched Western economies in terms of innovation. Unlike in Chapter 6, both the Soviet Union and Eastern Europe will be discussed here because the best available data are most abundant for the Soviet Union. Also unlike in Chapter 6, the discussion will be based primarily on detailed case studies, mainly derived from the steel industry. As we shall explain below, such an approach is more appropriate for the subject at hand.

To best analyze the comparative ability to commercialize technology, we shall address the three major aspects of what is generally defined as the innovative act. We shall begin by considering how willing CPE agents are to adopt new technologies relative to their market counterparts. Next we shall analyze possible differences between the market and central planning systems when it comes to the full-scope diffusion of a technology once it is adopted, particularly in terms of the speed of diffusion. Finally, we shall try to determine whether technological performance can be related to how CPE producers phase out (or extinguish) an existing technology.

WILLINGNESS TO INNOVATE: CASE STUDY EVIDENCE

As noted in Chapter 3, there are many methods of evaluating a system's ability to innovate. Many of them require information that is not easily available or is simply not generated by some economies so that certain cross-country comparisons are impossible. In general, there are fewer data of a broad nature on innovative processes than is the case with research activities. One solution is to turn to survey-type data with representative samples of enterprises from central planning and market systems. There are a number of Western studies to choose from, but only a very few for Eastern Europe and even fewer for the Soviet Union. This imbalance limits our analysis.

Studies by Szakastis (1974) in Hungary and Poznanski (1977) and Krajewski et al. (1978) in Poland are particularly useful for comparative purposes, partly because they apply concepts and methodologies used earlier by Western scholars. Specifically their approach is similar to the matching pairs of innovations used by Freeman (1974) in Great Britain and to the framework adopted by Myers and Marquis (1969) in the United States. The East European studies are comprehensive enough to enable a reconstruction of all the major features of technological change—the sources of technology, the motivation to innovate, the role of specific agents, and the bias in technical choice. Thus a broad comparison with the Western studies is possible.

Below we shall analyze the findings from Polish industry, mostly the results of the Krajewski et al. (1978) study (as reported in Poznanski 1980a). The study covers eighty-six cases of carefully described technological innovations in seven industrial sectors: textiles, consumer electronics, clothing, shoes, synthetic fibers and dyestuffs, automotive parts, and furniture. The study does not cover three important sectors of Polish industry—steel, shipbuilding, and machine tools—nor are any nonindustrial sectors included. The sample includes not only successful innovations, but also thirteen cases of projects which failed.

MECHANISMS OF CHANGE

Based on the survey data, one can try to reconstruct how innovation evolves under central planning relative to the market experience. As the 1978 survey shows, the main sources of new technologies of domestic origin introduced into industry are enterprises themselves, either their production departments or their own research establishments. Out of sixty-nine innovations based on domestic technologies, forty-two relied on such "in-house" sources (Freeman 1974: 170).* In contrast, in market economies the majority of domestic innovations are based on outside sources of new technology. In addition, when Polish enterprises reach out for external supplies of technology, their efforts are limited mostly to other enterprises or independent research institutes within the same associations or ministries. Among the twenty-seven external technologies incorporated into the domestic innovations discussed here, twenty-two came from within the same ministry. Since ministries in the CPEs are organized on the single-product principle, it implies that if technology exchange takes place, it is generally limited to organizations involved in similar types of manufacturing. In the West, on the other hand, new technology frequently crosses sectorial boundaries, with some industries very heavily relying on external supplies (e.g., textiles and household appliances).

Whether sources are in-house or not, the Polish studies show that in most cases innovations are developed by formal research establishments. Of the forty-two innovations based on in-house sources, twenty-seven were based on technology supplied by research departments within the innovating enterprises; the balance came from production and other nonresearch divisions. Almost equally high was the share of research establishments among the cases where external technologies were involved. Formal research does not seem to have such a dominant role in the West (Langrish and Poznanski 1981). This contrast certainly has something to do with the higher formalization of research activities in the CPEs, but other factors may be involved as well, such as the more passive behavior of production divisions in their role of technology suppliers.

The initiative to introduce a new technology in Polish industry comes from different sources, most often (as indicated in Krajewski et al. 1978) from the lower levels of the hierarchy. The latter were responsible for initiating fifty-seven innovations, of which forty-six were initiated by the innovating enterprises themselves. At the higher levels, responsible for the balance of the sample, the leading role was played by associations and the research establishments they supervise. Very few initatives came from industrial ministries. While in purely numerical terms low-level initiatives dominate, to determine

*The remaining innovations were based on license agreements with foreigners or on imported capital equipment.

the significance of that level one would have to establish whether these initiatives are of the same caliber as those coming from the upper levels. If the latter are of greater importance in terms of costs or results (as one could assume), then more weight should be attached to them. But even ignoring the weight of the respective initiatives, it is clear that the upper levels play a much more critical role in pushing for technological change than do their counterparts in the West.

It is important to note that regardless of where initatives begin, the chief promoters of change are the various research establishments. Krajewski et al. (1978) revealed that at least thirty-six initiatives originated in the research departments of innovating enterprises (twenty cases) or the research establishments supervised by associations (sixteen cases). Research departments in other than innovating enterprises played a marginal role in promoting changes, as did the research facilities directed by the industrial ministries. The passive role of the former may reflect the well-established fact that there is not much horizontal communication among enterprises even within the same association or ministry. However, the negligible role of the latter seems improbable and may stem from some limitations of the sample.

The Polish studies show that the major motive for enterprises to either attempt to innovate or give in to external pressures is the need to overcome various supply problems; it is not the need to adapt production to new market (i.e., demand) conditions. Krajewski et al. (1978) found that supply considerations were the primary motive for incorporating new technology in forty-two cases, while adaptation to new market conditions was responsible for thirty-three innovations. (The balance of the sample did not fall into either category.) This picture is just the opposite of that in market economies; where market needs are the driving force of innovations and where knowledge of customer demands is a prerequisite for successful changes in production (see Freeman 1974; Langrish and Poznanski 1981).

The two main motives of individuals working on the development of new technology seem to be (1) a desire to be creative and to satisfy their professional ambitions, and (2) a desire that their organization rank among the most modern (given their understanding of the economic needs of the innovating enterprise). The two main reasons given by enterprise employees in particular are (1) a conviction that participation is an employee's duty, and (2) a desire that their enterprise be among the most modern in its sector and achieve a good economic performance.

The prospect of individual financial benefits is rarely a motive. (Interestingly, Krajewski et al. 1978 found that the material motive was less important for people on production lines than for those working on the development of new technology.) One can argue that the relative unimportance of the material motive is due to weak financial incentives. However, to prove this we need to know whether the survey results are biased by the structure of the sample. The predominance of nonfinancial motives might be explained by the fact that a great number of innovations were small and participants did not expect any significant rewards for their contributions. Bias might also result from the methodology of the questionnaire (if steps were not taken to exclude answers which the respondents thought were expected of them or which presented an ideal picture instead of the real one).

Results from modified questions show that the most important factor discouraging individual innovation was that innovative effort does not greatly affect an employee's financial situation or promotion perspectives; moreover, benefits are not proportional to additional efforts or may be shared unfairly among participants (even nonparticipants). Answers to a modified question brought out the financial prospects of the participants and indicated that in fact the respondents were not trying to give an idealistic picture of their motivations by hiding the role of material benefits. We can conclude that financial incentives are weak and should be intensively studied in the near future.

It would be wrong, however, to conclude that innovations will be fully supported by enterprise employees only when every contribution is well rewarded. Even with more extensive (and proper) financial incentives, nonfinancial motives will still play a very important role in the motivation of individuals. Greater financial incentives cannot be considered a panacea for low motivation in the innovative mechanism of industry.

In the case of forty-nine innovations for which there were adequate responses, it was established that one or more financial incentives were used to remunerate individuals involved in thirty-six projects; only for thirteen innovations (including eight which failed) were no financial instruments used. The most frequent incentives were bonuses from a general fund that enterprises or research organizations are permitted to create as a fraction of their current profits.

In twenty-five projects enterprise employees were awarded such bonuses directly by their managements. In addition, rewards were provided by the ministers or directors of particular associations who are permitted to collect a part of the funds generated by enterprises. In many instances—sometimes in addition to these bonuses—incentives were provided from special funds designed exclusively for promoting innovation (see Chapter 1).

This high frequency of payments appears to contradict the statement above that the CPE system does not provide strong incentives for individuals. However, as Krajewski et al. (1978) indicate, it is not the frequency of payments but rather their magnitude and the fashion in which they are granted that determine individual behavior. In general, the former are inadequate; in particular, they are insufficient to counterbalance goals that stand in conflict with risky innovations and for which there are powerful incentives. In addition, only a small number of those involved in innovation are paid for their effort; the majority are in upper management, engineering, personnel, and research, while very few of them are from the lower levels.

An interesting aspect of the financial reward system is that in spite of the inadequate or incomplete fulfillment of projects (nearly one quarter of the forty-nine innovations discussed above was postponed or failed to fulfill every technical requirement), only in a very few cases was the original bonus reduced or withdrawn entirely. This can be partly justified bythe fact that in risky acivities such as innovations some deviations from the original plans are unavoidable and the participants are not to be blamed. Nonetheless, there is some evidence that enterprise managers—and those at higher levels of authority—prefer to go along with the promised rewards to avoid conflicts with interested parties. This may reflect a broader inclination of CPE managements to use positive incentives rather than sanctioning employees (as reflected in the well-documented uneasiness about firing employees who notoriously disrupt discipline or drink on the job, for example).

What emerges from the Polish findings—and is corroborated by results in other CPEs—is a mechanism in which state enterprises have very few incentives to innovate and research entities independently undertaking work on new technologies provide the pressure for innovation. This type of mechanism resembles the so-called supply-push model of technological innovation, well described in the theoretical literature and tested empirically as well (see Langrish and Poznanski 1981; Rosenberg and Mowery 1978). The evidence gathered for market economies clearly indicates that supply-push changes are outnumbered by demand-pull changes, where the initiative to innovate comes primarily from enterprises and the effort to develop appropriate technology follows.

It is a common perception in Western economics that the difference between the supply-push and demand-pull models is not purely formal. They differ in terms of effectiveness. Except for certain variants of innovation (many in military technology), the demand-upll mechanism is much more effective. As argued by Freeman (1974), for instance, when a change is initiated by an enterprise, it is more likely to succeed. If research establishments respond to specific requests by enterprises, their inventions will be more suitable to the needs of enterprises than if they develop new technology independently. In addition, when pressure from research establishments prevails, it is likely that less attention will be paid to economic risks than if an enterprise undertakes technological change first.

STRUCTURES OF INNOVATION

From the Polish studies we have cited, it is possible to ascertain specifically how innovations suffer under central planning. One piece of information comes from Krajewski et al. (1978), which examined the magnitude or caliber of innovations. It established that in the sample of eighty-six innovations 70 percent could be classified as minor changes of an adaptative nature, requiring relatively small resources and little organizational work (Poznanski 1980: 252-53). This share appears to be higher than that calculated for market enterprises. For instance, Myers and Marquis (1969: 22-23) demonstrated that for the United States this share was less than 60 percent. Thus a stronger resistance to technological change seems to be manifested in the preference of state enterprises for small, incremental improvements even when more radical options are available which would offer the same or better results with similar or lower total expense (e.g., an expected cost reduction owing to the application of a new production process).

Many explanations can be offered for this bias toward smaller innovations. It is likely that the pressure to innovate that comes from research establishments is not as effective as that stemming from market competition; the rejection of initiatives from research establishments does not necessarily involve organizational penalties, while a competitive enterprise could be eliminated if it did not comply with market forces. Even if a supervisory body puts pressure on an enterprise to innovate, the pressure may not be as strong as that exerted by the impersonal market, and there is a lot of room for relaxing or delaying it. As noted above, the continuously changing signals that state enterprises receive from planners regarding the availability or scarcity of particular inputs may lead to a shortening of the time horizons by enterprise managers, and thus a preference for small innovations.

Another piece of evidence concerns the relative share of product versus process innovations, of either an incremental or radical nature. Krajewski et al. (1978, cited in Poznanski 1980: 254) showed that 48 of the 86 innovations were process innovations. A 1977 study of 164 innovations in several Polish industries indicated that new processes clearly dominated technological change in the economy (Poznanski et al. 1977). In contrast, market enterprises are preoccupied mostly with new products. For example, Myers and Marquis (1969: 27) established that only 25 percent of the innovations in several sectors of U.S. industry involved process changes.

This bias against product innovation is a manifestation of the fact that state enterprises are more concerned with supply difficulties than with consumer demands. As noted, in the CPEs the manufacture of particular goods tends to be concentrated in a single enterprise or under the umbrella of one association. Therefore, the bargaining position of consumers is weak, and it is not critical that managers improve or differentiate their products. This situation is reinforced by the very loose link between economic efforts (including product strategies) and the financial conditions of enterprises, so that ignoring consumer demands does not necessarily lead to losses in disposable funds (e.g., wages, investment means).

The studies done in Poland also indicate that it is not uncommon for enterprises to introduce technological changes which increase costs or decrease quality. Some microeconomic evidence has been provided by Krajewski et al. (1978). However, this study did not identify such large-scale negative innovations because of the limitations of the sample analyzed. Polish professional periodicals provide examples of vast economic losses due to negative innovations. For instance, it has been proved beyond doubt that the so-called "house factories" introduced by the construction industry in the 1970s are much less efficient than traditional building methods—mostly because of higher transportation costs. (In the "house factory" method a majority of parts is prefabricated and then transported to the building site.) Nevertheless, the initial decision to switch to the new method—made at the central level—has never been reversed. More than forty gigantic "factories" now operate in the country.

Further evidence of negative innovations comes from a leading Soviet economist, A. Aganbegyan (1985), in a recent comment on robotization in the Soviet Union. In absolute numbers of robots either manufactured domestically or put into use, the Soviet Union seems to match many Western countries that can be considered advanced in this technology. (See the claim by Cooper 1984.) However, as Aganbegyan states, many of the Soviet robots are very unreliable; moreover, the labor they save is much below their production costs. Apparently, a large robot manipulator used for loading and unloading costs 40,000-50,000 rubles yearly, while wage savings amount to only 4,000 rubles.

The phenomenon of negative innovations has been recognized by Kornai (1980), who pointed out that some changes in production actually resulted in the deterioration of products. He calls such innovations "forced substitution" because they are mostly responses to shortages of higher quality materials and parts. It is not unlikely that some enterprises would make completely inefficient technological changes even without the severe constraints Kornai described. In other words, negative innovations are not immediately "killed" by standard enterprise procedures. Since rivalry between enterprises is rare in the CPEs, competition—unlike in the market system—cannot be counted on to eliminate negative changes (Balcerowicz 1978).

In sum, it appears that CPE enterprises are less interested in implementing new technology. The pressure exerted on them from either research establishments or supervisory bodies cannot compensate for the lack of powerful pressure from consumers. By and large CPE enterprises opt for technological change when they have failed to bargain for extra resources or lower output targets. Even if a state enterprise decides to innovate, it behaves in a much more cautious way than a market agent, replacing large-scale changes with small piecemeal ones and losing many opportunities for product changes.

DIFFUSION OF TECHNOLOGY: THE STEEL INDUSTRY IN THE CPES

SPEED OF DIFFUSION

Most of the quantitative evidence on diffusion under central planning comes from case studies of major Soviet industries and is persuasive (Amann, Cooper, and Davies, eds. 1977). The steel industry seems particularly suitable for a more extended systemic speed-of-diffusion analysis which would include direct data on Eastern Europe. Statistical data are scattered but sufficiently rich and available. Indeed there are few industries for which such long time series and such a broad cross-section of countries are available. The data provide information on basic process technologies that have been introduced over the last hundred years (e.g., on furnaces such as Bessemer and Thomas, open hearth, oxygen process, and electric arc as well as on the so-called continuous casting method), offering a unique opportunity to analyze the diffusion. In addition, the data permit the use of several different indicators of diffusion (e.g., number of mills, maximum capacity).

The diffusion of the oxygen process in the Soviet Union is particularly instructive here (Poznanski 1983). The industry initially adopted this technology in 1960, eight years after the pioneer, Austria. This should be considered a modest diffusion lag—especially considering that other major steelmakers (such as Great Britain, Belgium, and Luxemburg) began diffusion around the same time. However, Soviet industry has been considerably slower to further promote this process. It took the Soviet Union fourteen years to reach a 20 percent share, as against only five years for Japan and nine years for West Germany. The Soviet Union has not reached the 40 percent level of adoption after twenty-six years, whereas it took Japan seven years to reach this point, West Germany twelve years, and the United States fifteen years (see Table 1).

The picture for Eastern Europe is only slightly different from that for the Soviet Union, in part because the Soviet Union supplies Eastern Europe with most of the technology and construction work it needs (Poznanski 1983). The first East Europeans to adopt the oxygen process, Czechoslovakia and Poland, did so fourteen years after Austria, while East Germany introduced this technology with a twenty-one year lag. While Eastern Europe was slower in first adoption than the Soviet Union, it was faster in spreading the

Table 1

TIME LAG AND DIFFUSION SPEED OF OXYGEN PROCESS AND CONTINUOUS CASTING STEEL TECHNOLOGIES IN SELECTED COUNTRIES
(In years)

Oxygen Process

Country	Time Lag	Diffusion Speed		
		Twenty Percent Share	Forty Percent Share	From 10 to 50 Percent Share
Austria[a]	0	1	4	6
Canada	2	5	18	17
United States	2	12	15	7
France	4	13	16	9
Sweden	4	9	19	17
Japan	5	5	7	5
West Germany	5	9	12	6
Netherlands	6	1	1	4
Soviet Union	8	14	--	-
Great Britain	8	5	12	11
Belgium	10	4	7	5
Luxemburg	10	5	10	9
Spain	11	5	8	8
Italy	12	1	9	--
Poland	14	6	12	-
Czechoslovakia	14	7	--	-
Bulgaria	15	1	1	2
Romania	16	2	10	-
East Germany	21	--	--	--

Continuous Casting (Ingot Output)

		Five Percent Share	Ten Percent Share	Twenty Percent Share
Austria[b]	0	18	21	24
West Germany	2	15	18	21
France	2	19	21	22
Soviet Union	3	18	26	-
Canada	3	13	15	25
Great Britain	6	17	19	-
Italy	6	12	14	17
Japan	8	11	12	14
Spain	9	9	11	16
Hungary	9	--	14	16
United States	10	8	15	18
Czechoslovakia	10	-	-	-
Poland	12	-	-	--
Sweden	12	4	5	11
Belgium	13	13	16	15
East Germany	16	5	12	-

Source: Poznanski 1983: 315-16.

[a]Pioneer in 1952.

[b]Pioneer in 1952.

process (e.g., it took Czechoslovakia seven years to reach a 20 percent share and Poland six years).

Eastern Europe was nonetheless much slower than Western countries in both introduction and diffusion. Spain and Italy, both relatively less advanced among Western countries, are probably the best points of reference. As Table 1 shows, both Spain and Italy were a little faster in adopting the oxygen process than the first adopters in Eastern Europe. The contrast is sharper for the speed of diffusion. For instance, Spain needed only five years to reach a 20 percent share and eight years to reach a 40 percent share—faster than both Czechoslovakia and Poland (but slower than Bulgaria, which, however, is not fully comparable; see Poznanski 1983).

The above findings could be challenged on the grounds that an appropriate test would require a more refined method of data analysis—i.e., sophisticated econometric techniques instead of the conventional rough approach. It is true that most of the current studies on the diffusion of steel technology have employed the conventional methods. However, economic theory as well as many studies on technologies in industries other than steel provide more elaborate measurements. Beginning with Griliches's (1957) classic study and several in-depth case studies by Mansfield (1968), the tradition has been established of considering diffusion as following a logistic trend and of determining the speed of diffusion by fitting a logistic function to actual observation.

The following analysis of the speed of diffusion of the oxygen process is based on data gathered for twenty-four major steelmakers (Poznanski 1987). The sample includes eleven Western economies (including Japan, the United States, West Germany, France, and Great Britain), eight developing market economies (including three NICs—Mexico, Brazil, and South Korea), and six CPEs (including the Soviet Union, Poland, and Czechoslovakia). The data cover steel output during 1950-82, thus including the first world adoption (Austria, 1952) as well as the leveling of diffusion among the major steelmakers (1975-82).

Diffusion is measured here by the shares of two postwar technologies—oxygen and electric arc—in the total output of steel. The saturation point is assumed to be 100; this seems justified because the two older processes, Bessemer and open hearth, have essentially been eliminated. The parameters of speed (ϕ) are estimated for the linear version of the logistic function, specifically its log-transformation. (In this we follow the approach taken by Griliches 1957 and Mansfield 1968 for nonsteel technologies.) The logistic trend is fitted by both linear least squares and iterative (nonlinear) least squares, the latter (as argued by Oliver 1964) promising a better fit. Intercepts (μ) are estimated with these two methods as well, though they are not of special interest here.

The regression analysis shows that the iterative least-squares procedure produces a better fit for the logistic function than does the linear one (see Table 2). The correlation coefficients are generally higher for the nonlinear procedure than for the linear approach. In addition, in the majority of cases the correlation coefficients obtained from nonlinear regression were close to perfect. This is particularly so with respect to Western market economies, for which the most complete time series are available.

The choice of regression analysis is not neutral with respect to the estimation of numerical values of parameters. Regarding the speed parameter, both methods place the same groups of countries in the upper and lower ranges respectively. However, a precise country-by-country ranking with linear least squares shows substantial discrepancies with results obtained from iterative least-squares regression (confirming the general remark by Oliver 1964 on distortions caused by the linear method). Moreover, with the exception of values for the United States, Canada, Spain, and Bulgaria, the nonlinear least-squares regression produces lower values of the speed parameter than the linear procedure. For instance, the linear result for Japan is $\phi = 0.46$, compared to the nonlinear $\phi = 0.36$; the respective values for Belgium are 0.54 and 0.36.

Using the nonlinear least-squares regression as the more reliable of the two, we find that the leaders in diffusion in the West are Belgium, Japan, France, and West Germany. They have values for the speed parameter of at least 0.25. The United States falls among the modest performers at 0.22, while the slowest have been Austria, Canada, and Sweden, with $\phi < 0.15$. Austria and Canada rank relatively high in the earlier reported rough estimates but are at the bottom of the list derived from regression analysis.

The speed parameters for the developing countries are more or less in the range of those for the West. The most aggressive in diffusion have been South Korea and Spain—in the range of $\phi > 0.25$. At the other end of the spectrum has been Turkey, with $\phi = 0.11$, slightly above the speed reported by the slowest diffuser in the West (Sweden). Since the rough estimates provide little information on the developing countries, no comparison of the two methodologies is possible.

Table 2

DIFFUSION SPEED OF OXYGEN AND ELECTRIC ARC PROCESSES COMBINED IN SELECTED COUNTRIES

Region and Country	Linear Least-Square Regression ϕ	R^2	μ	Nonlinear Least-Square Regression ϕ	R^2	μ
Western Countries						
Belgium	.54	.87	10.5	.37	.99	7.6
Japan	.46	.81	6.0	.36	.99	4.7
France	.32	.89	6.5	.27	.98	5.8
West Germany	.25	.98	4.9	.26	.99	5.1
Netherlands	.38	.78	4.8	.23	.98	2.7
Great Britain	.35	.66	6.7	.23	.98	4.7
United States	.20	.97	4.0	.22	.98	4.4
Austria	.13	.94	1.0	.13	.94	1.0
Canada	.11	.86	2.0	.12	.85	2.1
Sweden	.17	.58	2.1	.10	.96	1.1
Developing Countries						
South Korea	.69	.48	15.0	.26	.80	3.5
Spain	.22	.98	3.7	.25	.99	4.3
Mexico	.19	.97	4.7	.19	.97	4.7
Argentina	.20	.83	5.0	.19	.84	4.8
India	.18	.86	5.7	.15	.86	5.0
Yugoslavia	.14	.97	4.0	.14	.97	3.9
Brazil	.15	.94	2.6	.13	.95	2.4
Turkey	.11	.75	2.5	.11	.70	2.3
CPEs						
Bulgaria	.12	.67	2.1	.16	.73	2.8
Poland	.14	.98	4.4	.14	.98	4.2
Romania	.15	.85	4.2	.14	.90	3.8
East Germany	.10	.88	3.8	.09	.90	3.4
Soviet Union	.09	.97	3.0	.08	.97	2.9
Czechoslovakia	.08	.74	2.8	.07	.76	2.6

The CPEs have speed parameters below 0.25. The fastest in diffusion has been Bulgaria, with $\phi = 0.16$, while the slowest, the Soviet Union and Czechoslovakia, recorded $\phi = 0.08$ and 0.07 respectively. The whole group lies outside the range determined for both Western and developing countries. The slowest among the Western and developing countries have had speed parameters in the upper range of the CPEs. The analysis here places the CPEs in a definitely lower range than do the rough estimates presented above.

Recent work by Thornton and Leary (1987) addresses the same issue as the regression analysis by Poznanski (1987). However, the former deals with the oxygen process alone, and consequently it is more appropriate for testing the data with independently estimated values of actual saturation points. These points very often deviate from a full output level, as indicated above in the comparison of the diffusion process in various economies. (Thus one may expect some bias in an analysis ignoring these deviations.) In addition, Thornton and Leary use not only the logistic function to regress the data, but also an alternative method—the so-called epidemic model.

Using the logistic function, Thornton and Leary conclude that there is no clear difference in the speed of diffusion in planned and market economies. These results are intriguing, but they do not necessarily contradict the findings by Poznanski (1987) because, given the methodological differences, they are not comparable. Moreover, using the epidemic model, Thornton and Leary conclude, as does Poznanski, that the CPEs are considerably slower in adopting the oxygen process.

FACTORS BEHIND SLOW DIFFUSION

The data presented above reveal that the CPEs are both slow to adopt a new technology and to diffuse it once it is adopted. This is in striking contrast to market economies, where late adoption is usually accompanied by faster diffusion. This phenomenon, called the "advantage of latecomers," has been detected in a number of studies on technology. For instance, Ray (1969) established that in five out of seven radical industrial innovations in the West (including the oxygen process) the latecomers were faster than the pioneer countries. Poznanski (1983) found this to be the case for Western economies with regard to the diffusion of continuous casting.

A convincing theoretical argument can be made that latecomers, whether countries or enterprises, should outperform the pioneers because they can avoid some of the initial difficulties and risks. In addition, they should benefit from the stable market relations developed by the pioneers (e.g., networks of suppliers, outlets for new products). However, the latecomers might suffer clear disadvantages as they face stiffer competition (rather than the "natural" monopoly of the pioneers).

To explain the slow diffusion of new technology in the CPEs, let us examine the role of economic structure in diffusion speed. One line of discussion in the literature is concerned with the impact of the concentration of production. Conflicting ideas have been aired in this respect, but most of the empirical evidence indicates that with an increasing concentration of production (and a decreasing degree of competition) diffusion slows down. For instance, Mansfield (1968) states that in the United States there is a correlation between the degree of concentration of production and the relative slowness of diffusion of the oxygen process. Adams and Dirlam (1968) provide additional evidence to that effect by showing that the largest steel companies were initially more reluctant to adopt the new process than were the smaller ones. Recent supportive arguments have been provided by Oster (1981) and Sumrall (1982). However, Maddala and Knight (1967) reject the argument that monopoly is a cause of slow diffusion. They admit that the large U.S. companies were slower in adopting the oxygen process than the smaller ones during the first years of diffusion, but they claim this did not have a significant impact on the country's relative performance. Rather they put the blame on late first adoption, which they do not link with the market structure of the industry but with such factors as an extremely dynamic demand for steel in the 1950s and the young age of capital equipment.

Another line of discussion concerns the possible impact of state intervention, an important consideration given the widespread nationalization of steel industries in the postwar years. By and large state intervention is deemed detrimental to diffusion. Maddala and Knight (1967) point out that state involvement, with its rigidities and decisionmaking lags, seems to be responsible for both delays in first adoption and slowness of further applications. They found this factor particularly relevant for diffusion in developing countries and the CPEs. The U.S. Federal Trade Commission (1977) also found a negative correlation between the degree of nationalization and the speed of diffusion.

An in-depth analysis of Soviet steelmaking by Cooper (1979) illustrates how state bureaucracy may hamper technological change. Initially the Soviet Union proved capable of developing technology for the oxygen process (almost simultaneously with Austria, the pioneer), mostly through an independent effort. However, due to conservatism and vested interests in the upper levels of the bureaucracy, applications of the new technology proceeded very slowly for more than a decade, and the strong preference of Soviet bureaucrats for the quantitative growth of output rather than the quality of steel or cost reductions has worked in the same direction.

In contrast, Aylen (1980) shows that the 1967 nationalization of a large share of the British steel industry (under the British Steel Corporation) had a strong positive impact on the diffusion of the oxygen process. Great Britain had been lagging far behind other Western nations in diffusion. With nationalization the industry gained access to government financing, restoring the opportunity to invest. Within a decade of nationalization all the major integrated steelmills were based on oxygen furnaces. Aylen's study does not necessarily contradict Cooper's. The British proceeded with nationalization in a generally competitive environment, while almost the entire Soviet steel industry is state-regulated and leaves very little room for competition.

Interesting lessons can also be drawn from our comparison of the CPE industries and major steel producers among the NICs. The regression analysis reported above indicates a much higher speed of diffusion for the NICs even though their industries are only slightly less nationalized than in the CPEs (e.g., 95 percent nationalization in South Korea and around 80 percent in Brazil, but 100 percent in the CPEs sampled). It can be argued that the major differences between the two groups are that the steel sectors in the NICs operate in an environment where some market forces are given play and that NIC steelmakers are less protected from foreign competition than in the CPEs, where imports are completely licensed by the state (see Nyers 1982).

While the CPE system seems to be in large part responsible for the slow diffusion of new technology, additional factors should be taken into account. One is the usefulness of and access to the information possessed by a pioneer innovator. While in theory latecomers should benefit from the initial efforts of pioneers (as noted), there is no evidence to that effect in the case of the diffusion of the oxygen process in the steel industry. It may be that latecomers are unable or unwilling to take advantage of the knowledge and experience accumulated by their predecessors. Indeed some studies indicate that only a limited amount of information gathered by the pioneers may be useful to latecomers owing to differences in both the production process (e.g., scale of operation, structure of fixed assets) and the type of markets supplied. In an analysis of over five hundred innovations, Myers and Marquis (1969: 27) found that at most one in three or four innovations introduced by an enterprise was a simple takeover of a predecessor's technology; all others required adaptations which often increased operation costs above those experienced by the innovators. (This observation should apply to an economy as a whole: it can benefit from outside information to only a limited extent.) Moreover, for latecomers to gain an advantage over the early innovators, there must be effective channels for transmitting information from pioneers to latecomers. Again some studies show that such channels often malfunction, either because predecessors knowingly conceal information (e.g., via patent protection or industrial secrecy), or because latecomers have a limited ability or desire to absorb external information. The latter could be a result of economic backwardness, which makes the identification of potentially useful information difficult or deprives the latecomer entirely of some channels of communication. Political factors may interfere as well (e.g., embargoes imposed by technology leaders or a less developed country's refusal to negotiate with leaders on the grounds of "exploitation" or "cultural invasion"; Poznanski 1984).

The lack of well-established communications—a flow of both pure information and goods incorporating new technology—seems to be in part responsible for the much slower diffusion of new steel technologies in the CPEs, in spite of their late adoption. Until the late 1960s the East European steel industries were operating very much independently of technology generated by the West. There were some transfers of information and limited purchases of machinery and equipment for steel production—for instance, the Soviet Union imported an entire plant from Austria in 1963 (Amann, Cooper, and Davies, eds. 1977: 98) to help Soviet engineers solve some technological problems with the oxygen process; for the same reason China purchased an Austrian steel mill in 1965 (Aylen 1980). The major source of CPE technology, however, was domestic research, especially that conducted by the Soviet Union, which dominates the steel industry in the region. In addition, some contributions were made by Czechoslovakia, Poland, and Romania (UN Economic Commission for Europe 1979: 62). The Soviet Union was also the major producer of machinery and equipment for the steel industry in the area. Although the Soviet Union's technological capacity in steel production is highly regarded by international specialists, the limited access to Western technology probably had some negative impact on the ability of the CPEs to modernize their steel industries as rapidly as in the West.

Whereas the generally slow diffusion of new technologies in the CPEs can to some extent be explained by their limited communication with Western countries, it seems that an improvement in relations since the late 1960s has helped to accelerate these processes during the past several years. Data show not only that CPE imports of steel machinery and equipment from the West have increased dramatically during the past several years, but also that the diffusion of new steel technologies has accelerated at the same time. Poland is a good case in point, with a sharp increase in imports of machinery and equipment mostly from Western countries and a radical change in the use of the oxygen process during the last decade.

The speed of diffusion could also be influenced by cost considerations, including a difference in the magnitude of investment necessary to replace physically unserviceable capital. In his study of the diffusion of the oxygen process in the United States and Canada during 1959-69, Bauman (1973: 6) proved that the higher the level of expenditure on the replacement of old capital, the better are the opportunities for the application of new technologies. Of a large group of economic variables which could influence diffusion speed in these two countries, the difference in the level of depreciation of fixed capital was the most significant determinant. According to Bauman a relatively slower propagation of the oxygen process in the United States was probably caused mainly by the fact that the initial implementation of this process took place after a long period of rapid buildup of production capacities based on other technologies.

Numerous technological refinements introduced in the Soviet Union and Czechoslovakia—e.g., natural gas and heavy oil firing and oxygen blowing—have enabled the CPEs to surpass the West in the productivity of open-hearth furnaces by more than 100 percent while the West has emphasized the oxygen process. However, is it these improvements in the open-hearth process that have discouraged CPE planners from giving priority to the oxygen process, or have they been deterred by a general opposition to major change? We are inclined to believe that difficulties in developing the new technology to the point of successful commercialization—plus planning conservatism—have stimulated additional efforts to improve old technology even beyond economic reasons. Even with the refinements, the open-hearth process still lags behind the oxygen process in terms of both production unit costs and output quality.

Finally, we should consider the relative availability of productive inputs that go into the steelmaking processes in various countries. The validity of our comparisons could be questioned—at least in the case of the Soviet Union—on the grounds that the primary reason for slow diffusion has been a relative lack of scrap metal. This argument seems sound since it has been proved that the availability of scrap is critical for the speed of diffusion (e.g., Bauman 1973). To determine whether such a nonsytemic factor explains the sharp differences in diffusion, we should analyze a technology which is not so affected and is also not complementary to the oxygen process. Continuous casting of steel is such a technology.

The Soviet Union introduced the continuous casting technology in 1955, three years after the pioneer, Austria—much earlier than Great Britain or the United States. However, it took it twenty-six years to move from the first application to a 10 percent share, compared to twenty-one years for France, nineteen years for Great Britain, eighteen years for West Germany, and fifteen years for the United States. As late as 1980 the Soviet Union had not reached a 20 percent share (meaning that it will take it more than twenty-six years to get to this level), while it took West Germany twenty-one years and the United States eighteen years. Again, the Soviet Union was slower in the speed of diffusion than its major Western counterparts (Table 1).

Eastern Europe has been both very late in initial adoption and relatively slow in the diffusion of the continuous casting technology (as with the oxygen process). Czechoslovakia, probably the first adopter among the East Europeans, showed a ten-year lag, compared with six years for Italy and nine years for Spain. East Germany was again very late, with a sixteen-year lag. Czechoslovakia, Poland, and East Germany had not reached a 20 percent level of diffusion by 1980, but Italy and Spain had (Spain in sixteen years). By 1980 continuous casting represented 1.7 percent of total ingot output in Czechoslovakia; thus it will take several more years for its industry to attain a 20 percent level.

In sum, the CPEs seem unable to capitalize on the knowledge accumulated by the pioneers in a given technology. Apparently owing to the institutional deficiencies of central planning, they often—or generally—do not reap the advantages of latecoming. Their failure is related in particular to the high risk-aversion of planners, the politicization of economic issues, and the overconcern of CPEs with quantitative growth. In addition, slower diffusion is the price the CPEs pay for their isolation from information channels to technology leaders—for all practical purposes the West.

ELIMINATION OF OBSOLETE TECHNOLOGY: A REEXAMINATION OF THE STEEL INDUSTRY

We argued in Chapter 3 that the adoption of new technology alone does not determine how successful an economy will be, but that success also depends on terminating obsolete technologies. Very little research has been done on the CPEs (or indeed any economy) along the lines of this argument, but in this section we shall provide some supporting evidence by reexamining our data on the steel industry. As in the preceding section, we shall begin with the determination of time patterns in a group of centrally planned and market economies (including those in the developing world) and then turn to an analysis of some causal factors to better understand the role of the systemic variable (also see Slama 1981).

PATTERNS IN THE EXTINGUISHING PROCESS

The first dimension of the extinguishing process to be determined is when a country began to eliminate old steel technologies—i.e., the Bessemer and open-hearth processes. Table 3 shows that the maximum threshold points for individual countries are widely dispersed over time for the two decaying technologies. For the Bessemer process in Western countries, developing countries, and the CPEs, they range over the period 1950-71, with slight concentrations around 1962 and 1970. Similarly, for the open-hearth process the thresholds range between 1960 and 1981. The long time-span implies that the countries in the sample differed in one type of innovativeness—i.e., the ability to phase out an obsolete technology. In the West the clear lead in both processes belongs to Japan and West Germany. The United States was among the first in the world to

Table 3

TIMETABLE OF THE EXTINGUISHING PROCESS OF OLD TECHNOLOGIES IN THE STEEL INDUSTRY FOR VARIOUS COUNTRIES, 1982

Region and Country	Bessemer Process			Open-Hearth Process		
	Maximum Threshold	Total Elimination	Cycle (*Years*)	Maximum Threshold	Total Elimination	Cycle (*Years*)
West						
Austria	n.a.	1977	n.a.	1968	cont.	n.a.
Belgium	1969	1978	9	1960	1977	17
Canada	n.a.	n.a.	n.a.	n.a.	n.a.	n.a.
France	1970	cont.[a]	>12	1964	cont.	>18
Great Britain	1964	1981	17	1966	1980	14
Italy	1963	1977	14	1970	1982	12
Japan	1954	1966	12	1965	1977	12
Netherlands	n.a.	n.a.	n.a.	1963	1977	14
Spain	1962	1970	8	1971	cont.	>11
Sweden	1962	1973	11	1967	1982	15
United States	1950	1967	17	1967	cont.	>15
West Germany	1958	1977	19	1965	cont.	>17
Developing Countries						
Argentina	1970	cont.	12	1972	cont.	>10
Brazil	1971	cont.	11	1975	cont.	>7
India	n.a.	n.a.	n.a.	1979	cont.	>3
Mexico	n.a.	n.a.	n.a.	1975	cont.	>7
CPEs						
Bulgaria	n.a.	n.a.	n.a.	1978	cont.	>4
Czechoslovakia	n.a.	n.a.	n.a.	n.a.	n.a.	n.a.
East Germany	n.a.	n.a.	n.a.	1982	cont.	>0
Hungary	n.a.	n.a.	n.a.	1981	cont.	>1
Poland	n.a.	n.a.	n.a.	1978	cont.	>4
Romania	n.a.	n.a.	n.a.	1981	cont.	>1
Soviet Union	1966	cont.	>16	1981	cont.	>1

[a]Process still in use.

begin the elimination of the Bessemer process but relatively late in removing the open-hearth technology. Belgium was just the opposite: first in open-hearth and very late in Bessemer. Our data on the Bessemer process are not sufficient to compare the abilities of the three blocs of countries, although the developing countries and CPEs included in the sample clearly lagged behind most of the Western steelmakers. The Soviet Union began to eliminate the Bessemer process only in 1966, and Argentina and Brazil in 1970 and 1971 respectively.

Sharp cross-country differences appear, however, in the open-hearth case. The countries in the sample can be classified into four groups in terms of their readiness to phase out this technology. The fastest countries, all in the West, began the elimination process between 1960 and 1965 (i.e., Belgium, the Netherlands, Japan, West Germany, Great Britain, and France). Between 1966 and 1970 the remaining Western countries began the process. Steelmakers from the developing countries began the extinguishing process during 1972-75. The clear laggards were the CPEs (excluding Czechoslovakia for lack of data), where the elimination process began as late as 1979-81, with East Germany the latest in the group. Thus the CPEs began to phase out the open-hearth process about fifteen years after the majority of Western steelmakers.

The literature on diffusion processes often suggests that the expansion of a new technology immediately begins to force the old technologies out. However, except for Belgium, where output from open-hearth furnaces began to fall shortly before the first oxygen-process installations were built, in the first years of the expansion of the oxygen process, open-hearth output increased or remained stable. In Hungary the gap was very short (i.e., one year), but Hungary could be considered a special case because it was the last to adopt the oxygen process (in 1980). If Belgium and Hungary are excluded from the sample, the average period during which production from both old and new technologies was increasing or stable amounts to around eleven years. Even if we exclude one extreme case in which the time-span was very long (twenty-one years), the average is still ten years. Clearly, effective substitution does not immediately follow the introduction of a new technology.

A comparison of individual countries suggests that Western countries which were among the first to implement the oxygen process went through a longer period of parallel production increases from old and new technologies than the latecomers. For example, in Austria (the pioneer in the oxygen process) the period ran sixteen years, and in the United States (the second adopter) it was thirteen years. In the Western countries that started implementing the oxygen process in the 1960s, the period did not exceed eight years.

Cross-country comparisons show that the periods of parallel production increases or stability were generally shorter in the West than in the CPEs, where (excluding Hungary for the reasons mentioned above) these periods were close to or much above the average, with the Soviet Union reporting a twenty-one-year span. This is true even though Eastern Europe (but not the Soviet Union) introduced the oxygen process much later than the West (see Poznanski 1983). This finding reinforces our observation that the CPEs appear to be less prepared than market economies to make optimal use of available technologies.

Only in a few cases was the introduction of a new technology accompanied by an even faster growth in production using old technologies. Among these is France, where Bessemer output increased for more than eight years parallel with the expansion of the oxygen process. In Sweden the situation was just the opposite. Open-hearth output increased by half as much as that from oxygen-process installations during the first ten years of the latter. Obviously the upward trends led to a flatter initial stage of the diffusion curve for oxygen-process steel measured in relative terms.

The average period for totally extinguishing old technologies has been found to be thirteen years for the Bessemer process (sample of seven countries) and fourteen years for the open-hearth process (sample of six countries). If the countries that had not completed the extinguishing processes by 1982 are taken into account, the two averages rise substantially. The truncated cycles (i.e., up to 1982) for most of these countries turn out to be longer than the average for the full cycles for the remaining countries. Moreover, in some of these countries the elimination of one or both technologies is far from complete. The averages should probably be adjusted upwards by at least two years.

Some individual cases stand out. One is the Soviet Union, which appears to be going through the most extended extinguishing cycle for the Bessemer process. In 1982 sixteen years had passed since output from the Bessemer process had started declining—much above the average of all the countries sampled and close to the longest full cycles of Western steelmakers (i.e., Great Britain and West Germany). However, the elimination of this process seems far from complete. If the rate of output reduction during 1978-82 continued, full elimination would take place around 1989-90—a total of twenty-three years.

The United States is another interesting case because it appears very slow in removing the open-hearth process. By 1982 the United States was one of very few Western steel producers with open-hearth installations still in operation. (The only other significant exceptions were Canada and West Germany, the latter appearing to be close to final elimination.) The United States was likely to complete the extinguishing process by 1985-86 at the earliest, making the full cycle for its industry one of the longest (if not the longest) among Western producers.

BASIC CAUSAL RELATIONSHIPS

In this section we shall try to determine what economic factors are responsible for the extinguishing patterns and country differences discussed above. In particular we shall be interested in the timing of the maximum threshold point and the length of the extinguishing cycles. Again we want to separate systemic factors (the focus of this analysis) from other variables, having established the empirical relationships in our discussion of the diffusion process. Below we shall look into the role of one nonsystemic factor—business conditions—and one system-related variable—trade openness.

From what is known about the economic aspects of technological change, it would seem that the phasing out of an old technology should in some way depend on business conditions, such as the state of demand. The link has been considered on many occasions by economists working on diffusion processes—with limited success, however. As yet, there is not much quantitative evidence to support the view that an improvement in business conditions (e.g., an upward movement in demand) either helps diffusion or indeed retards it. Thus an analysis of the relationship between the extinguishing process and business conditions would be particularly useful.

An old technology is eliminated when its current costs of production are higher than the current costs of a new substitute. The old technology, at least partially amortized, has the advantage of lower capital costs because to build a similar capacity with a new technology as a rule requires higher capital inputs. Given the comparative total (i.e., current and capital) costs of both the old and new technologies, strong product demand should make an industry more interested in prolonging the life of the old technology, while weak demand would probably lead to elimination.

To investigate whether there is a link between business conditions and the extinguishing process, let us consider whether or not the maximum threshold point for the open-hearth process was preceded by a change in the total output of steel. If total output declined and/or stagnated before the maximum threshold point was reached, we could reasonably argue that poor business conditions led to a reduction in the output from the open-hearth process. The opposite result would suggest that no relationship exists, unless it was determined that the end of expansion led to an accelerated elimination of the old technology (a possibility calling for separate analysis).

In most cases the maximum threshold point for open-hearth output was earlier than the endpoint of expansion in total output. On average, the countries sampled began to eliminate the open-hearth process eight years before total production stagnated or declined in absolute terms. (This is a low estimate based on a sample of ten countries for which the points have been identified and the sequence established.) In a few cases the elimination of the old technology took place with a continuously increasing total output of steel, but in the majority the extinguishing process at least for a period paralleled a stagnating and/or declining total production of steel. The process was phased out in the expanding steel industries of Italy, Argentina, Brazil, and Mexico—all latecomers to the steel industry, a fact which at least provisionally explains why they were exceptions. The comparison of the relative timing for total production and open-hearth output also reveals that only in the CPEs did total production drop before some reduction in open-hearth output took place. In Bulgaria, Hungary, Romania, and the Soviet Union, an average of five years passed from the time total production ceased to increase and open-hearth output began to drop.

A closer analysis reveals that changing business conditions have some impact on the extinguishing process once the demand for steel has begun to decline. To measure the immediate effect of a decline in total demand, we have gathered data on the rate of growth in output from the open-hearth process before and after the turning point in demand for ten Western countries. An acceleration in the decline of output from the old process could be interpreted as an indication of the direct influence of business conditions upon the pace of the extinguishing process. In five cases (France, Great Britain, Spain, Sweden, and West Germany) the turn in total demand for steel led to a faster elimination of technologically obsolete installations. In Austria and Japan the rate of decline in open-hearth output remained the same after the turn in business conditions, and in Belgium, the Netherlands, and the United States the extinguishing process was actually faster before the collapse of total demand than after. One is tempted to conclude that a worsening in business conditions stimulates the elimination of an old technology. However, it could be that the faster phasing out of the open-hearth process following a turn in total demand results less from temporary overcapacity than from the growing obsolescence of the technology, which is by then close to total elimination anyway.

Now let us consider whether there is a relationship between the time patterns of the extinguishing process and the openness of an economy—i.e., the extent to which foreign agents enjoy the same rights as domestic agents. It is widely recognized by economists that the more open and export-oriented a country, the stronger are the pressures for technological modernization. Supposedly, openness in an economy provides its industries with information on relative price trends and demand evolution and places them in a competitive environment which promotes a readiness to innovate. We shall test this hypothesis below.

The ten Western countries for which we have data have been ranked according to their export orientation, measured in terms of the share of steel exports in total production (for 1975, chosen arbitrarily). This ranking generally matches the ranking of these countries according to the time they began eliminating the open-hearth process. Belgium and the Netherlands appear at the top in both cases, while Spain and the United States rank at the bottom. The only important deviations are Austria and Japan.

Even stronger appears the correlation between the readiness to eliminate an old technology and absolute steel exports, treated as another measure of export orientation. In this case all five countries ranked in the top half in terms of absolute exports (i.e., Japan, West Germany, Belgium, France, and the Netherlands) also rank high in terms of when the extinguishing process began. While the correlation is not perfect, none of the deviations can be called sharp.

The simple ranking procedure does not show a correlation between a country's magnitude of changes in export orientation during 1963-84 and its readiness to extinguish the open-hearth process, however. The ranking for the Netherlands, France, Great Britain, and the United States is quite consistent, but for Japan, West Germany, Sweden, and Austria it is completely random. (Two countries had to be excluded from the original sample.)

The appropriate measure for the degree of export orientation may well not be a country's share of exports in its total production but rather its share of world exports. It is possible that a country which supplies a substantial part of the world market will be more concerned with its exports (i.e., more likely to follow market signals and accept competition) than a smaller supplier, even if the latter devotes a larger share of its total production to exports.

From the above analysis we can make some general observations about the extinguishing process in the steel industry. For one thing, the reduction of output from obsolete technologies does not begin immediately after a new technology is introduced, but after a lengthy time lag. For another, it takes a considerable amount of time for obsolete technologies to be completely eliminated. Moreover, the countries which first introduced the oxygen process seem to have been relatively slow in eliminating the open-hearth process. Finally, the CPEs have been the last to begin eliminating the old technologies, lagging far behind both Western steelmakers and those from developing nations. The CPE conservation of older technologies cannot be attributed to specific demand conditions—unmet needs of the user industries—but rather to the lack of competitive forces (or substitute institutions).

There is ample evidence that the persistent lag of the CPEs behind Western technology is related not only to their limited access to technology (as argued in Chapter 6), but also to the inability of state enterprises to implement technology. It takes much more to persuade CPE enterprises to innovate than competitive market enterprises, and there is less assurance that innovations, if pursued, will exploit all avenues of cost reduction or quality improvement, or that negative changes will either be prevented or eliminated if they appear. Innovations detrimental to the general welfare seem in particular to separate the CPEs from the market systems.

Our analysis also reveals that the CPEs are not only slower in first adoption when compared to the West, but also that they are less effective in pursuing technological changes with which their enterprises have already successfully experimented. Unlike Western latecomers, the CPEs do not take advantage of pioneer efforts and experience to establish a stable market for new or improved products. Their systemic deficiencies are a key factor in such behavior. Their lack of contact with Western technology leaders is a factor as well; it leaves them without much practical information on effective ways to commercialize technology.

Finally, the CPEs are demonstrably more conservative in their policy of phasing out old technology. We consider this another critical reason for the long-lasting East-West technology gaps. It appears that the comparative profitability of old and new technologies is of less concern in the CPEs than in the market economies, so that inferior older technologies remain or even expand, long after new substitutes are available. This is in part responsible for the slower diffusion of new technologies because some of the available scarce resources are assigned to older technologies.

The above comparison of innovative behaviors does not draw from the experience of non-Western market economies (i.e., the developing world); however, it is likely that if included, this experience would also point to the inferiority of the CPE mechanism. Additional research will be required to fully substantiate this hypothesis, but some fragmentary quantitative evidence presented in this chapter suggests that the hypothesis is correct. If it turns out that evidence supports the hypothesis, one could claim that the poorer technological performance of the CPEs vis-à-vis the Latin American and Far Eastern NICs is related not only to the CPEs' limited access to foreign technology, but also to their reluctance to introduce and diffuse new technologies.

Chapter 8

ALTERNATIVE THEORETICAL EXPLANATIONS

In Chapters 6 and 7 we established that the behavior of technological agents in the CPEs and market economies differs substantially in terms of effectiveness. In this chapter we would like to explore what makes the CPEs less effective. To do so we shall determine the most essential feature of the planning mechanism that leads to inferior technological behavior instead of assessing all the specific instruments used by planners. Three major theoretical perspectives of the planning mechanism will be outlined here and analyzed from the point of view of their adequacy.

THE RISK-REWARD EXPLANATION

There is a long tradition in the economic literature of blaming the CPE resistance against technological changes on the highly uncertain environment in which enterprises have to operate (see Berliner 1976). It is argued that even though enterprise managers do not face many market-type risks (e.g., sudden changes in consumer taste, a switch in demand to a product's close substitute), they are subject to other risks, specific to the central planning system, which are the sources of more intense uncertainty.

One reason for the high uncertainty, it is claimed, is that CPE managers are continually confronted with pressures from central planners to exactly fulfill annual targets for total production and the output of some goods. Because of such pressures managers wish to avoid the uncertainties typically associated with major technological changes. These put state enterprises in a riskier situation than market enterprises, which have a wide range of acceptable outcomes, with output less important than input. According to Berliner, the most critical source of high risk is the uncertainty over supplies (i.e., parts and materials).*

*"The consequences of the unreliability of the system are more severe for innovator than for non-innovator. . . . The avoidance of innovation is a device for minimizing uncertainty over supply" (Berliner 1976: 72-73).

Another feature of central planning that some economists claim makes technological change particularly risky is the tendency among planners to demand uninterrupted increases in the volume of production and in the supplies of some specified goods. According to Grossman (1966: 118-29), plan targets for upcoming periods are generally extrapolations of previous performance, so that enterprises performing well in one plan period are likely to be given new targets demanding an increase in production of at least the magnitude reached in the previous period.* Faced with this planning practice, enterprise managers may be unwilling to introduce even technologies that pose little difficulty, for if an enterprise achieves a higher output level owing to such a low-risk change, a more difficult target can be imposed upon it in the next plan.

A corollary to the argument on excessive risk is that state enterprises do not take risks because the rewards are insufficient.† Even though numerous, the rewards offered to Soviet enterprises for innovation are small compared with the bonuses for other endeavors, which are often in direct conflict with the innovative effort (Berliner 1976). It is also sometimes stressed that an enterprise's record on innovation is considered less important than other indicators of performance for promotions and wage increases.

It follows from the above discussion that obstacles to innovation could be eliminated if there were more flexibility in target planning and if financial bonuses were increased. This contention is explicitly made by Berliner, who accordingly puts considerable weight on the ongoing reforms in the Soviet economic system, which he sees as a proper vehicle for making central planning more efficient in stimulating technological change.**

*Grossman sums up as follows: "Complex in its many details, the matter [of obstacles to innovation] is essentially quite simple: given the success indicators and the system of bonuses to management, the "taut" plans, and the "ratchet principle" of raising plan targets on the basis of most recent performance, management has little to gain and much to risk by espousing new products or processes" (1966): 121).

†Berliner puts it as follows: "Innovation involves both great risk and great effort, and both need to be rewarded. The point itself has never been in dispute. What has been the bone of contention is the size of the reward needed to elicit various quanta of innovational activity. I believe the evidence is mounting that the rewards have been far too small in the socialist economies to elicit the desired rate of innovation" (1976: 158).

**Berliner states the following: "With a different set of policies and structural [i.e., systemic] properties the socialist economy may well be able to

The problem with the risk-reward model as an explanation for low innovation is that it is based on something of a caricature of central planning. It implies a degree of planning rigidity which does not exist. In fact, enterprises sometimes operate with no clear plan targets, particularly when there is a delay in setting goals for an upcoming plan period. More important, confirmed targets are subject to revision by industrial ministries and higher authorities when there are indications that a plan will not be fulfilled or that increases in production are possible. In some cases—such as Poland in 1976-79—planning is so soft that it is more random than rigid.

Interestingly enough, it was Berliner (1952: 342-65) who in a seminal paper demonstrated that the Soviet planning system was much less rigid than was usually assumed at the time. Berliner enumerated some informal mechanisms that managers used to help meet plan targets (volume of output in particular), in the process breaking official rules. Among them were safety factors (e.g., excess demand for supplies and so-called hoarding); simulation (e.g., underrepresentation of production capacities, assortment manipulations); and personal influence. Berliner considers these informal procedures not marginal but absolutely essential for the Soviet and, one can assume, any other CPE system.

In his analysis Berliner does not discuss plan target modifications during a given plan period; rather he focuses on how already fixed objectives are met. He gives the impression that managers put all their efforts into meeting deadlines instead of trying to negotiate them, even when a good case can be presented for extension. Moreover, Berliner states that bonuses for fulfilling original output targets—which can be as much as one third of monthly wages—are not paid at all if the actual output figure is even one percent short of the planned figure (a situation which is more the exception than the rule in CPE practice).

The consequences of not meeting production targets are not as severe as assumed in the risk-reward explanation. The strongest sanctions for failure involve personnel changes in upper management. However, there is not much evidence that top managers are always punished for failing to meet plans, regardless of the reason (be it an unsuccessful innovation or a more trivial mistake or just bad luck in routine activities). In most cases, the rules of the party

eliminate the perpetual disequilibria that give rise to the uncertainties in supply. . . . The fault is in the state of disequilibrium rather than in the socialist base of property ownership" (1976: 62).

nomenklatura prevent severe punishments of managers who have failed. At worst, these managers are rotated to other, often equally respectable, positions.

The risk-reward explanation also underestimates the ability of enterprises—with their monopoly on most of the information on production—to present their failures as successes. Moreover, enterprises can redefine failures as successes, however socially inefficient this may be. One way of doing so is by negotiating additional resources and pouring them into a bad project for as long as necessary to make it look good. Enterprises are also frequently in a position to make prices cover manufacturing costs, which again helps to avoid the risks of failure through innovation.

If enterprises can manipulate information to their advantage, then the bonuses attached to technological performance become a minor or secondary issue. Clearly there is no guarantee that even a competitively high reward would make the economic agents struggle for rapid technological change. In addition, it is difficult for the central authorities, despite all the bureaucratic procedures, to assure that rewards would be granted for a serious innovative effort rather than for sham improvements. Such problems were apparent in the case of the experimental Polish fund for implementation effects described above. An effort to increase innovation by offering higher bonuses is bound to fall short of expectations.

Rewards for enterprise managers are not a key issue for another reason as well: as Bergson (1978b) has shown, given the proper economic environment, the bonuses that would have to be paid to make managers of any state enterprise take necessary risks—from the point of view of reaching Pareto optimality—would not be particularly high. Except for some extreme cases—e.g., the so-called asymmetric "career function" calling for severe penalties when losses are incurred and offering no rewards for above-minimum performance—the bonuses would not have to exceed wages and would not pose any ideological problem for the CPEs, given that the existing income inequalities are quite substantial and do not cause much social frustration.

THE ZERO-PRICE EXPLANATION

INSTITUTIONALIZED INEFFICIENCY

In this section we shall argue that it is not the uncompromising pressure from the state for growth, but rather its permissiveness that creates an obstacle to technological change in the CPEs. In other words, the real reason for the low level of technological change is not in enterprise fears of failing with innovations in production (thus upsetting plan fulfillments), but rather a lack of economic incentives for enterprises to innovate owing to planners' readiness to accept excessive inputs (of labor, capital, and materials), as well as a failure to meet customer needs.

Any enterprise which behaves rationally, regardless of the economic system under which it operates, will introduce some technological changes. However, full-speed innovation is possible only if an enterprise is forced into it because changes in production are more demanding than routine procedures and bear higher risks as well. Only if an enterprise's survival depends on a continuous reduction in unit costs and on its ability to market its output will it take every opportunity to introduce technological (or other) changes. Any relaxation of these criteria will provide an excuse for ignoring potential technological improvements.

In a competitive market, enterprises are coerced into making a maximum effort for fear of being outpaced by rivals and of going bankrupt if they fail to match other producers over a long period of time. This is also true for any economy in which the state interferes with market forces but does not help enterprises in a systematic way, so that managers cannot ever predict whether they will be bailed out or not. In the West, and to a lesser degree among the NICs, the majority of enterprises cannot count on being rescued. To survive they have no other choice but to innovate.

In contrast, the CPEs (as noted) are characterized by an extensive safety net that the state continuously provides to all enterprises, either through a relaxation of plan targets or by allowing changes in the relationship between the fulfillment of objectives and rewards. As a result, even if productive resources are formally priced, these prices are not a serious consideration for enterprises. For example, bank credit can be made to carry interest rates which are then not collected by the banks. This zero-price situation permits the inefficient use of inputs to be a permanent feature of the CPEs—a condition to which we shall refer as "institutionalized inefficiency." It removes pressure from CPE enterprises to fully engage in innovation.

It follows that for the CPEs to attain technological capability comparable to that of the market economies, a reinstitution of bankruptcy will be necessary. This idea has been occasionally discussed in some of the CPEs, but only Hungary has started to argue openly for it. Thus far bankruptcy legislation in Hungary has been soft. According to the law, a state enterprise can be pronounced bankrupt only after it has been given time for "rescue adjustments." First, a warning has to be delivered to the management of an unsuccessful enterprise, and some financial concessions have to be made to help it in its adjustments. If these measures fail, the planners (i.e., the ministry of finance and relevant industrial ministry) have to come up with a "reconstruction program" which they can force upon the enterprise. Only when these steps have led nowhere can the decision be made to dissolve the enterprise and transfer its assets to a more viable concern. However, no precise time-frame is set by the legislators for this bankruptcy procedure. (Similarly a Yugoslav effort in this direction has failed to produce unambiguous legislation.)

The administration in Hungary does not use its right to declare even a chronically deficient enterprise bankrupt very often. Such enterprises receive generous direct subsidies and tax exemptions—up to 40 percent of production costs in most industries (Szabo 1974: 7). This helps many inefficient enterprises to show profits, so they do not qualify for bankruptcy even though they deserve it. In such a permissive environment only 10 enterprises out of 1,735 showed a loss in 1980, a crisis year in Hungary. Eleven enterprises were ordered to merge with others, and 13 were liquidated. These figures were higher than in any preceding year but still too low considering the real losses incurred by poorly managed enterprises (Kornai 1983).

There is some evidence that the full reinstitution of bankruptcy has many opponents within the Hungarian leadership. Moreover, enterprise managers are accustomed to a paternalistic relationship with central planners, who as a rule bail them out during periods of financial difficulty. The Hungarian trade unions, which enjoy more freedom from party control than their counterparts in other countries of the region, are not sympathetic to this idea either, for they worry about the fate of workers in enterprises which would be forced to go out of business.

Even if the Hungarian regime (or any other among the CPEs) pursued bankruptcy procedures more vigorously, it is doubtful that it would make much difference in terms of improving efficiency. While a fear of bankruptcy might work as a stimulus for both managers concerned with their professional image and workers who are proud of their plants, the institution of bankruptcy cannot possibly offer more than such psychological motivation. In short, bankruptcy not in a formal but in a real sense, as it exists under the market system, and central planning are clearly not compatible.

The logic of bankruptcy under the market system is that it allows an inefficient enterprise (i.e., one earning less than average profit rates) to regain efficiency either by reducing capital costs or forcing workers to accept lower wages. The choice of one of these alternatives will be determined (among other things) by technological factors—namely, whether a given enterprise's capital is usable in other sectors of industry or whether workers' services (i.e., skills) are usable outside the sector in which their enterprise operates. Thus, for instance, if capital is usable in other sectors but the skills are not, the workers will have to bear the costs of "adjustment through bankruptcy."

It is hard to imagine how such mechanisms of adjustment could possibly work under central planning. The state owns almost all the capital, so that it would have to bear the costs of capital losses; moreover, the resale of capital would be difficult to monitor, given the lack of real capital markets in the CPEs. Managers would continue to be immune to capital losses, so that their efficiency (i.e., interest in making profit- or revenue-maximizing decisions) would hardly be affected by bankruptcy. Under these circumstances it would be unfair to ask the workers to bear the costs of adjustment since it would not be their fault that an enterprise was doing badly. In addition, given the special status of workers in the CPEs, it is difficult to imagine any regime enforcing an adjustment at the expense of the workers without jeopardizing its political future.

Thus we are led to conclude that it is the ownership structure and not the specific instruments activated by the state apparatus which makes for such permanent behavioral characteristics of central planning as the lack of real prices for productive inputs.* While the existing CPE systems are reformable, as long as the system of property rights is not changed, the systems have to allow for the less

*As I see it, this is also the central thrust of Kornai's (1981) theory of the CPEs. He refers to the "paternalistic" nature of these societies rather than to ownership itself, but the difference is only in wording and not in substance. In this sense, the theory follows in the footsteps of von Mises (1932), who considered property rights to be the essence of any economic system and argued that rational prices are not separable from the profit-maximization behavior of private individuals. By the same token, this theory, shared by the author, goes against Lange's (1936) claim that market rationality (and efficiency) can be assured in a system where resources are owned by the state because planners should be able to simulate prices and therefore properly value inputs.

efficient behavior of enterprises than under the market system. This could be one of the reasons why the indicators in this volume do not show that the only decentralized CPE, Hungary, has in any large measure been more effective in pursuing technological change than the other CPEs (see also Marer 1985).

PERMANENT SHORTAGES

The zero-price model, focusing on the lack of real prices for inputs as a source of low innovation, is closely related to Kornai's (1981) theory. When Kornai refers to the "soft-budget constraint" as a distinctive feature of the CPEs, he implies that enterprises are permitted to waste productive resources in the expectation that the state will rescue them from difficulties. However, the lack of incentives for the efficient use of inputs is not the focus of Kornai's theory. Rather, it is the specific imbalances (different from those in market economies) that are caused by permissive planners—a phenomenon which we find of less importance than institutionalized inefficiency, as we shall demonstrate.

According to Kornai, the most important implication of the soft-budget constraint is that it allows enterprises to express an unlimited demand for goods. As a result, there is a permanent excess of demand over supply of productive inputs. The same is true with consumer goods, even though consumers face hard-budget constraints because enterprises are in a stronger position to absorb the available supplies of double-use goods. Consequently, Kornai calls the CPEs "shortage economies." In contrast, in the market economies, all enterprises (and consumers of course) face hard-budget constraints, so that another type of imbalance evolves— namely, excess supply. Accordingly, Kornai labels these "slack economies."

The fact that shortage is a central category in Kornai's analytical model is reflected in his explanation of lower innovation in the CPEs. Unlimited enterprise demand for inputs means that suppliers have secure outlets. Thus they have little motivation to satisfy the quality demands of customers and even less reason to use new products as an instrument for boosting demand. Kornai considers that it is the insufficient supply of product innovations which distinguishes the CPEs from the market economies, where quality improvements are crucial for survival.* Thus Kornai sees low

*The CPEs may expend a considerable effort (though not necessarily comparable to that of market-type economies) toward process innovations for

innovation as a direct result of excess demand, while in the zero-price model this phenomenon is linked directly to institutionalized inefficiency.

There is overwhelming evidence of a permanent gap between demand and supply of consumer goods in Hungary (Kornai et al. 1971: 242-44). In the case of automobiles, for example, only 22 to 33 percent of the orders placed in 1968 were met. For telephones the figure was around 33 percent, and for most clothing and shoes it ranged between 70 and 94 percent. A similar analysis for the late 1970s indicated that this gap had diminished, but it continues to be substantial. The waiting period for apartments was seven years in 1979 (in Poland, ten to twelve years). For passenger cars the lag between initial (or full) payments and delivery was five years in 1979 (Kornai 1983).

These permanent shortages are also reflected in a time-consuming buying process. An analysis of the time budgets in a sample of Polish families indicated that shopping for food and other necessities took an average of two to three hours a day. Faced with a lack of the most desired articles, many consumers settled for less popular substitutes. In Hungary Kornai's (1983) study shows that more than half of women buying shoes were forced to purchase models that were not the most desirable. They had to buy winter shoes in the summer and accept styles and colors other than the ones they desired at the time of purchase.

There is also some evidence that shortages on the consumer goods market tend to be more severe than for investment goods. In the constant struggle for goods, enterprises seem to win over consumers, as indicated by the well-known practices of central planners to limit resources in the consumer sector when the building of a consistent "material balance" requires some reallocation of resources (Montias 1960). Moreover, in the economic cycles consumption seems to serve as a buffer for many major difficulties, such as excess investment or balance-of-payments crises (Bauer 1978). The consumer goods sector seems to benefit mostly after a society openly shows its frustration or a new leadership strives for popularity, but the positive impact by and large does not last long.

The above cannot be considered ultimate proof that Kornai's theory of shortage is valid. In fact, starting from different assumptions,

expanding production, to which enterprises are strongly committed even without pressure from planners.

some economists argue that, contrary to Kornai's claim (at least with respect to consumer goods), there is no systemic reason for shortages to be permanent (see Gomulka 1986). Shortages could be eliminated in the consumer goods sector if central planners were only willing to raise prices sufficiently to eliminate the accumulated imbalances and then to take care of other distortions by further raising prices (all this assuming that the state would not correct incomes upward at an even faster rate). If this has not been practiced thus far in the CPEs, it is most likely due to the conservatism of the planners.*

The above argument does not take into account some distributive aspects of a flexible pricing policy (and possibly continued open inflation) within the framework of the CPEs. If prices were indeed allowed to clear consumer markets, they would further upset the income equity intended by the regimes and most likely supported by a majority of the citizens even without accepting the economic system in its entirety. Lower-income people, who now spend more time standing in lines and therefore have better access to shortage goods, would lose this advantage with flexible prices, and more goods would be shifted to the upper-income groups. Of course, without knowing how much the lower-income groups gain due to their greater willingness to search for goods, one cannot exactly predict the distributive impact of such a policy shift.

Under a policy of shortage elimination there would also be the problem of how to treat the special access to supplies by dignitaries, a situation permitted by almost all the CPEs. Special shops or purchase coupons (distributed by higher levels of the party organization and central administration) offer a better selection of goods for prices generally below those prevailing in open sales. Buying goods in such protected enclaves is a problem too, though of a different magnitude. To eliminate imbalances here would require price increases that could be only partially mitigated by relatively larger supplies. In other words, the requirement of shortage elimination would put strong constraints on the ability of the regimes to provide selected members of the political establishment with a subsidized supply of goods.

Under the market-clearing policy any instance of the state planners trying to distribute consumer goods without a concern for

*As Gomulka points out, such a pricing policy has successfully operated in Yugoslavia, which in some ways resembles the CPEs. Whether this example is sufficient proof is not clear.

demand signals would lead to price differentiations for identical goods. If (say) all consumers exhibited equal price elasticities of demand, then whenever one group was given preferences in supplies, a lower price would have to be charged to assure local equilibrium. The special shops and coupons for dignitaries are not the only instances of the segmentation of consumer "markets" in the CPEs. With large, so-called flagship plants, priority construction projects, highly demanded professionals, many "culture-workers" (e.g., writers, painters), and others enjoying better access to goods as well, the application of the flexible pricing policy would lead to a substantial differentiation in prices which could provide the masses with a more transparent picture of the actual inequality levels.

Full price flexibility would most likely not cause a supply response by enterprises, but rather simply suppress revealed demand. While shortages would be eliminated, the hunger for consumer goods—or the feeling that consumption was being neglected—would not. Owing to their institutional powers, enterprises would continue receiving a disproportionately larger share of the available goods. In addition, even with a fully balanced market for consumer goods, enterprises would not have to pay much attention to quality or timely deliveries because under the prevailing system it is not up to the consumers but to permissive planners to judge the economic performance of managers. Thus any strengthening of incentives for efficiency at the enterprise level is not likely to be accomplished by allowing flexible pricing.

There is also the possibility of a negative reaction to price increases—namely, that enterprises will reduce their supplies. This would result in a negatively sloped supply curve, which Kornai calls a "shortage-maintaining supply-curve" (1985: 53). If such reactions are frequent enough, then the inflationary balancing of supply and demand on the consumer market will fail. Generally such a situation would occur only if state planners were not consistent in their policy of clearing the market so that when faced with an easing of shortages in one area of production (due to higher prices), they reallocated resources away from that particular area (feeling that other areas needed them more, on the grounds of a relative degree of shortages).

It is doubtful whether required price adjustments would be feasible because a technical issue arises of how the planners would handle all the adjustments without leaving the job to market forces. Slow reactions by managers to a sudden increase in consumer demand would call for an immediate upward correction in prices, as would a breakdown in the supply of goods. In the past CPE pricing agencies have proved very inefficient in making slow and isolated price adjustments (for a few products at a time); thus they would probably be unable to cope with the much more demanding task of making prices fully flexible (very much in line with what Lange's [1936] model of decentralized socialism called for).

As a result of flexible price policies, consumers would have to add the misery of rapid and unpredictable price changes to perceptions that consumption is underplayed in order to either satisfy bureaucrats' industrial ambitions or cover for their lack of efficiency. This is probably too great a political cost for the regimes to allow it to happen. Moreover, given the organizational constraints on the pricing apparatus, shortages would continue to exist, very likely on a smaller scale than under the traditional pricing policy, but still more severe than in the market economies; thus the systemic difference stressed by Kornai regarding the degree of shortages on the consumer market would not cease.

The most likely outcome of an effort to eliminate shortages through price adjustments in the investment goods area is an uncontrolled inflation in investment goods which would sooner or later spread to the consumer sector, quickly causing planners to reverse the pricing policy. What seems to be at least theoretically possible with respect to the formal balancing of consumer markets (more appropriately, the demand/supply relation) is not achievable in terms of determining managerial behavior in the investment goods market (a fact basically acknowledged by Gomulka 1986). Our argument is that as long as central planners have to make up for all losses incurred by enterprises, the policy of raising prices for productive factors will not prevent managers from asking for investment goods (or labor) in excessive amounts—i.e., above the minimum efficient requirements. Clearly elastic price increases would result only in even faster growing budgetary appropriations to meet enterprise demands without making them insolvent.

While we find Kornai's claim of the inevitability of shortages in the CPEs well founded both empirically and theoretically, we do not consider this phenomenon the essence of central planning. Nor do we view the presence of shortages a primary source of low CPE technological abilities (though excess demand certainly has something to do with them, including the mechanism identified by Kornai). We believe that it is institutionalized inefficiency that truly characterizes the planning system and explains the technological inferiority of the CPEs as well.

No doubt there are at any point a number of markets (or submarkets) where demand and supply are in equilibrium. Moreover, there are goods for which planners should be able to assure equilibrium at some reasonable price levels. Still, even in these instances some measure of inefficiency will remain. With all the confusion stemming from arbitrary prices, multiple subsidies and taxes, and administrative constraints on managerial decisionmaking, it is only by accident that the maximum efficiency postulate is satisfied in equilibrated markets; such is most likely also the case with all goods where shortages occur.

Kornai's preoccupation with shortages seems only to detract from the critical issue—i.e., , the lower efficiency of central planning as compared to the market system. This point can be derived from Kornai's analysis, as we have indicated, however. In its underlying philosophy, Kornai's theory corresponds with the basic postulate of von Mises (1932), who claimed that it was impossible to make rational choices, or to fully economize on productive resources, under central planning. Kornai's theory not only provides a set of analytical tools that affords a more rigorous exposure of the key deficiencies of central planning, but it is also understandable for those (a clear majority) working with the modern tools of microeconomics.

In conclusion, without a stimulus for cost minimization or for meeting real demands, state enterprises do not need to innovate—at least not to undertake cost-reducing changes or meet desirable standards and levels of quality. In other words, it is not so much a fear of failing with innovation—the assumption of the risk-reward model—as it is a lack of pressure to economize that turns enterprises away from innovation. For the same reason, if efforts are made, they do not have to be optimal. While the risk-reward model fails to explain irrationality, the zero-price model explains both the reasons for the low frequency of innovation and the factors behind inefficient technological changes.

THE CLOSED ECONOMY EXPLANATION

As described above, the zero-price model and the related theory of shortage by Kornai abstract from foreign trade transactions.

Built in a microeconomic tradition, they focus purely on the relationships between domestic agents. For instance, when the models address the issue of the real prices of inputs as opposed to the zero-price situation, they refer to domestic scarcities and not to world market prices as an ultimate measure of opportunity costs. Furthermore, when they address the importance of competition, it is again without mentioning the opening of an economy to the world market.

In fact, the majority of authors writing on technological change in the CPEs give little attention to the determining role of the foreign trade system. The work by economists in Eastern Europe and the Soviet Union—as well as in the West—is full of ideas on how to invigorate CPE industries technologically. Recommendations include (among others) breaking ministerial (i.e., branch) monopolies in production, commercializing the banking system so that investments carry real prices, and allowing upper flexibility in prices for consumer goods so that excess demand is eliminated. However, there is very little discussion of the potential technological progress in opening the CPEs to the world market.

Not only are the technological aspects of an opening ignored, but also the whole issue of building normal links with the world system is played down in the CPEs. Unlike in the West, where even the most pro-intervention economists view an open economy as the best system, in the CPEs it is much easier to opt for a reduced involvement of the state in domestic affairs than to question the state monopoly in trade and other institutions of the closed economy. In the CPEs the world market is perceived mainly as a source of economic plagues: fluctuations and inflation. It is also seen as a threat to economic sovereignty—specifically that free trade allows stronger, more advanced countries to take advantage of others (for example, via the imposition of production structures that are suitable primarily to the needs of the strong and not the weak nations). Consequently, a very limited role is ascribed in the CPEs to the world market. While the planners have moved far from the original insistence on self-sufficiency, the world market is nonetheless seen primarily as a buffer to absorb excess domestic supplies or provide goods lacking on the domestic market. There has also been an understanding in theory that the world market should be used as a source of so-called competitive imports to introduce some pressure on domestic enterprises to economize on resources, but the policy has remained on paper. The only other important role ascribed to the world market is pricing, where—after years of efforts to design an independent system of valuation—the CPEs have adopted the idea of using world market prices as a permanent point of reference for the bureaucratically determined prices in intra-CMEA trade.

The lack of an international dimension in the zero-price and shortage models—as well as in a systemic discussion in general—would be of no relevance if such a dimension did not have any impact on changes in technology. However, one of the most critical points of this volume is that trade arrangements play an important determining role in technological change. The lack of an international dimension would also be of no significance if the CPEs and market economies did not differ in their systemic arrangements for foreign transactions. However (as indicated above), one of the characteristics of the CPEs is their deep institutional isolation, more excessive even than in the most protective market economies.

The CPEs operate all the institutions of a closed economy. One of them is the state monopoly in trade which excludes enterprises from decisionmaking on transactions with outside partners and makes foreign agents unable to freely spend their earnings on goods made in the CPEs. This isolation is further amplified by the fact that CPE currencies are not convertible, thus complicating the financing of trade transactions. Since domestic currencies are not traded, the state has to set their value administratively. In addition, there are multiple exchange rates—i.e., they are different for various sectors of industry or even for individual enterprises within one industry. Moreover, prices are based on cost-plus formulas, and an extensive mechanism of state taxes and subsidies on trade operates.

Given the above, we have to seek a more appropriate body of theory than that offered by the risk-reward and zero-price models. One analytical possibility is to work within these two models by adding the external relations of domestic agents, including state planners. Thus one could add export-import transactions to the risk-reward explanation and claim that planner pressures for uninterrupted increases in exports or improvements in the export-import balance are also responsible for the insufficient pace of technological changes, and that noncommensurate rewards for taking risks discourage managers as well. The zero-price explanation (as well as Kornai's approach) could also be extended to foreign transactions because here too planners must make up for enterprise losses so that the motivation for technological changes in export production is weakened.

Instead of modifying these models, however, we prefer to advance a separate framework that makes the focal point of explanation the degree to which an economic system is open to the world market. While we agree with the main thrust of these models, we believe that openness is a more critical factor in the mechanism of technological change, as well as in determining the competitiveness of an economy. The postulates derived from the models described can be fully satisfied as much in a closed economy as in an open one. In an open economy other postulates (to be specified) are met as well, making an open economic system much better equipped to promote technological change.

DOMESTIC DRAWBACKS

In this section we shall discuss the most important drawbacks to technological change in the CPEs stemming from their closed economic systems. Many of them have already been signaled in the analysis above, but here we would like to both systematize and complete the picture. Specifically, we shall distinguish a group of negative impacts related to the fact that domestic agents in the CPEs lack certain sources of information and types of economic pressures necessary for rapid technological change. We shall call these domestic impacts, and we shall identify two sorts: the reduced ability of enterprises to pursue changes in technology and the related (but not synonymous) reduction in technology import potential.

Regarding the first domestic impact, we must accept that there is always some "learning process" involved when a domestic agent pursues foreign transactions, since potential sellers have to provide technical information on the goods they offer (for example, on maintenance). Many empirical studies indicate that this sort of information is one of the major preconditions of successful innovations (see Langrish and Poznanski 1981). Thus the more frequent the contacts, the more information can be acquired, particularly if domestic agents and foreign sellers cooperate in production so that contacts are more open. CPE enterprises are by and large excluded from direct contacts with foreign partners and gain access mostly through the state administration (including foreign trade enterprises), making it difficult for them to acquire full technical expertise; thus their ability to promote changes in production is diminished.

Another potential advantage of the world market is that it provides signals on the desirable directions of technological change.

World prices indicate the relative scarcities of various inputs, thus pointing to the type of technologies that are most appropriate in terms of input savings. Moreover, they indicate the growth potential of specific products and the time for their replacement by newer models. Most of this information does not reach CPE enterprises in time. When it arrives, it is very often distorted because (as noted) CPE domestic prices are very loosely connected with world market prices. The CPEs have been trying to compensate for this limitation by putting large labor resources into special agencies collecting and disseminating nonprice information on technological trends, but this can hardly be considered an effective substitute for direct price signals from the world market.

The world market can also serve as a source of additional pressure on enterprises to promote technological change. By extending the number of parties involved in the economic rivalry for customers, it encourages domestic enterprises to use innovation as a means of survival. This pressure may be particularly helpful when, to take advantage of the so-called economies of scale, a country has to allow a high concentration of production so that not much internal competition is left. However, if an economy (or some of its sectors) is immature, then external competition, if excessive, may only damage its internal technological capability, and some temporary protection may be necessary. In the CPEs not much external competition is permitted—even from other members of the CMEA—so pressure has to come either from rudimentary domestic rivalry or the state apparatus, which (as we have already argued) is not ready to use all its administrative powers for this purpose.

Regarding the second domestic aspect, in addition to the advantages already mentioned, the world market offers a stimulus for exports, enhancing an economy's capability to purchase foreign technology. This is particularly important in small economies—such as most of the East European countries—which are limited by minimum scale requirements so that some sort of research specialization is unavoidable. It is also particularly applicable to the economies that lag behind the technological leaders. (All the CPEs fall into this category.) As indicated, latecomers can benefit from the sources of technology accumulated by the leaders by substituting them for their independent efforts and thus making possible a savings on resources. Moreover, by importing technology more advanced than it could produce itself, a latecomer can achieve a higher rate of change in the domestic technological level than the leader; thus the initial gap can eventually be closed, as can the related wage differential. Indeed importing advanced technology is the only practical way for a follower to achieve these goals. The independent reinvention of a leader's technology by a domestic research sector will not necessarily lead to a closing of the gap because the follower's potential to develop technology is inferior. Copying (i.e., reverse engineering) is not a solution either, particularly if such an effort takes as much time as it takes a leader to invent new vintages of technology.

The CPEs do not allow the world market to encourage exports, nor do they have a substitute mechanism. At first glance the CPEs seem to be well equipped at least to force domestic enterprises to export, and in many instances—particularly when faced with severe balance-of-payments difficulties—they have shown a remarkable ability to accelerate sales abroad. However, upon closer scrutiny this ability turns out to be illusory, as is well demonstrated by an equally well-documented phenomenon—namely, the short durations of export expansions and quick regressions to severe trade deficits. The key characteristic of the CPE economies is a chronic shortage of foreign currencies. It is not so much related to the excessive demand of domestic agents—driven by the same forces as those we described when analyzing institutionalized inefficiency—but rather to the small quantities of goods available for export.

The CPEs do not enforce an orientation toward exports for a number of reasons. One is that within their political systems there is very little incentive for any group to advocate sales abroad. Most of the political struggle revolves around the allocation of resources to specific regions because by acquiring more productive inputs (including those from imports), local party units or factories improve their self-esteem as well as gain leverage in future political negotiations. There is much less interest in the maximization of output, despite ever-present pressing needs, and even less interest in promoting outputs for exports. For one thing, supplies that are directed to the domestic market can serve as a means of direct (often informal) barter with producers of scarce goods, whereas such transactions are not generally possible with export goods. In addition, there is not much potential for a group to enhance its internal position by building close trading ties with any foreign country except the Soviet Union (Staniszkis 1987).

INTERNATIONAL DRAWBACKS

Here we shall discuss a group of international negative impacts related to the fact that a closed economy discourages foreign nationals from participating in its technological effort. The earning of export revenues is not the only precondition for getting access to external technology; certain types of direct operations by foreigners in a host economy provide such an opportunity as well. The presence of foreign agents enhances the host economy's potential to absorb foreign technology and stimulates the domestic research sector at the same time. In many ways the latter mode of technology acquisition appears superior to the former, so that they cannot be seen as simple substitutes. As we shall see, this applies in particular to foreign direct investment—i.e., investment that involves production control by a multinational company or other forms of production ventures with multinational corporations.

The most obvious advantage of foreign direct investment is that it provides a host economy with capital assets—and opportunities to embody new technologies—that otherwise would have to be financed through export expansion. (This is true assuming that such investment does not draw from the domestic capital market or that the outflow of profits does not exceed domestic spending by the foreigner.) The capital benefits of foreign direct investment are particularly valuable for countries that lag far behind the technological leaders and therefore experience difficulties in securing export revenues sufficient to finance the purchases of necessary foreign technology. During the initial stage, foreign direct investment may easily substitute for export promotion, but in the longer run, with the declining ability to place goods in the market of the host economy, a good export showing by the host economy is essential for the continued interest of foreign investors.

Another critical advantage of foreign direct investment is that in most cases it involves a transfer of technology. Generally it is the foreign investors' technological superiority which enables them to install production in environments which are culturally unfamiliar or hostile (owing to unequal support from local governments to domestic and foreign agents). Indeed investments by multinational corporations have proven to be the major vehicle for technology transfer in the world economy (Romeo 1983). To turn their technological lead into a competitive weapon, multinationals must of course have control over their own technologies. The more effective is such control, the more eager will foreign investors be to transfer their latest technologies. This is one of the reasons why, as shown by Mansfield et al. (1979), the newest technologies are transferred almost exclusively via fully owned foreign direct investment, secondarily via joint ventures (with limited control), and least often via license agreements.*

In addition, foreign direct investment provides host countries with invaluable technical expertise. When a foreign agent sells a license, only a limited amount of knowledge can be transferred because certain types of information can be transmitted only through personal contact. The buyer of a license can contract for consulting services or training programs to acquire this sort of information, but these are almost never as effective as having a foreign supplier of technology oversee a project himself. With foreign direct investment the supplier is much more strongly motivated to use all his technical expertise to make a project succeed because his own profits are at stake.†

Finally, foreign participation can provide a host country with access to the marketing networks and service facilities of the technology suppliers. In many areas of world trade a well-developed network for sales and maintenance is required for exporting new products (for evidence, see the case study of Hungarian exports by Murrell 1981: 352-66); most often such networks are controlled by multinational companies. To export a product based on imported technology, an economy may be forced to enter such a network. This may apply to domestic sales as well if the economy does not

*Consequently, the more hostile an economy is to foreign direct investment, the less likely is its acquisition of the most advanced technologies available. Evidence is provided by Coughlin (1983), who has demonstrated that there is a substantial difference in the time lag of technology acquisition depending on the permissiveness or restrictiveness of local regulations on foreign direct investment. Thus in one of the most liberal host economies, West Germany, the average lag during 1945-85 between the appearance of a new technology and its transfer to West Germany was 8.9 years for product innovations and 11.4 years for process innovations, whereas in a relatively restrictive host economy, Yugoslavia, the respective lags were 14.1 and 15.8 years. (All the figures calculated by Coughlin are from the data base generated by Davidson and Vernon 1979.)

†This is one reason why the choice of projects is by and large more rational and the absorption of technology is faster in a host economy when foreign direct investment rather than another mode of transfer is involved. This phenomenon is demonstrated in the comparative diffusion of technology in several industrial sectors in Hong Kong (Chen 1983: 309-21).

have enough experience to set up a network internally. Foreign agents are not willing to open their networks to competitors, so that the only practical way to gain such access is to allow these agents to invest in an economy. In most cases foreign investors will make their networks available to only strictly specified segments of the world market, so that there is no unnecessary competition. It follows that by allowing direct investment, a host country will gain not only network access, but will also avoid direct competition with the more powerful suppliers of technology from abroad.

Currently it is almost impossible for the Soviet Union and Eastern Europe (as well as China, which is not a focus of this book) to benefit from foreign direct investment. In part this is because foreign direct investment regulations in the CPEs (as argued in Chapter 6) are both less established and not as attractive as those in other countries. However, this is not the most important reason. As we see it, the most critical reason is that central planning is so rigid—and so different from the market system to which multinational companies are accustomed—that it is virtually impossible for foreign investors to run an efficient operation.

If one accepts the notion that foreign direct investment is probably the single most important factor behind successful technological development—particularly in a small and/or less advanced economy—then it becomes apparent that CPE barriers against it are the primary or at least one of the most critical explanations for the lackluster CPE technological performance since World War II.* Phrased differently, more than anything else it is the isolation of the CPEs—plus the factors stressed in the risk-reward and zero-price models—which makes them less able than most market economies

*The CPEs have been most successful in promoting capital transfers within the CMEA. These are usually bilateral or multilateral projects which—unlike foreign direct investment—do not involve ownership control by those who provide resources except for the country in which a project is located. The major purpose for such investment for the nonhost participant(s) is to secure the supply of certain products. Thus far, the majority of projects has been in primary sectors, particularly energy and ores. These investments have been almost exclusively in the Soviet Union and at Soviet insistence. The key reason for the Soviet interest in "joint investments" has been its leaders' concern with high capital-intensity projects in primary sectors and the supposedly lower than world market prices charged to East Europeans. While these investments have benefited the CMEA members in some ways (e.g., relaxing supply difficulties), they cannot be considered an important stimulus for overall technological progress and are by no means a substitute for the potential benefits from direct investment by Western multinationals (see Csaba 1985: 227-43).

to change production. The most detrimental aspect of this isolation is the barriers to foreign direct investment and other forms of involvement (e.g., industrial cooperation) by foreign nationals.

The opening of the CPEs to the world market would be very difficult and is extremely unlikely in the near future. During the lengthy period of economic reforms in the CPEs, very little has been done with respect to foreign trade compared to other areas. Even in the most decentralized economy, Hungary, enterprises have only a small margin of discretion in dealings with foreign partners. Access to foreign currencies remains very difficult, and directives (particularly related to export obligations covered by the CMEA specialization programs) cover at least one third of the intrabloc trade. While domestic price rules have been relaxed in Hungary more than in the other CPEs, the pricing system still bears only a very loose relationship to world market prices, and its informative role is further diminished by extensive financial transfers (i.e., taxes and subsidies) to domestic importers and exporters.

The low likelihood of any immediate radical changes in the CPE foreign trade institutions has its roots in the ideological sphere. The persistence of state regulation of external transactions reflects more than just the intellectual tradition of Marxism which (as we noted) presents the world market as a source of even more aggravating stresses than those generated on national markets. It also reflects important political factors, including the impossibility of the East Europeans opening their economies without upsetting the Soviet leaders. Such an opening would allow countries other than the Soviet Union to increase their leverage over Eastern Europe and encourage the development of local interest groups not identifying themselves with the Soviet Union. In addition, domestic elites in Eastern Europe are not very sympathetic to opening because it could be implemented only at the expense of their monopoly over economic control.

In sum, the degree of openness of an economy to foreign trade, including transfers of capital (and of other productive resources as well), plays a critical role in how its agents perform in technological terms. Specifically, in a more open economy, all other factors being equal, pressure for changes in production is stronger and direct investment—which we see as a major vehicle for the transfer of the most advanced technologies—more likely. We also argue, that, while the lack of pressure to economize on resources reduces the motivation for technological changes, the isolation of the CPEs is probably the most important explanation for the region's difficulties in promoting technological change, and consequently for its lack of success in catching up with the West and losing its former technological edge over the NICs in several key areas.

Three competing theoretical approaches address the factors determining the low technological capability of the CPEs. One, here called the risk-reward explanation, focuses on excessive risks of innovation to enterprises or lack of sufficient rewards for taking on additional risks. Another theory, called the zero-price explanation, links their lackluster performance to the state's willingness to rescue failing enterprises by providing additional resources to pay wages or to complete delayed or misguided investment projects. Finally, the closed-economy explanation relates their incapacity to the autarkic nature of CPE systems, reducing enterprises' exposure to foreign competition and limiting the inflow of foreign direct investment.

In one restricts discussion to internal matters, the zero-price theory appears to be the most plausible. Where a permissive state offers help to any unfortunate or mismanaged enterprise, it weakens interest in efficiency and in pursuing innovations whose purpose is to economize on resources. The risk-reward explanation loses force if one assumes the presence of a permissive (or paternalistic) state, because it implies little real risk for managers, which makes the size of rewards for innovative actions rather irrelevant.

However, one can scarcely be satisfied with a discussion of the factors behind the lackluster performance of the CPEs that remains within the framework of a national economy. Technological changes in contemporary economies are highly international, so that developments in one country are very dependent on those occurring elsewhere. Therefore the most useful theory is the closed-economy explanation. What most undermines the CPEs' efforts is their limited degree of openness to the world market, which is not compensated for by their extensive—but bureaucratized—trade with one another.

CONCLUSIONS

From the analysis we have presented, several points stand out concerning the ability of the CPEs to improve their trade competitiveness in the world market and to keep up with technological changes elsewhere. Most of them seem well supported by the evidence presented throughout this book, but further enquiries will be worthwhile. Particularly valuable would be additional research on the comparative performance of the CPEs and market (or quasi-market) economies in the rapidly growing regions of Latin America and the Far East.

(1) During the last decade and a half, the CPEs have gone through a series of economic reforms that have modified their institutional setup for technological progress in the hope of improving their competitive stand. These changes equipped central planners with more refined instruments of control over basic agents, research establishments, and state enterprises, while increasing the flexibility of the latter two. However, the core elements of the system, such as the central allocation of inputs and setting targets for the agents, have remained untouched, as has the logic of the technological changes (i.e., their supply-push character).

(2) Prior to these reforms the CPEs—or at least the Soviet Union—did not show any success in reducing their historical lag behind Western technology, a point convincingly demonstrated in the study of Soviet technology in the 1960s by Amann, Cooper, and Davies (1977). As our analysis shows, the CPEs have proved unable to reduce this lag after the reforms as well, a fact reflected both in comparative technological levels of major industries and in the trade performance of exports from the Soviet bloc and those from the industrialized West.

(3) The CPE performance during the last several years has been lackluster even though their efforts have been supported with unprecedented large-scale imports of Western technology. The relative scale of total imports by individual CPEs has made some difference. The most aggressive borrowers of technology, such as Hungary and Poland, demonstrated a faster pace of technological modernization than many other East Europeans—at least until the most recent

adjustments. (In Poland this process was dramatically upset, or indeed reversed, by the 1979-82 crisis and the illusive recovery that followed; Poznanski 1986c). The economies which based their modernization efforts in particular sectors on Western technology seem to have experienced greater success than those trying to use domestic designs and equipment. The case of passenger cars is a good example, with aggressive importers such as Poland and the Soviet Union outperforming passive Czechoslovakia and East Germany (the two major exporters of cars).

(4) The CPEs have skillfully utilized the latest intensification of technology trade to support their jointly conducted domestic efforts in strategic technologies such as computers. Faced with Western restrictions on technology exports and concerned with national security, the CPEs, with strong backing by the Soviet Union, have adopted and redesigned a host of Western technologies—acquired either legally or through unofficial channels—to launch their own family of advanced computers. Both the acceleration of computer production and the CMEA-wide specialization in the manufacture of specific models (and peripherals) are impressive. However, the effort has not brought the CPEs closer to the frontier technology; it has helped only to prevent them from falling further behind the West.

(5) Recent efforts by Eastern Europe (and to a lesser extent the Soviet Union, which relies less on the export of manufactures) to accelerate the exports of manufactures to Western markets on the basis of Western technology imports have met with an unforeseen challenge in the rapidly expanding exports of similar goods by the NICs. In some export categories the NICs had already surpassed the CPEs in the late 1960s—mostly consumer goods, such as garments, radio receivers, and television sets, to which the CPEs had allocated little investment in earlier years. Currently the NICs lead in a large number of intermediate and capital goods categories as well, though many of these enjoy strong CPE planner support (e.g., steel, ships).

(6) The seriousness of the NIC challenge results not only from their proven ability to manufacture the same goods which dominate CPE supplies to the West, but also from the fact that the CPEs do not show any superiority in advanced goods such as computers, peripherals, or synthetic drugs, nor with respect to other goods.* If

*The weakness of Eastern Europe is in part reflected by the fact that its market position in the West has been eroded in the last years. In 1970 Eastern Europe accounted for 0.9 percent of the OECD imports of medicinal and

the situation in other technologically complex products is no different from that in computers and synthetic drugs, one can argue that, at least in the short run, the CPEs (particularly resource-poor Eastern Europe) have no choice but to compete with the NICs in the area of unsophisticated products, where the NICs have already proven more successful. The inability to quickly replace traditional manufactures with advanced products fundamentally distinguishes the CPEs from most of the industrial countries of the West, where trade in traditional manufactures—also threatened by the NICs— is gradually giving way to more advanced products.

(7) The NICs have been technologically outpacing the East Europeans despite the latter's substantial advantage in domestic research effort as reflected in research expenditure and foreign patents per capita. We have demonstrated that the smaller NIC involvement in the production of technology, both original and imitative, has been continuously offset by more extensive imports of Western technology. The lesson seems to be that for successful catching-up with the technology leaders, followers have to expand economic links with the more advanced economies rather than imitate them through domestic research.

(8) One of the most critical differences between the CPE and NIC approach to the importation of Western technology has been that the latter have aggressively promoted direct foreign investment by Western multinational corporations to acquire advanced technology, a channel which is hardly exploited (and is often prohibited) by the CPEs. The significance of this difference can be properly understood only if one takes into account that (as argued here) the newest and most strictly protected Western technology is by and large—and in some industries exclusively—transferred through multinationals.

(9) The trends in the East European exports of manufactures to Western markets documented here (as well as those of the Soviet Union; see Poznanski 1987) clearly contradict most earlier projections indicating that the West was going to be flooded with cheap manufactured goods produced in Eastern Europe with the help of Western technology and financing. Even if there were no trade squeeze and reorientation (i.e., a switch to the Soviet market) as is taking place now, Eastern Europe would be in no position to

pharmaceutical products, but in 1980 the share was only 0.4 percent. This contrasted with a substantial improvement for the NICs from 1.1 percent in 1970 to 2.5 percent in 1981.

flood the Western market in the coming years because the precondition for a large-scale export expansion by Eastern Europe is not just a sufficient surplus of goods (the lack of which was traditionally seen as a primary obstacle to East-West trade), but also the ability to compete with NIC exporters. As we have shown, Eastern Europe clearly lacks this ability (as does the Soviet Union).

(10) The CPEs will very likely remain at a disadvantage as exporters of manufactured goods because (as noted) they do not seem prepared to integrate more closely with multinational corporations, which in practice do most of the trade in manufactures. While the current NIC export offensive benefits greatly from the presence of Western multinational subsidiaries, with their distribution and service networks, the CPEs continue to rely mostly on their own narrow channels. Instead of opening up to direct investment, they promote buy-back agreements, which can hardly be considered an adequate substitute due to the inflexibility of such arrangements and their conflictual nature. (They are strongly opposed by the European Economic Community and the OECD as a threat to free trade; OECD 1981a).

(11) The outcome of the competition between the CPEs and the NICs will depend not only on supply factors (e.g., access to credit and investment capital), but also on the ability of these groups of countries to develop favorable trade arrangements with Western countries. There is no doubt that the CPEs have been unable to negotiate conditions as good as those enjoyed by the NICs, particularly in the case of the United States and Japan, two of the most vital markets for manufactures supplied by "newcomers."* As a result of recent decisions (e.g., U.S. temporary suspension of most-favored-nation status for Poland and exclusion of Romania from the Generalized System of Preferences) the situation has deteriorated for Eastern Europe. Nor is the region in a position (at least for the time being) to assure that it will be treated equally in the recent round of quota reductions affecting such crucial exports as steel and garments.

(12) Our analysis provides an additional argument for the superiority of the export-oriented—and one should add (not

*Recent moves by the U.S. government have reduced the amount of imports from the NICs which are granted duty-free entry to the United States under the Generalized System of Preferences (Lachica 1984: 37).

without certain reservations) foreign investment-oriented*—economies over those geared to import substitution and to an autarkic policy of economic growth. It has been demonstrated elsewhere that an export-oriented policy has enabled the NICs to perform better than the non-oil and gas rich countries of the developing world which embarked on an import-substitution policy; India and Pakistan are good cases in point (see Krueger 1983: 7). The evidence presented here indicates that the recent NIC record is also superior—at least in technological terms—to that of Eastern Europe, which has recently tried to depart—slightly and rather inconsistently—from its deeply rooted autarkic tendencies (Marer 1981).

(13) Considering the nature of the obstacles to the CPE trade with the West, we can argue that the policy experiments of the CPEs and Western countries in the 1970s have by and large lost much of their practical value and need reevaluation. Trade concessions by Western countries, although important, are not essential any more, nor is the limited CPE liberalization of foreign trade procedures. To reverse the current and unfavorable trends in exports, more fundamental changes are needed, particularly ones which could better integrate the region with the international financial and capital markets (i.e., direct investment). All require at least a partial reinstitution of a uniform exchange rate system and convertibility on the part of the CPEs, as well as a debureaucratization of the economic system.

(14) Without reforming, the CPEs may find it increasingly difficult to support a rapid sustained growth of their economies. These economies are and will continue to be critically dependent on Western sources of imported technology, as these cannot be substituted with other sources. To assure growth rates similar to those of the NICs, the CPEs would have to reverse their declining shares of the Western markets and match the performance of their counterparts in the developing world. If the leaders of the CPEs

*Not all the NICs can be said to rely heavily on foreign direct investment. Certainly such investment has been critical for Singapore, while Mexico (for example) has been more inclined to rely on freign borrowing. Moreover, foreign direct investment does not always have to be accompanied by an export-oriented strategy. Mexico geared its program of foreign direct investment to domestic demand more than to exports, while in Singapore such investment was expected (or required) to help the country in export expansion. We refer here to the combination of export-oriented strategy and foreign direct investment geared to exports. (See an assessment of particular strategies in Tyson 1986.)

decide to settle for lower rates of growth, then even an inferior trade performance could turn out to be sufficient. In any event, in the planning of economic growth, the CPEs have to take into account the competitive challenge of the NICs on the Western market for manufactures.

(15) The isolation of Eastern Europe and the Soviet Union is the crucial but not the only reason for low innovativeness of the CPEs. Technological change is also hindered by what we call institutionalized inefficiency. Poor performance by enterprises is tolerated by the state, and managers are not pressed to take advantage of opportunities for improving quality by introducing new products and reducing costs of manufacturing by altering processes.

(16) State planners would like enterprises to execute their production assignments perfectly and increase output in each plan period. If planners were able to enforce their objectives, experiments with new technology could become very risky for managers by jeopardizing current plan targets and ability to show future improvements. In these circumstances, to encourage innovations the state would have to offer very high, perhaps politically unacceptable, bonuses to managers. The past record shows, however, that planning in the CPEs is far from rigid, and that failures with innovations do not necessarily lead to difficulties with target fulfillment.

(17) Though shortages, which are a permanent feature in all the CPEs, make buyers willing to accept obsolete or poor quality goods, so that suppliers feel little need for improving their products, they are not primarily responsible for enterprises' lack of interest in altering manufacturing processes. The primary cause of low innovativeness—both in products and processes—is the state's willingness to tolerate cost-overruns and wastage in industry. Shortages are simply another consequence of that tolerance.

(18) The state's permissiveness is also responsible for the CPE tendency to extend the life-span of products and processes beyond any economic justification. Even if substitutes superior to the older technology are introduced, the state often allows older products to continue to be used because it would rather absorb economic losses than permit the outdated enterprises to go bankrupt or dismiss their employees.

BIBLIOGRAPHY

Adams, W., and Dirlam, J. 1968. "Big Steel, Invention, and Innovation." *Quarterly Journal of Economics* 80 (May).

Aganbegyan, A. 1985. Statement in "Sojuz mysli i dela." *Pravda*, 13 July.

Altman, F., and Clement, H. 1979. *Die Kompensation als Instrument im Ost-West Handel.* Munich: Osteuropa Institut.

Amann, R., and Cooper, J., eds. 1982. *Industrial Innovation in the Soviet Union.* New Haven: Yale University Press.

Amann, R.; Cooper, J.; and Davies, R. W., eds. 1977. *The Technological Level of Soviet Industry.* New Haven: Yale University Press.

Amann, R., and Slama, J. 1976. "The Organic Chemicals Industry in the USSR: A Case Study in the Measurement of Comparative Technological Specification by Means of Kilogram." *Research Policy*, no. 5.

American Machinist. Various years.

Aylen, J. 1980. "Innovation in the British Steel Industry." In *Technical Innovation and British Economic Performance*, ed. K. Pavitt. London.

Balazsy, S. 1979. "Financial Regulating System and Technical Development." *Acta Oeconomica* 22, 1-2.

Balcerowicz, L. 1978. "Niektore problemy innowacji technicznych w gospodarce socjalistycznej." Warsaw: Central School of Planning and Statistics; mimeo.

Baranson, J. 1979. *Automotive Industries in Developing Countries.* Baltimore: Johns Hopkins University Press.

Bauer, T. 1978. "Investment Cycles in Planned Economies. *Acta Oeconomica*, no. 3.

Bauer, T., and Soos, K. 1979. "Interfirm Relations and Technological Change in Eastern Europe: The Case of the Hungarian Motor Industry." *Acta Oeconomica* 23, 3-4.

Bauman, H. 1973. "The Diffusion of the Basic Oxygen Process in the U.S. and Canadian Steel Industries, 1955-1969." University of Western Ontario; mimeo.

Bentley, B. 1981. "Technical Change in the GDR." University of Sussex (December); mimeo.

Bergson, A. 1978a. *Productivity and the Social System: The USSR and the West.* Cambridge, Mass.: Harvard University Press.

_________. 1978b. "Managerial Risk and Rewards in Public Enterprises." *Journal of Comparative Economics*, no. 2.

________. 1983. "Technical Progress." In *The Soviet Union Toward the Year 2000*, ed. A. Bergson and H. Levine. New York: Columbia University Press.

Berliner, J. 1952. "The Informal Organization of the Soviet Firm." *Quarterly Journal of Economics* 66 (August).

________. 1976. *Innovation Decisions in Soviet Industry*. Cambridge, Mass.: MIT Press.

Biuletyn Statystyczny. 1985. Warsaw.

Boguszewski, T. 1981. "Wachstrum und Produktivitat in der Industrie und ihren Hauptbereichen in der BRD, Oesterreich, Polen und Ungarn in Zeitraum 1960-1972." Vienna Institute for Comparative Economic Studies.

Bornstein, M., et al. 1980. "The Planning and Management of Industrial Research and Development in the USSR." Washington, D.C.: SRI, International Strategic Studies Center report; mimeo (June).

Campbell, R. 1976. "Issues in Soviet R & D: The Energy Case." In *Soviet Economy in a New Perspective*. Washington, D.C.: Joint Economic Committee of the U.S. Congress (14 October).

Cave, M. 1977. "Computer Technology." In Amann, et al., eds., pp. 383-84.

Chen, E. 1983. "Multinational Corporations and Technology Diffusion in Hong Kong Manufacturing." *Applied Economics*, no. 15.

China, People's Republic of. 1980. *Monthly Bulletin of the Republic of China*, no. 174 (June).

Chudnovsky, D. 1982. "The Changing Remittance Behaviour of United States Manufacturing Firms in Latin America." *World Development* 10, 6.

Conference Board, Investment Data Department. Various issues. *Global Investment Flows*. New York.

Cooper, J. 1984. "Is There a Technological Gap between East and West?" Paper for conference on The East-West Economic Relationship in a Changing World Economy. Canadian Institute of International Affairs, Toronto, 13-14 June.

Coughlin, C. 1983. "The Relationship between Foreign Ownership and Technology Transfer." *Journal of Comparative Economics* 7, 4 (December).

Crane, K., and Gilliot, A. 1981. "MNCs in the Aircraft Industries in Brazil and Poland." Paper for conference on Multinational Corporations in Latin America and Eastern Europe. Bloomington: Indiana University (March).

Csaba, L. 1985. "Joint Investments and Mutual Advantages in the CMES—Retrospection and Prognosis." *Soviet Studies* 36, 2 (April).

Dahlman, C. J. 1982. "Foreign Technology and Indigenous Technological Capability in Brazil." Washington, D.C.: World Bank; mimeo (May).

Dahlman, C. J., and Sercovich, F. 1984. "Exports of Technology from Semi-Industrial Economies." Washington, D.C.: World Bank; mimeo (June).

Davidson, R., and Vernon, R. 1979. *Foreign Production of Technology-Intensive Products by US-Based Enterprises*. Washington, D.C.: National Science Foundation, 15 January.

Davis, N., and Goodman, S. 1978. "The Soviet Bloc Unified System of Computers." *Computing Surveys* 10, 2 (June).

DDR Handbuch. 1985. Cologne.

Deutschen Bundesbank. 1984. *Statistisch Berichte zu den Monatsberichten der Deutschen Bundesbank*, Reihe 3.

Dezsenyi-Guellette, A. 1983. "The Utilization and Assimilation in Hungary of Advanced Technology Imported from the West." *Soviet Studies* 2, 35 (April).

Economic Bulletin for Europe. 1986.

Edwards, I., and Fraser, R. 1977. "The Internationalization of the Eastern European Automotive Industries." In *East European Economies Post-Helsinki*, pp. 390-419. Washington, D.C.: Joint Economic Committee of the U.S. Congress (25 August).

European Economic Community (EEC). Various years. *Eurostat, Foreign Trade, Analytical Tables* (NIMEXE). Brussels.

Fallenbuchl, Z. 1983. *East-West Technology Transfer: Study of Poland 1971-1980.* Paris: OECD.

Fernhout, T. 1978. *The Soviet Chemical Industry and Its Role in East-West Trade*. Washington, D.C.: U.S. Department of Commerce, Office of East-West Trade and Planning (4 August).

Freeman, C. 1974. *Economics of Industrial Innovation.* Baltimore: Penguin.

Freris, A. 1984. *The Soviet Industrial Enterprise.* New York: St. Martin's Press.

Gajewski, E. 1983. "Czy rynek na tym skorzysta." *Tygodnik polski* (November).

Glikman, P., and Poznanski, K. 1976. "Finansowanie dzialalnosci inwestycyjnej w nowym systemie ekonomicznym." *Gospodarka planowa*, no. 6.

Gomulka, S. 1971. *Inventive Activity, Diffusion and the Stages of Economic Growth* Aarhus: University of Aarhus.

_________. 1985. "Soviet Equilibrium Technological Gap and the Post-1975 Productivity Slowdown." Paper for conference on Technological Progress in the Communist World, Hoover Institution, 20-21 July.

_________. 1986. *Growth, Innovation and Reforms in Eastern Europe.* Madison: University of Wisconsin Press.

Goodman, S. 1979a. "Computing and the Development of the Soviet Economy." In *Soviet Economy in a Time of Change.* Washington, D.C.: Joint Economic Committee of the U.S. Congress (10 October).

_________. 1979b. "Soviet Computing and Technology Transfer: An Overview." *World Politics* 30, 4 (July).

_________. 1984. "Technology Transfer and the Development of the Soviet Computer Industry." Washington, D.C.: Georgetown University, CSIS Task Force on Trade, Technology and Soviet-American Relations.

Griliches, Z. 1957. "Hybrid Corn: An Exploration in the Economics of Technological Change." *Econometrica* 25, 4 (October).

_________. 1985. *R&D, Patents, and Productivity.* Chicago: Univ. of Chicago Press.

Grossman, G. 1966. "Information and Innovation in the Soviet Economy." *American Economic Review* 6, 2 (May).

Gustafson, T. 1981. *Selling the Russians the Rope? Soviet Technology Policy and US Export Controls.* Santa Monica: RAND Corporation (April).

Gutman, P. 1980. "East-West Industrial Cooperation in the Automotive Industry and the International Division of Labor." *ACES Bulletin* 22, 3-4 (Fall/Winter).

Hanson, P. 1981. *Trade and Technology in Soviet-Western Relations.* New York: Columbia University Press.

________. 1982. "The End of Import-Led Growth? Some Observations on Soviet, Polish and Hungarian Experience in the 1970's." *Journal of Comparative Economics* 6, 2 (June).

________. 1984. "Soviet Assimilation of Western Technology." Paper for conference on Trade, Technology and Soviet-American Relations. Center for Strategic and International Studies, Georgetown University, 16-17 April.

Hill, M. 1984a. "The Soviet Quality Attestation and Market Quality System." Loughborough University of Technology, Department of Management Studies, Working Paper No. 84.

________. 1984b. "Soviet Product Quality and Soviet State Standards: The Case of Machine Tools." Loughborough University of Technology, Department of Management Studies, Working Paper No. 87.

Hirsch, S. 1965. "The United States Electronics Industry and International Trade." *Economic Review*, no. 34: 92-97.

Hotzer, L. 1980. "Innovation in the Hungarian Engineering Industry." *Acta Oeconomica* 24, 1-2.

Hungary, KSM. 1971. *Ausztria, Csehoszlovakia, Franciaorszag e Magyarorszag ipari termelikeny segenek osszehosonlitasa.* Budapest.

Industry of Free China. Various years.

International Monetary Fund (IMF). Various years.

Jacobsson, S. 1985. "Technical Change and Industrial Policy: The Case of Computer Numerically Controlled Lathes in Argentina, Korea, and Taiwan." *World Development* 13, 3 (March).

Juhasz, T. 1980. "Some Aspects of the Adaptation of the Most Advanced Technical Achievements in Hungary." *ACES Bulletin* 22, 1 (Spring): 98.

Khorzov, C. 1982. "Reserwy koncentracji proizwodstwa." *Planowoje chozjaistwo*, no. 11 (November); original in Russian.

Kim, A. 1981. "Economic Development and External Links." *Journal of East Asian Affairs* 1, 1.

Kieser, J. W. 1977. *Report on the Potential for Technology Transfer from the USSR to the United States.* Washington, D.C.: U.S. Department of State.

Kiss, E. 1980. "Problems in Technology Transfer in the Hungarian Pharmaceutical Industry." *ACES Bulletin* 22, 1 (Spring): 85-86.

Koo, B. 1982. "The Role of Foreign Direct Investment in Recent Korean Economic Growth." Ithaca, N.Y.: Cornell University; mimeo.

Kornai, J. 1980. *Economics of Shortage.* Amsterdam: North-Holland.

________. 1983. "Comments on the Present State and the Prospects of Hungarian Economic Reform." *Journal of Comparative Economics*, no. 3.

________. 1985. "Gomulka on the Soft Budget Constraint: A Reply." *Economics of Planning* 19, 2.

Krajewski, S., et al. 1978. "Fotografie przedsiewziec innowacyjnych: Raport z badan." University of Lodz; mimeo.

Krueger, A. 1983. "The Effects of Trade Strategies on Growth." *Finance and Development* (June).

Lachica, E. 1984. "U.S. to Cut Duty Breaks to Mexico, Taiwan, and South Korea, Expand Other Benefits." *Wall Street Journal*, 28 March.

Lange, O. 1936. "On the Economic Theory of Socialism." *Review of Economic Studies* 4, 1 (October).

Langrish, J., and Poznanski, K. 1981. "Studia nad innowacjami w przedsiebiorstwie kapitalstycznym: Proba rekapitulacji." In *Innowacje w przemysle: Wyniki badan impirycznych*, eds. J. Muzjel and K. Poznanski. Warsaw: PWE.

Levcik, F., and Skolka, J. 1984. *East-West Technology Transfer: Study of Czechoslovakia.* Paris: OECD.

Lloyd's Register of Shipping. Various years. Annual Summary of Merchandise Ships Completed (Launched) in the World. London.

Machlup, Fritz. 1962. *The Production and Distribution of Knowledge in the United States.* Princeton: Princeton University Press.

Maciejewicz, J., and Monkiewicz, J. 1982. "Technology Exports from Poland." *Economics of Planning* 18, 1.

________, and ________. 1983. "Trends in Technology, Exports from the Socialist Countries." *Yearbook of East European Studies*, Band 10.

Maczynska, E. 1984. "Finansowanie postepu naukowo-technicznego w Bulgarii." *Finanse* 34, 2 (February).

Maddala, G., and Knight, P. 1967. "International Diffusion of Technical Change: A Case Study of the Oxygen Steelmaking Process." *Economic Journal*, September.

Maly Rocznik Statystyczny. 1983. Warsaw: GUS.

Mansfield, E. 1968. *Industrial Research and Technical Innovation.* New York: Norton.

Mansfield, E., et al. 1979. "Foreign Trade and U.S. Research and Development." *Review of Economics and Statistics* 61, 1 (February).

Marer, P. 1981. "Eastern European Economies: A Region in Crisis." Paper for the annual meeting of the Association for Comparative Economic Studies, Washington, D.C., 29 December.

________. 1984a. "Joint Ventures in Hungary, 1972-1983." Bloomington: Indiana University, School of Business (January); mimeo.

________. 1984b. "The Political Economy of Soviet Relations with Eastern Europe." In *Soviet Policy in Eastern Europe*, ed. S. M. Terry. New Haven: Yale University Press.

________. 1985. *East-West Technology Transfer: Study of Hungary, 1968-1984.* Paris: OECD.

________. 1986. *Dollar GNPs of the USSR and Eastern Europe.* Baltimore: Johns Hopkins University Press.

Marrese, M., and Vanous, J. 1983. *Soviet Subsidization of Trade with Eastern Europe.* Berkeley: Institute of International Studies.

________, and ________. 1984. "Soviet Trade Relations with Eastern Europe, 1970-1984." December; mimeo.

Martens, J. 1986. "Quantifications of Western Exports of High-Technology Products to Communist Countries." In *East European Economies: Slow Growth in the 1980s.* Washington, D.C.: Joint Economic Committee of the U.S. Congress (28 March).

Martin, J. 1983. "Japanese Agree to Transfer Steel Expertise to South Korea." *Financial Times*, 2 December.

Monkiewicz, J. 1980. "Licencje." *Zycie gospodarcze*, no. 16.

Montias, J. M. 1962. *Central Planning in Poland.* New Haven: Yale University Press.

________. 1983. "Observations on Recent Trends in East-West Trade." Yale University (June); mimeo.

Motor Vehicle Manufacturers' Association of the U.S. 1986. *Facts and Figures.*

Mujzel, J. 1981. "Ceny w procesie innowacyjnym." Department of Economics, University of Lodz. Mimeo.

Murrell, P. 1981. "An Evaluation of the Success of the Hungarian Economic Reform: An Analysis Using International Trade Data." *Journal of Comparative Economics* 5, 4 (December).

Myers, S., and Marquis, D. G. 1969. "Successful Industrial Innovation." In *Factors in the Transfer of Technology*, eds. W. H. Gruber and D. G. Marquis. Cambridge, Mass.: MIT Press.

National Machine Tool Builders' Association. Various years. *Economic Handbook of the Machine Tool Industry.* McLean.

Nolting, L. 1976a. *The Financing of Research, Development and Innovation in the USSR by the Type of Performer.* Washington: Department of Commerce.

________. 1976b. *The 1968 Reform of Scientific Research, Development and Innovation in the USSR.* Washington: Department of Commerce (September).

Norwegian Shipping News. 1982.

Nyers, J. 1982. "Hungarian Ferrous Metallurgy in International Competition." *Acta Oeconomica* 29, 1-2.

Nyitrai, V. 1977. "A Comparison of the Austrian and Hungarian Industries." *Acta Oeconomica* 19, 3-4.

OECD. 1979. *Technology Transfer to Developing Countries.* Analytical Study No. 2: *The International Flows of Technology to Developing Countries.* Paris, 22 October.

________. 1981a. *East-West Trade, Recent Developments in Counter-Trade.* Paris.

________. 1981b. *Technological Balance of Payments and International Competition: The Case of West Germany.* Workshop on the Technological Balance of Payments; Geneva, 14-15 December.

________. 1981c. *Technology Transfer and the Technological Balance of Payments.* Note by the Italian Delegation, Workshop on the Technological Balance of Payments; Geneva, 14-15 December.

________. Various years. *Foreign Trade by Commodities.* Paris.

Oechsler, R. 1981. "GDR Trade with the Industrial West since 1975: Performance and Prospects." In *East European Assessment.* Washington, D.C.: Joint Economic Committee of the U.S. Congress (27 January).

Oliver, F. R. 1964. "Methods of Estimating the Logistic Growth Function." *Applied Statistics* 13.

Oster, S. 1981. "The Diffusion of Innovation among Steel Firms: The Basic Oxygen Furnace." *Bell Journal of Economics.*

Parker, W. 1980. "The Soviet Motor Industry." *Soviet Studies* 32, 4 (October): 522-23.

Pavitt K. 1983. "Patent Statistics as Indicators of Innovative Activities: Possibilities and Problems." Conference paper, American Association for the Advancement of Science, Detroit, 30 May.

Pavitt, K., and Soete, L. 1980. "Innovative Activities and Export Shares: Some Comparisons between Industries and Countries." In *Technical Innovation and British Economic Performance*, ed. K. Pavitt, pp. 38-66. London.

Posner, M. 1961. "International Trade and Technical Change." *Oxford Economic Papers* 13: 323-41.

Poznanska, J. 1987. "Import-Led Strategy and Export Promotion: Lessons from the Foreign Trade Adjustment." Saratoga Springs, N.Y.: Skidmore College, Department of Economics; mimeo.

Poznanski, K. 1977. "Planowanie postepu technicznego w zwiazku radzieckim." *Gospodarka planowa*, no. 11.

________. 1980. "A Study of Technical Innovation in Polish Industry." *Research Policy*, no. 9.

________. 1981. "Dzialalnosc innowacyjna przemyslu w swietle analiz mikroekonomicznych." In *Innowacje w przemysle: Wyniki badan empirycznych*, ed. J. Mujzel and K. Poznanski. Warsaw: PWE.

________. 1982a. "Ekonomiczny mechanizm innowacji w gospodarce Wegierskiej." *Ekonomista*, no. 1-2.

________. 1982b. "New Dimension in International Trade: East-South Competition in the West." Cornell University, Department of Economics (December).

________. 1983. "International Diffusion of Steel Technologies: Time Lag and the Speed of Diffusion." *Technological Forecasting and Social Change*, no. 23.

________. 1984. "Technology Transfer: West-South Perspective." *World Politics*, October.

________. 1985. "The Impact of Western Technology on Importing Economies." Paper for conference on Technological Trends in the Communist World. Hoover Institution, Stanford, Calif., 20-27 June.

________. 1986a. "Competition between Eastern Europe and Developing Countries in the Western Market for Manufactured Goods." In *East European Economies: Slow Growth in the 1980s*, vol. 2: *Foreign Trade and International Finance*. Washington, D.C.: Joint Economic Committee of the U.S. Congress (28 March).

________. 1986b. "The Extinguishing Process: A Case Study of Steel Technologies in World Industry." *Technovation*, no. 4.

________. 1986c. "Competitiveness of Polish Industry: 1970-1985." In *Creditworthiness: Can Poland Regain It?*, ed. P. Marer and W. Siwinski. Bloomington: Indiana University Press.

________. 1987. "Diffusion Performance of Major Steel-making Countries: Cross-System Comparison." Department of Economics, Northwestern University; mimeo.

Poznanski, K., et al. 1977. "Fundusz efektow wdrozeniowych jako narzedzie integrowania zaplecza badawczo-rozwojowego przemyslu z jednostkami produkcyjnymi." Warsaw: Institute of Planning; mimeo.

Quarterly Economic Review. 1980. London; no. 3. Economic Intelligence Unit: Czechoslovakia, East Germany.

Radovsky, Y. 1979. "Computer Co-operation in CMEA." *Soviet Exports*, May.

Ray, G. 1969. "The Diffusion of New Technology." *National Institute of Economics Review* 48.

________. 1984. *The Diffusion of Mature Technologies*. Cambridge: Cambridge University Press.

Rice, C. 1984. "Defense Burden Sharing." In *The Warsaw Pact: Alliance in Transition?*, ed. D. Holloway and J. Sharp. Ithaca: Cornell University Press.

Rjatsow, J. 1982. "Uprawlenije nauczno-techniczeskim progressom i rost effectivnosti proizwodstva." *Planowje chozjaistwo*, no. 4 (October); original in Russian.

Rocznik Statystyczny Handlu Zagranicznego. 1981. Warsaw.

Roman, Z. 1980. "Selection of Indicators for Comparison of Productivity Levels." *Acta Oeconomica* 22, 3-4.

Romeo, A. 1983. "Direct Foreign Investment and Technology Transfer." Paper for conference on International Technology Transfer: Concepts, Measures, and Comparisons. New York: Social Science Research Council, 2-3 June.

Rosegger, G. 1980. "Diffusion of the BOF Process in the United States 1954-1974." In *Evaluating Technological Innovation: Methods, Expectations and Findings*, eds. B. Gold, G. Rosegger, and M. G. Boylan. Lexington Books.

Rosenberg, N., and Mowery, D. 1979. "The Influence of Market Demand upon Innovation: Critical Review of Recent Studies." *Research Policy*, no. 2.

Rushing, F. 1976. "Soviet Chemical Industry: A Modern Growth Sector." In *Soviet Economy in a New Perspective.* Washington, D.C.: Joint Economic Committee of the U.S. Congress (14 October).

Saunders, C. 1984. "Comparative Advantage and Competitiveness in East-West Relations." Conference paper, International Economic Association meeting, Budapest/Vienna, 8-12 October.

Scherbina, D. 1979. "From Electronic Components to Computer Systems." *Soviet Exports*, May.

Schmookler, J. 1966. *Invention and Economic Growth.* Cambridge, Mass.: MIT Press.

Schroeder, G. 1979. "The Soviet Economy on a Treadmill of Reforms." In *Soviet Economy in a Time of Change.* Washington, D.C.: Joint Economic Committee of the U.S. Congress (October).

Skoczny, T. 1982. *Wielkie przedsiewziecia nau ikowo techniczne europiskich krajach socjalistycznych.* Warsaw: PGN.

Slama, J. 1981. "Das Innovationsverhalten der Lander und der Wirtschaftssysteme." Munich: Osteurope-Institut München; Miszelen No. 7 (January).

Soete, L. 1981. "A General Test of Technological Gap Trade Theory." *Weltwirtschafticues Archiv* 117.

Spaeth, A. 1984. "Korean Companies Set Expensive Plans to Make Microchip Plants Competitive." *Wall Street Journal*, 9 February.

Staniszkis, J. 1987. "Mechanizmy uzalezniania." University of Warsaw, Department of Sociology, May (mimeo).

Statisticzeska Rocenka CSSR. Prague.

Stoneman, P. 1980. "The Rate of Imitation, Learning and Profitability." *Economic Letters*, no. 6.

Sumrall, J. 1982. "Diffusion of the Basic Oxygen Furnace in the U.S. Steel Industry." *Journal of Industrial Economics* 30, 4 (June).

Sutton, A. 1971/1973. *Western Technology and Soviet Economic Development.* Stanford: Stanford University Press.

Svejnar, J., and Smith, S. 1982. "Economics of Joint-Ventures in Centrally Planned and Labor-Managed Economies." *Journal of Comparative Economics* 6: 148-72.

Szabo, B. 1974. "Economic Management, Regulation, Incentives." *Valosag* (November).

Szakastis, G. 1974. "The Adoption of the 'Sappho' Method in the Hungarian Electronic Industry." *Research Policy*, no. 3.

Szuprowicz, B. 1982. "Poland's DP Industry Experiencing Dog Days.'" *Computerland*, 11 October.

Tardos, J. 1982. "The Increasing Role and Ambivalent Reception of Small Enterprises." Round table on the Hungarian economy, Indiana University, Bloomington, 21-24 March.

Tasky, K. 1979. "Soviet Technology Gap and Dependence on the West: The Case of Computers." In *Soviet Economy in a Time of Change.* Washington, D.C.: Joint Economic Committee of the U.S. Congress (10 October).

________. 1981. "Eastern Europe: Trends in Imports of Western Computer Equipment and Technology." In *East European Economic Assessment.* Washington, D.C.: Joint Economic Committee of the U.S. Congress (10 July).

Thornton, J., and Leary, N. 1987. "Are Socialist Industries Inoculated Against Innovation?: An Experimental Test." Department of Economics, University of Washington, mimeo.

Tigre, P. 1983. *Technology and Competition in the Brazilian Computer Industry.* New York: St. Martin's Press.

Tyson, L. 1986. "The Debt Crisis and Adjustment Responses in Eastern Europe: A Comparative Perspective." *International Organization* 40, 2 (Spring).

United Nations. Various years. *Bulletin of Statistics of World Trade in Steel.*

________. Various years. *Bulletin of Statistics on World Trade in Engineering Products.* New York.

________. Various dates. *Monthly Bulletin of Statistics.* New York.

________. Various years. *Yearbook of Industrial Statistics.* New York.

________. 1982. *Statistical Yearbook.* New York.

________, Center on Transnational Corporations. 1983a. *National Legislation and Regulations Relating to Transnational Corporations.* New York.

________, ________. 1983b. *Transnational Corporations and Development.* Third Survey, New York.

UNCTAD. 1980. *Legislation and Regulations on Technological Transfer: Analysis of Their Effects in Selected Countries.* Geneva.

________, Economic Commission for Europe. 1979. *Structural Changes in the Iron and Steel Industry.* New York.

________, ________. Various years. *The European Steel Market.*

United States. Various years. *Statistical Abstracts of the U.S.* Washington, D.C.

United States, Department of Commerce. 1974. *Polymerization Processes and Related Production Equipment: A Market Assessment in the USSR.* Washington, D.C. (June).

________, ________. Various years. *Survey of Current Business.* Washington.

________, Federal Trade Commission. 1977. *The U.S. Steel Industry and Factors Determining International Competitiveness.* November.

________, Patent and Trademark Office. 1981. *Indicators of the Patent Output of U.S. Industry.* Washington, D.C.

Von Mises, Ludwig. 1951. *Socialism: An Economic and Sociological Analysis.* New Haven: Yale University Press.

Wharton Econometrics. 1984. *Centrally Planned Economies. Current Analysis. Chemical Trade between the CPEs and the EEC*; part 2: *Prices and Market Shares*, vol. 4, no. 86-87 (26 November).

WIPO. Various years. *Industrial Property Statistics.* Geneva.

Wolf, T. 1982. "Optimal Foreign Trade for the Price-Insensitive Soviet-Type Economy." *Journal of Comparative Economics* 6: 54-67.

World Automotive Market. Various years. *Automobile International.* New York.

World Bank. 1982. *Brazil Industrial Policies and Manufactured Exports.* Report no. 3766-82 (2 July).

Zaleski, E. 1976. "Planning and Financing of Research and Development in the USSR." In *Soviet Science and Technology*, eds. J. B. Thomas and U. Kruse-Vancienne. Washington, D.C.

Ziech, M. 1983. "Kto pozwala firmom polonijynm." *Glos wybrzeza*, 7 November.

INDEX

KAZIMIERZ Z. POZNANSKI is Associate Professor of Economics at the Henry M. Jackson School of International Studies at the University of Washington, Seattle. He has previously taught at Cornell University and Northwestern University. He specializes in the study of comparative systems, international economics, and the economics of technological change. He has published articles in *World Politics*, *International Organization*, *World Development*, and other leading journals.

INSTITUTE OF INTERNATIONAL STUDIES
UNIVERSITY OF CALIFORNIA, BERKELEY

215 Moses Hall Berkeley, California 94720

CARL G. ROSBERG, *Director*

Monographs published by the Institute include:

RESEARCH SERIES

1. *The Chinese Anarchist Movement.* R.A. Scalapino and G.T. Yu. ($1.00)
7. *Birth Rates in Latin America.* O. Andrew Collver. ($2.50)
16. *The International Imperatives of Technology.* Eugene B. Skolnikoff. ($2.95)
19. *Entry of New Competitors in Yugoslav Market Socialism.* S.R. Sacks. ($2.50)
20. *Political Integration in French-Speaking Africa.* Abdul A. Jalloh. ($3.50)
21. *The Desert & the Sown: Nomads in Wider Society.* Ed. C. Nelson. ($5.50)
22. *U.S.-Japanese Competition in International Markets.* J.E. Roemer. ($3.95)
24. *Urban Inequality and Housing Policy in Tanzania.* Richard E. Stren. ($2.95)
25. *The Obsolescence of Regional Integration Theory.* Ernst B. Haas. ($6.95)
27. *The SOCSIM Microsimulation Program.* E. A. Hammel et al. ($4.50)
28. *Authoritarian Politics in Communist Europe.* Ed. Andrew C. Janos. ($8.95)
31. *Politics of Oil Pricing in the Middle East, 1970-75.* R.C. Weisberg. ($4.95)
32. *Agricultural Policy and Performance in Zambia.* Doris J. Dodge. ($4.95)
34. *Housing the Urban Poor in Africa.* Richard E. Stren. ($5.95)
35. *The Russian New Right: Right-Wing Ideologies in USSR.* A. Yanov. ($5.95)
37. *The Leninist Response to National Dependency.* Kenneth Jowitt. ($4.95)
38. *Socialism in Sub-Saharan Africa.* Eds. C. Rosberg & T. Callaghy. ($12.95)
39. *Tanzania's Ujamaa Villages: Rural Development Strategy.* D. McHenry. ($5.95)
40. *Who Gains from Deep Ocean Mining?* I.G. Bulkley. ($3.50)
43. *The Apartheid Regime.* Eds. R. Price & C. Rosberg ($12.50)
44. *Yugoslav Economic System in the 1970s.* Laura D. Tyson. ($5.95)
45. *Conflict in Chad.* Virginia Thompson & Richard Adloff. ($7.50)
46. *Conflict and Coexistence in Belgium.* Ed. Arend Lijphart. ($10.50)
47. *Changing Realities in Southern Africa.* Ed. Michael Clough. ($12.50)
48. *Nigerian Women Mobilized, 1900-1965.* Nina E. Mba. ($12.95)
49. *Institutions of Rural Development.* Eds. D. Leonard & D. Marshall. ($11.50)
50. *Politics of Women & Work in USSR & U.S.* Joel C. Moses. ($9.50)
51. *Zionism and Territory.* Baruch Kimmerling. ($12.50)
52. *Soviet Subsidization of Trade with East Europe.* M. Marrese/J. Vanous. ($14.50)
53. *Voluntary Efforts in Decentralized Management.* L. Ralston et al. ($10.00)
54. *Corporate State Ideologies.* Carl Landauer. ($5.95)
55. *Effects of Economic Reform in Yugoslavia.* John P. Burkett. ($9.50)
56. *The Drama of the Soviet 1960s.* Alexander Yanov. ($9.50)
57. *Revolutions & Rebellions in Afghanistan.* Eds. Shahrani/Canfield. ($14.95)
58. *Women Farmers of Malawi.* D. Hirschmann & M. Vaughan. ($8.95)
59. *Chilean Agriculture under Military Rule.* Lovell S. Jarvis. ($11.50)
60. *Influencing Political Behavior in Netherlands and Austria.* J. Houska. ($11.50)

LIST OF PUBLICATIONS *(continued)*

61. *Social Policies in Western Industrial Societies.* C.F. Andrain. ($12.95)
62. *Comparative Social Policy.* Harold Wilensky et al. ($7.50)
63. *State-Building Failure in Ireland and Algeria.* I. Lustick. ($8.95)
64. *Social Legislation in Middle East.* Eds. Michalak/Salacuse. ($15.50)
65. *Foreign Politics of Richard Nixon.* Franz Schurmann. ($18.50)
66. *State, Oil, & Agriculture in Nigeria.* Ed. Michael Watts. ($16.95)
67. *Apartheid in South African Town.* Martin West. ($9.50)
68. *International Politics of Telecommunications.* D. Blatherwick. ($8.95)

POLICY PAPERS IN INTERNATIONAL AFFAIRS

1. *Images of Detente & the Soviet Political Order.* K. Jowitt. ($1.25)
2. *Detente After Brezhnev: Domestic Roots of Soviet Policy.* A. Yanov. ($4.95)
3. *Mature Neighbor Policy: A New Policy for Latin America.* A. Fishlow. ($3.95)
4. *Five Images of Soviet Future: Review & Synthesis.* G.W. Breslauer. ($5.50)
5. *Global Evangelism: How to Protect Human Rights.* E.B. Haas. ($2.95)
6. *Israel & Jordan: An Adversarial Partnership.* Ian Lustick. ($2.00)
7. *Political Syncretism in Italy.* Giuseppe Di Palma. ($3.95)
8. *U.S. Foreign Policy in Sub-Saharan Africa.* Robert M. Price. ($4.50)
9. *East-West Technology Transfer in Perspective.* R.J. Carrick. ($5.50)
11. *Toward Africanized Policy for Southern Africa.* R. Libby. ($7.50)
12. *Taiwan Relations Act & Defense of ROC.* Edwin K. Snyder et al. ($7.50)
13. *Cuba's Policy in Africa, 1959-1980.* William M. LeoGrande. ($4.50)
14. *Norway, NATO, & Forgotten Soviet Challenge.* K. Amundsen. ($3.95)
15. *Japanese Industrial Policy.* Ira Magaziner and Thomas Hout. ($6.50)
16. *Containment, Soviet Behavior, & Grand Strategy.* Robert Osgood. ($5.50)
17. *U.S.-Japanese Competition-Semiconductor Industry.* M. Borrus et al. ($8.50)
18. *Contemporary Islamic Movements in Perspective.* Ira Lapidus. ($4.95)
19. *Atlantic Alliance, Nuclear Weapons, & European Attitudes.* W. Thies. ($4.50)
20. *War and Peace: Views from Moscow & Beijing.* B. Garrett & B. Glaser. ($7.95)
21. *Emerging Japanese Economic Influence in Africa.* J. Moss & J. Ravenhill. ($8.95)
22. *Nuclear Waste Disposal under the Seabed.* Edward Miles et al. ($7.50)
23. *NATO: The Tides of Discontent.* Earl Ravenal. ($7.50)
24. *Power-Sharing in South Africa.* Arend Lijphart. ($10.00)
25. *Reassessing the Soviet Challenge in Africa.* Ed. M. Clough. ($8.00)
26. *Why We Still Need the United Nations.* Ernst Haas. ($8.50)
27. *Impact of U.S. Policy in El Salvador.* M. Diskin & K. Sharpe. ($6.50)
28. *American Military Strategy.* Samuel P. Huntington. ($4.95)
29. *International Debt Threat.* Vinod K. Aggarwal. ($5.95)
30. *Nuclear Competition in South Asia.* R.R. Subramanian. ($5.50)
31. *Newly Industrializing Asia in Transition.* T. Cheng/S. Haggard. ($8.50)
32. *Asymmetries in Japanese-American Trade.* S.D. Krasner. ($6.50)

Modernization & Bureaucratic-Authoritarianism: Studies in South American Politics. Guillermo O'Donnell. ($9.50) [POM Series No. 9]